Cruel to be Kind

CATHY GLASS

Cruel to be Kind

Saying no can save
a child's life

HARPER
element

Certain details in this story, including names, places and dates,
have been changed to protect the family's privacy.

HarperElement
An imprint of HarperCollins*Publishers*
1 London Bridge Street
London SE1 9GF

www.harpercollins.co.uk

First published by HarperElement 2017

1 3 5 7 9 10 8 6 4 2

A catalogue record of this book is
available from the British Library

ISBN 978-0-00-825955-6

Printed and bound in the United States of America by
LSC Communications

Find out more about HarperCollins and the environment at
www.harpercollins.co.uk/green

ACKNOWLEDGEMENTS

A big thank you to my family; my editors, Carolyn and Holly; my literary agent, Andrew; my UK publishers HarperCollins, and my overseas publishers who are now too numerous to list by name. Last, but definitely not least, a big thank you to my readers for your unfailing support and kind words. They are much appreciated.

PROLOGUE

Since I began writing my fostering memoirs ten years ago, the number of children in care in the UK has risen to an all-time high of 70,000. Children come into care for many reasons, including physical, emotional and sexual abuse, neglect or a crisis in the family where there is no one to look after them. It is always very sad when a family is separated, and of course the child suffers. This is the story of one of those children: Max.

CHAPTER ONE

A BAD START

'H is mother is in hospital having two toes amputated and there have been complications.'

'Oh dear. I am sorry,' I said.

'Max is going to be very upset when I tell him he won't be going home,' Jo, Max's social worker, continued. 'It will be the first time he's been in foster care, although his family are known to the social services. I'm anticipating collecting him at the end of school and then bringing him straight to you, so I'm afraid he'll just have what he stands up in.'

'Don't worry, I've got plenty of spare clothes.' I already knew that Max was six years old.

'Good. Hopefully I'll be able to get some of his belongings tomorrow. I'm going to see his mother, Caz, this evening after I've brought Max to you. She wants him to visit her in hospital.'

'This evening?' I asked, aware that it would be late and Max would already be very unsettled.

'Yes.'

'And you want him to go to school tomorrow?' I needed to know so I could make arrangements to take him.

1

'I don't see why not. I'll let you know the name and address of his school and the other information you'll need when I see you later.'

'OK. Thank you.'

We said goodbye.

It was now 2 p.m. and I went straight upstairs. I'd been fostering long enough to have accumulated spare clothes for emergency use for children of most ages. Sometimes I had plenty of notice when a child was being brought into care and could prepare for their needs, even meet the child if it was a planned move, but many children just arrived – as Max was going to – with very little notice.

I went first to the airing cupboard where I took out a fresh set of towels, and then continued into my bedroom and to the ottoman where I kept the spare clothes. Lifting the lid, I rummaged through until I found pyjamas, socks and pants for a six-year-old. I didn't have any spare school uniforms so I'd have to wash and dry what Max was wearing. From a drawer in my room I also took out a child's toothbrush and hairbrush. I put the towel and toothbrush in the bathroom, ready for later, and then carried the clothes into what would shortly be Max's bedroom. I'd already thoroughly cleaned and vacuumed it and put on fresh bed linen after the last child had gone. Since Alex (whose story I tell in *Nobody's Son*) had left two weeks previously, I'd looked after a child on respite for ten days who'd now returned to live with his carer.

Satisfied I was as prepared as I could be at such short notice, I returned downstairs to telephone Jill, my supervising social worker from Homefinders, the agency I fostered for. Jill's role was to supervise, monitor and support me in fostering so that the child received the best possible care. She had telephoned me an hour before to say that Max was being brought into care and to ask if I could look after him. Although she'd asked me, it is generally assumed that a foster carer will accept the child referred to them. It's not a pick-and-choose situation. The child coming into care needs a home, so unless there is a very good reason why a carer can't take a particular child then they are expected to do so. From the little I knew, I was happy to accept Max and had no reservations. Jill had given me a brief outline of his home situation and why he was now coming into care. Although Max hadn't been in care before, his family had come to the attention of the social services when some support had been put in, and now, while Max's mother was in hospital, his three teenage sisters were supposed to be looking after him, but last night they'd gone out partying instead. A neighbour had alerted the social services when Max had knocked at her door asking for dinner and she'd taken him in. I also knew from Jill that Max was being brought into care under Section 20 (of the Children's Act), also known as Accommodated. This is when parents 'agree' to place their child in care voluntarily, rather than going to court and risking a care order, which would mean they would lose their parental rights. Around 30 per cent of children who come into care are placed under Section 20. Jill had said she was hoping to be with me when Max arrived, and I now phoned her to let her know the time.

'OK, see you later,' she said.

I began a quick tidy-up of the living room and also took food from the freezer for dinner later. I knew from experi-ence that when a child first arrived with their social worker there was a lot to get through, and also Jo was expecting me to take Max to visit his mother in hospital, so time would be short.

Adrian, my seven-year-old son, would be pleased to have another boy staying with us, I mused as I worked, although in truth he and my three-year-old daughter, Paula, usually got along with any child we looked after. They'd grown up with fostering, so having someone else living with us was the norm. Also the norm, although it saddens me to say so, was that I was now a single parent, as my husband, John, had left us eighteen months before. I'd taken a short break immediately after he'd gone and then a few months later, with the children's agreement, I'd resumed fostering. I enjoyed fostering – caring for and helping the children while they were with me. It gave another dimension to my life and the small payment I received, together with the part-time work I did from home, paid the bills. At present Adrian was at school and Paula was playing at a friend's house. I would collect her on the way to meet Adrian from school.

I'm always a bit anxious just before a new child arrives, wondering how they will settle and if they will like my family and me, but once they're here I'm so busy that there isn't time to worry. I just concentrate on looking after them and meeting their needs to the best of my ability. This afternoon, however, ten minutes before I was due to leave to collect Adrian and Paula, my anxiety level rose to a new height. The phone rang and I answered it in the hall, expecting Jill or Jo with some more news about Max or a last-minute change of plan, which happens a lot in fostering. However, a rather gruff woman's voice I didn't recognize demanded, 'Is that Cathy Glass?'

'Yes,' I said tentatively. 'Who's calling?'

'Max's mum, Caz. I'm warning you, lay one finger on my boy and you'll be sorry. Do you understand? I might be in hospital but his dad isn't, and he don't stand any nonsense.'

CHAPTER TWO

MAX

My heart began to race and my mouth had gone dry. 'Of course I'll take good care of Max,' I reassured his mother, ignoring her slight, and trying to keep my voice even. I appreciated that parents who've just had their children taken into care are often angry and upset, but threatening me before I'd even met the child was a first. However, as worrying as this was, of more concern was how his mother, Caz, had got my number. 'Who gave you my telephone number?' I asked.

'His social worker. Our solicitor told her she had to give it to us, as he's in care voluntarily, or I wouldn't have agreed to him going.' Sometimes the parents of children in care under a Section 20 are given the contact details of the carer, but usually the carer is asked first, and it's in cases where there is no animosity and the parents are working with the social workers and the foster carer in the best interests of the child. I didn't dare ask if she had my address too.

'Make sure you give Max what he wants to eat,' she continued in the same confrontational tone. 'I'll be asking him when I see him what he's had, so it better be good. No cheap rubbish.'

'I always give the children good food, and a balanced diet,' I said. 'When they first arrive I ask them what they like and dislike.'

'Max likes everything and plenty of it, so give him whatever he wants. I've told Jo, the social worker, I'll want to see him every evening. You gonna be bringing him?'

'I expect it will be me,' I said. 'I'm seeing Jo later when she brings Max to me, so she'll tell me about the contact arrangements then.' For even when a child is in care voluntarily it's usual to have a timetable of contact.

'I've told her,' she said. Then, 'You haven't got any dogs, have you? Max don't like dogs. He's been scared of 'em since he got bit.'

'No, we just have a cat, Toscha.'

'That don't bite, does it?'

'No, she's very placid.' And long-suffering, I thought but didn't say.

'Make sure you look after him proper. Understand? When I see him I'll ask him how you've been treating him.'

'He'll be well cared for,' I said evenly. 'Now I'm going to have to go to collect my children. Thank you for phoning.'

'If those stupid girls had done what they were supposed to, none of this would have happened. Silly bitches,' she fumed.

I assumed she meant her teenage daughters. I didn't comment but rounded off the conversation as politely as I could. 'I hope you feel better soon.'

'What do you care?' she snapped, and the phone went dead.

* * *

I left the house to collect Paula and Adrian, agitated, worried, and annoyed with Jo for giving Max's mother my telephone number without mentioning it to me or advising her on when to use it. Telephone contact between the child and their family is often part of the contact arrangements, but it has to be regulated or it can become a nuisance for the foster family, and upsetting for the child when they are trying to settle in. It's certainly not supposed to be used to harass and threaten the carer. I'd raise it with Jill and Jo when I saw them later, out of earshot of Max. The poor child, I thought. It's so important for any child coming into care to see their parents getting along with the foster carer and working together with them – it helps the child come to terms with what has happened.

This certainly wasn't the best start. There is so much more to fostering than just looking after the child, which is often the easiest and most pleasant part. However, I consoled myself that Caz was angry that her child was coming into care, and hopefully things would settle and improve as time went on. I had no idea how long Max would be staying with me, but that's often the case in fostering. Perhaps it would just be for the time his mother was in hospital, although the social services would need to be certain he would be well cared for and safe before they returned him home.

Half an hour later I'd collected Paula from her friend's house and Adrian from school, and as we walked home I was telling them about Max. It was the beginning of July and the day had turned very warm, so I was carrying their jerseys as well as Adrian's school bag; he had his games kit to carry.

'Max is a nice name,' Paula said, giving a little skip and already excited at the prospect of a new playmate.

'Yes, it is,' I agreed.

'Can we play in the garden when Max arrives while you and the social worker talk?' Adrian asked, aware that the adults did a lot of talking when a child was first placed.

'Yes, if Max wants to,' I said. 'But remember, he might be shy and uncertain to begin with. He'll be missing his family and everything will be new and strange to him.' However, if Max did want to go into the garden to play with Adrian and Paula while the social worker and I talked, it would make discussing his situation considerably easier. She would need to share information about Max, his family and home life with me and it's not usually appropriate to do so in front of the child, so if Max could be entertained in the garden, so much the better.

'He could have an ice cream if he's upset,' Adrian suggested cannily.

'And me,' Paula said. 'It's not fair if just Max has an ice cream. Adrian and me should have one too.'

'I think that's what Adrian meant, isn't it?' I said, throwing him a knowing smile.

'Doh!' he said to Paula. 'As if Mum would just give Max an ice cream and leave us out.' There was ice cream and similar sweet desserts in the freezer, but generally I liked the children to have dinner first.

'Yippee! We're going to have fun and an ice cream,' Paula said, delighted. Dropping my hand, she began hopscotching along the pavement.

I hoped that some of their enthusiasm for having Max to stay would help him. I'd found in the past that often the child I was fostering bonded with my children first before me, and once a child starts playing, their anxiety begins to lift.

Although, of course, I guessed that Max, like most of the children I'd fostered, was going to be upset to begin with at being separated from his family and having to live with strangers, albeit well-meaning ones. I was expecting tears and sleepless nights at the start. But usually by the end of the first week, when the child is more familiar with their foster family and the new routine and is seeing their parents regularly at contact, they are less anxious.

Once we were home I made the children a cold drink and a snack and then I went with them into the garden to unlock the shed where I kept the outdoor toys. It's part of every foster carer's safer caring policy that sheds and similar outbuildings are kept locked. We took out a selection of toys for them to play with, including Adrian's bicycle, the spare bike for Max, Paula's tricycle, the doll's pram, skateboard and a football. The mini goalposts were still up at the end of the garden and the covered sandpit sat closer to the house. Adrian immediately began practising goal shots while Paula rode her tricycle. I returned indoors to prepare dinner so we could eat as soon as Jo and Jill had left. They were expected around five o'clock and from experience I was anticipating them staying for at least an hour, possibly much longer, when placing a child.

I could see the children from the kitchen window and as I worked, I glanced up regularly to make sure they were all right. My thoughts went repeatedly to poor little Max who at this moment was being told by his social worker that he wouldn't be going home. What a dreadful shock – to go to school in the morning as normal and then not be allowed home at night. My heart went out to him. How was he coping?

About half an hour later, hot from playing, Adrian and Paula came in and sat in the cool living room where Toscha, our cat, was already spread out on the floor by the toy box. I'd put some games and toys in there in case Max didn't want to go outside. Most children can't resist toys, and Adrian and Paula began doing some puzzles. After about ten minutes, just as I'd finished preparing the dinner for later, the doorbell rang and it was Jill. She greeted me with a warm smile and, 'Hi, Cathy, how are you?'

'We're good, thank you. Would you like a drink?'

'A glass of water, please.'

I asked her to come with me into the kitchen, as I needed to tell her something. She called hi to Adrian and Paula as she passed the living-room door and once in the kitchen I quickly told her of the phone call I'd received from Max's mother.

'That's not on,' she said. 'I'll raise it with Jo. She should have asked you or me first before she gave out your details. She'll need to speak to his mother and explain that's not acceptable. Are you all right taking Max to the hospital to visit her?' Foster carers are expected to transport the child or children they look after to and from contact.

'Yes, although I'll have to take Adrian and Paula with me. I can't leave them with a sitter every time. Do we know how long Max will be seeing his mother for each evening? Visiting is two till eight.'

'I don't know yet. We'll raise it with Jo, and also find out if you have to stay on the ward with him. There's a café in the hospital with a children's play area. It would be better if you could wait there.'

'Yes, thanks. That would be useful. I doubt if there'd be time for me to come home.'

I handed her the glass of water and we went into the living room and settled on the sofa and chair. Jill asked Adrian and Paula how they were.

'Very well, thank you,' Adrian said politely. Paula went into shy mode and came over and sat on my lap, even though she knew Jill from previous visits.

'Are you looking forward to meeting Max?' Jill asked, making conversation and trying to put them at ease.

Paula managed a small nod, while Adrian said a rather formal, 'Yes, thank you.'

Jill smiled. 'It's a lovely day,' she said, glancing towards the garden.

'They're hoping Max will want to play outside,' I said. The patio doors were slightly open and through them came the warm air and the sounds of summer.

'I'm sure he will,' Jill said. 'You've got a nice big garden to run and play in.'

A few minutes later the doorbell rang. 'That'll be Jo with Max,' I said, lifting Paula from my lap and standing. Toscha also looked up.

Paula slipped her hand into mine and came with me, while Adrian stayed with Jill. I opened the front door with a warm, welcoming smile. 'Hello, I'm Cathy.'

'Hello, Cathy, I'm Jo, and this is Max.'

My gaze went to the child standing beside Jo and I had to hide my shock. Dressed in a light blue shirt and navy trousers from his school uniform, he was sweating profusely. Beads of sweat stood on his forehead and ran down his face. His hair glistened and his shirt was wringing wet. He had one hand resting on the wall to support himself, as an elderly person might, and he was struggling to catch his breath. Yes, it was a warm day, but that didn't account for Max's obvious distress. What was responsible – and what no one had thought to mention – was that Max was dreadfully overweight.

'He needs to sit down,' Jo said, coming in. 'He's got an inhaler in here somewhere.' She began undoing the school bag she was holding as Max took hold of the doorframe and heaved himself over the doorstep into the hall.

'Sit down here, love, until you get your breath,' I said, directing him to the chair we kept in the hall by the telephone.

He dropped into it as Jo took his inhaler from his school bag, shook it and passed it to him. 'Do you know how to use it?' she asked.

Max nodded, gave it another shake, put it to his mouth, took a deep breath, held it and then exhaled. Jo looked as worried as I was.

'I didn't know he had an inhaler,' I said to her. The foster carer should be told of any medical conditions during the first phone call about the child.

'I didn't know either until I collected him,' Jo said, clearly stressed. Max took a second breath from his pump.

'Has he got asthma then?' I asked. Clearly I needed to know so I could be prepared.

'I'm assuming so. I'll find out when I see Caz later.'

Max had administered the second pump and now returned the inhaler to Jo. 'It's just two pumps?' she asked him.

'Yes,' he said, his voice husky.

Jill appeared at the end of the hall. 'Is everything all right?' I could tell from the look on her face that she hadn't been informed of Max's asthma or obesity either. Paula had taken a few steps back and was looking at Max from a short distance, very concerned. In addition to the drama of him needing his asthma pump and Jo's and my concern, this clearly wasn't the child Paula had been expecting. He wasn't simply chubby or what one would describe as a bit overweight; my guess was that he was at least twice the size he should have been, over-fed to the point where it was obviously affecting his health and quality of life.

'Shall we go into the living room?' I suggested to Max now his breathing had settled. 'I'll fetch you a drink.'

The poor child heaved himself off the chair and not so much walked as waddled down the hall towards Jill. I always try not to judge, but seeing him in so much obvious discom-fort, I thought that, assuming he didn't have a medical condi-tion, whoever had allowed him to get into this state, presumably his mother, was as guilty of child abuse as if he'd been beaten. This hadn't happened overnight; it had taken years of over-eating – probably all his life – for him to get like this.

CHAPTER THREE

AMAZED

I saw Adrian do a double take as Max entered the living room, but to his credit he quickly recovered and said a welcoming, 'Hi, I'm Adrian.'

Max nodded and lumbered over to the sofa where he heaved himself onto the seat and sat back. Jo sat beside him as Jill took one of the easy chairs. 'What would you like to drink?' I asked Max.

'Cola,' he said in a husky voice.

'I'm afraid I haven't got any of that,' I said. Like many parents and carers, aware of how bad sweet fizzy drinks were for children's teeth I limited them to special occasions. 'You could have water, fruit juice, milk or squash,' I offered.

'Juice,' he said.

'Jo, what would you like?' I asked.

'A black coffee, please.'

Paula came with me to make the drinks and was clearly worried. As soon as we were out of earshot she said quietly to me, 'What's the matter with Max?'

'He got a bit out of breath. He'll be all right soon when he's sat quietly and had a drink.' But I knew that wasn't the only reason for Paula's question. It was impossible even for a young child (who are generally very accepting of differences) not to notice Max's size.

'Will he be able to play with us?' she asked as I made Jo's coffee.

'Yes, of course, love.'

'How will he ride the bike we got out for him?'

'We'll find some games he can play,' I said positively. 'Now, come on, stop worrying. We'll take him his drink.'

I poured Max's juice and carried it with Jo's coffee into the living room where Jo and Jill were chatting lightly to Max, trying to put him at ease. Adrian was on the floor by the toy box, stroking Toscha. Paula went over and joined him. I gave Jo and Max their drinks and sat in another easy chair. Then a horrendous thought occurred to me. I looked at Jo. 'Animal fur doesn't affect Max's breathing, does it?' It is for reasons like this that any medical condition should be discussed with the foster carer at the time of the referral, not once the child has arrived. Children with allergies to animal fur generally have to be placed in foster families where there are no pets.

'Not as far as I know,' Jo said, taking a grateful sip of her coffee. 'But I wasn't aware he had asthma or was using an inhaler until today. I'll ask his mother when I see her this evening.' Then, looking at Max: 'You have a cat at home, don't you?'

'Two,' Max said. 'Tiger and Smokey.'

'Those are nice names,' I said, relieved.

'And they don't make your breathing bad?' Jill asked him.

'No,' Max said.

'Best keep an eye on it, though,' Jill said. Then to Jo: 'Will he be having a medical?'

'That's something else I'll need to discuss with his mother,' she replied, setting her cup in its saucer. When a child first comes into care they usually have a medical. If the child is in care under a Section 20 then the parent's permission is sought. 'Caz told me he'd had some teeth out earlier this year,' she added, 'but I don't know of any other medical conditions.'

Max had already finished his drink, having swallowed it straight down. 'Would you like another drink?' I asked him, as he was clearly thirsty. He nodded. 'What would you like?'

'Juice.'

I took his glass and went into the kitchen where I poured another glass of juice, aware that even pure juice has a high calorie content from the fructose sugar. Not a good idea for a child who is already badly overweight. Returning to the living room I passed the glass to Max and he drank down half of it in one go and then sat with the glass resting on his stomach.

'Here's the paperwork you need,' Jo said, handing me the essential information and placement forms.

'Thank you.'

'Could you send a copy to the agency too,' Jill said. 'So we have it on file.' This was normal practice.

'Yes, of course,' Jo said. 'Sorry, I should have realized. It's been a busy day.' She took a notepad from her bag and made a note.

'It's a nice house, isn't it?' Jill said encouragingly to Max. He nodded.

'I'll show you around later,' I said.

'I'm hoping to send some of his belongings over tomorrow,' Jo now said. 'One of his sisters might be able to drop them off. She passes by the end of your road most days on her way to college.'

I looked at Jill. 'I think we'll need to discuss that,' Jill said, nodding pointedly towards Max. For clearly discussing any issue in respect of Max's family was going to be difficult in front of him. There was an awkward silence.

'Now Max has recovered, perhaps he'd like to go in the garden with Adrian and Paula?' I suggested. 'There are some toys out there and a bench in the shade of the tree,' I said to him.

'That sounds nice,' Jo said, appreciating my suggestion. 'Let's take a look, shall we?' She set her cup and saucer on the coffee table and stood. Max, who'd been leaning right back into the sofa, began struggling to get off, shuffling forward but finding it difficult. Jo instinctively offered her hand and helped him off, as one would an elderly person. It was pathetically sad and another indication of just how being badly overweight was blighting his life. Most children would have leapt off the sofa and been down the garden in an instant.

I looked at Max as he waddled towards the patio doors. Of average height for a six-year-old, he had short brown hair, a pleasant face, round and open, and seemed quite placid in nature. I wondered how he coped with the inevitable name-calling in the school playground. My heart went out to him. Children can be cruel and anyone who deviates from the norm can easily become the object of bullying.

Just outside my patio doors there is one small step that leads onto the patio. It's not high and is easily navigated by even small children, but Max now held onto the edge of the door to support himself as if worried he might lose his balance and topple. He carefully turned sideways and tentatively lowered one foot and then the other, as a toddler might.

Outside, we all crossed the patio and went onto the lawn where the toys were.

'What would you like to play?' Adrian asked sensitively. 'It's a bit hot for football.' Indeed, Max was perspiring again, although the sun was starting to lose its strength.

'I'll watch while you play,' Max said quietly. 'Like I do at school.' I could have wept. The thought of the poor child having to sit and watch while his friends played instead of joining in touched me. Whether his non-participation was from not being able to run and keep up, discomfort if he tried or a fear of being laughed at I didn't know – possibly a little of each – but it was desperately sad.

Adrian and Paula were looking a little awkward, not sure what to do for the best. 'You can play,' I said to them. 'Max can join in if he wishes or sit on the bench. It's up to him.'

'I'll sit,' he said, and lumbered towards the bench in the shade. Toscha had followed us out of the house and strolled over to join him.

'I'll sit with you,' Paula said to Max, suddenly losing her shyness. I think she felt sorry for him.

'So will I,' Adrian said. I saw Jill smile.

Max heaved himself onto the bench and Adrian sat on one side and Paula the other. Toscha sprawled at their feet.

'I'll leave the patio door open so you can come in when you want,' I said for Max's benefit. Jo, Jill and I then returned to the living room.

I was now expecting Jo to start talking about Max's obesity, including details of the diet he must surely be following and any appointments at the health clinic. But, draining the last of her coffee, she opened her notepad and said to Jill, 'What was the issue with Max's sister bringing his clothes here?'

'Cathy received a rather unpleasant telephone call from Max's mother earlier this afternoon,' Jill said evenly. 'She wasn't aware her contact details had been given to the family. We usually ask our carers first.'

Jo raised her eyebrows. 'His mother wanted the phone number of where Max would be staying and I didn't see a problem in giving it to her. He *is* in care voluntarily.' It sounded as though it was me who had the problem.

'It was quite a threatening call,' I said. 'Caz told me to give Max whatever he wanted or I'd have his father to answer to.'

Jo nodded dispassionately and made a note. 'I'll mention it to her when I see her later.'

'Does the family have Cathy's address too?' Jill asked.

'I'm not sure. I might have mentioned it but I think I just told her the area. She was quite insistent on a number of points before she agreed to Max going into care.'

'Given the nature of the phone call this afternoon, if she doesn't already have the address perhaps we could withhold it for now?' Jill suggested diplomatically. 'We can always review that later.'

'All right,' Jo said, and made another note.

I was grateful for Jill's support. I felt that Jo, like many social workers, didn't fully appreciate how worrying it could be for a carer to have an irate parent phoning or turning up on their doorstep. Social workers don't have this worry, as the families they deal with don't know their home address. While it's often appropriate for the parents of a child in care to have the foster carer's contact details, it didn't hurt to err on the side of caution to keep everyone safe.

Jill took a pad and pen from her bag. 'What are the contact arrangements?' she now asked.

'Caz wants to see Max every evening while she's in hospital, as she has been doing. His sisters have been taking him, but I assume Cathy will be taking him now?'

'Yes,' I said.

'Perhaps his sisters could take his bag to the hospital and Cathy could collect it from there?' Jill suggested.

'That would be good,' I added.

'I'll mention it tonight,' Jo said, making another note. 'Hopefully they can arrange it for tomorrow. It's too late this evening. They'll be on their way to the hospital now – they use the bus.'

'How long will Max see his mother for each evening?' Jill asked.

I picked up my fostering folder and pen so I had them ready to write down the contact arrangements. I start a new folder for each child.

'Caz said they have been visiting between five-thirty and seven, so I think keep to that.'

'Is that all right with you?' Jill asked me.

'I'll have to give the children their dinner before we go or it will be late by the time we get home,' I said, thinking aloud.

'OK,' Jill said. 'See how it goes. Max may be tired after an hour. It's a long time for a child to be on a ward. Do you want Cathy to stay on the ward with Max? She'll have Adrian and Paula with her, so it would be better if they could go and wait in the play area by the café.' A good support social worker is invaluable in clarifying arrangements and making sure they are practical for the carer.

'That should be all right,' Jo said. 'It's not supervised contact. But please be on hand in case Max wants to leave early.'

I wrote the times of contact on a sheet of paper in my folder. 'Will this start tomorrow?' I asked, mindful of the time. 'It's already five-thirty now.'

Jo glanced at the clock on the mantelpiece. 'Caz was expecting him this evening, but I take your point. I'm not going to be finished here for a while.'

'Perhaps Max could phone and speak to his mother this evening?' Jill suggested.

Jo nodded. 'I'll speak to Caz once I get there.'

'Will Max be seeing his mother at the weekend too?' I asked.

'Yes,' Jo said, as if it was taken as read. All very well, but that would mean any of our outings at the weekend, including visits to my parents, would need to be curtailed so we were back in time to take Max to the hospital. However, I knew this wasn't negotiable, as contact arrangements take priority over the carer's arrangements. Foster carers get used to fitting in.

'Will you be applying for a Full Care Order?' Jill now asked.

'Not at this stage,' Jo said. 'As long as I have Caz's cooperation, there shouldn't be any need to. She's cooperated in the past.'

'What have been the concerns?' Jill asked, meaning why were the social services already involved with Max's family.

'They've been mainly around the girls. They weren't going to school and two of them have been in trouble with the police. Caz was finding it a struggle to cope. She has various health issues, including type 2 diabetes and a heart condition, so we put in some support.'

'Is Max's weight due to a medical condition?' Jill asked.

'No, I don't think so,' Jo said lightly. 'His mother and sisters are all a bit chubby like Max. They like their food.'

I looked at her, amazed.

CHAPTER FOUR

A HEALTHY APPETITE?

In my view, there is a big difference between being 'a bit chubby' or carrying a few extra pounds and being clinically obese. Jo carried a few extra pounds, as did Jill and I, and many other adults of our age. Aware of this and the need not to add more extra pounds, and hoping to lose a few, I limited the amount of sweet foods I ate, as I know Jill did too. I was astounded that Jo could dismiss Max's size as 'chubby' and liking his food. Most of us like our food, but with so many enticing choices and food so easily available, we often have to moderate our intake for the sake of our health. However, it didn't seem appropriate to raise the issue now, as Jo had dismissed it, so other than asking her if Max was following a diet – he wasn't – I didn't say anything further on the matter at this stage. There was a lot to get through and Jo was going to the hospital after she left us.

'I'm anticipating Max will remain in care while his mother is in hospital,' Jo continued, 'and possibly for a while after she returns home, until she is able to cope again. But she's not being discharged yet. She had toes amputated two weeks ago and her foot isn't healing as it should. She can't manage on crutches yet. When I saw her yesterday her blood pressure was up, so she won't be discharged until that is under control again.'

Jill and I both nodded. 'Is the children's father living at home?' Jill now asked.

'Yes, although he doesn't have much involvement in the day-to-day running of the home or looking after the children. That falls to Caz. Max's sisters are older and reasonably self-sufficient, but obviously he needs looking after at his age.'

'Does Max have any allergies?' Jill asked, going through a mental checklist of issues that the carer needs to know.

'Not as far as I'm aware, but I'll check with Caz this evening,' Jo said, and made a note.

'Is Max up to date with his dental and optician check-ups?' Jill asked. Again, another standard question. If the child isn't up to date with these check-ups then the carer will usually book the necessary appointments and take the child to them.

'Dentist, I would think so,' Jo said, 'as Max had some teeth out not so long ago, but I'll ask Caz about the opticians.' She made another note. 'Now, school,' she said, moving on. 'The details are on the essential information form. His school is about a ten-minute drive from here. Max usually goes to breakfast club and Caz wants that to continue. She says he has a bowl of cereal before he leaves in the morning and then has a proper breakfast at school. It's already paid for, as are his school dinners, as the family are in receipt of benefits. Max has been staying at after-school club until around four-fifteen, but that's flexible. One of his sisters has been taking him to school and collecting him, but I'm assuming you'll do that now?'

'Yes,' I said. That Max went to breakfast club and after-school club would help me enormously, for it meant I could take him to school first and then go on with Adrian and

Paula. Then, at the end of the day, I'd do the reverse. The logistics of the school run are sometimes very difficult and I could find myself having to be in two places at the same time.

'His sisters went to the same school as Max,' Jo continued. 'Although there's a big age gap, some of the staff taught the girls so they know the family. Max is doing well at school and likes to read. His teacher, Mrs Marshall, is very nice and was a big help earlier when I had to tell Max he wouldn't be going home.'

'I'll introduce myself tomorrow,' I said.

Jo then went quickly through the essential information forms to see if there was anything she'd missed. I followed in my copy; I'd look at it again later in more detail. The box for information on cultural and religious needs showed that Max was British and nominally Church of England, and in the box for details of any challenging behaviour the word *None* had been written. Coming to the end of the form, Jo told Jill she'd make sure she was sent a copy and then passed me the place-ment agreement form to sign. This contained the consent I needed to legally look after the child and required my signa-ture to say I would foster the child in accordance with the foster-carer agreement and fostering regulations.

'I'll put copies of this in the post to you both,' Jo said as I handed it back. 'I think that's everything.' She looked again at the clock. 'Let's show Max around and then I'll be off.' It's usual for the social worker to see the foster carer's home when the child is placed, and specifically the child's bedroom.

I went into the garden and to the children. Max and Adrian were still sitting on the bench beneath the tree, talking quietly. Paula was now on the grass, stroking Toscha. 'All right, love?' I said to Max. 'Jo is going soon so we'll show you around the house before she leaves. You two can stay here if you want, as you know what the house looks like.' Adrian obliged me with a smile.

Max heaved himself off the bench and plodded towards me. 'I'm hungry,' he said.

'We'll have dinner just as soon as Jo has gone, all right, love?'

He nodded. 'Paula said we could have an ice cream.'

'Yes, after dinner.' It was a bit close to dinner now to have it before, I thought.

'I like ice cream,' Max said.

'So do Adrian and Paula.' I offered him my hand, as I would any young child, for comfort and reassurance, and he took it. Because of Max's size it was easy to forget he was only six. Rotund, he looked more like a portly little gentleman – Dickens's Mr Pickwick – rather than a small child. I could picture him in a waistcoat with a pocket watch.

Max also used my hand for a degree of support. I felt his weight, a pull, as we trod over the lawn towards the patio, then even more so as he hauled himself up the step. Taking hold of the edge of the patio door with one hand, he kept a grip on me with the other and levered himself into the living room with a small sigh, then dropped my hand.

'How are you doing?' Jo asked him.

'OK,' he said.

'It's a nice big garden, isn't it?' Jill said brightly.

Max nodded dispassionately, for of course the appeal of a garden to a child is that they can run and play in it, but Max's running and playing was so severely compromised that the garden would probably be just another hurdle to overcome, rather than a means of having fun.

'Cathy is going to show us around the house now, and then I'm going to see your mother at the hospital,' Jo said. 'As it's getting late I'll suggest to your mum she speaks to you on the phone tonight, rather than you visiting her. Is that OK?'

I was expecting a reaction – 'I want to see my mummy' or similar – as was Jill from the way she was looking at Max. But he just nodded stoically, apparently as accepting of this as he appeared to be of most things.

Jo and Jill now stood and I began the tour. 'This is the living room,' I said, addressing Max. 'We use this room the most and often sit in here in the evenings to play games or watch some television.' He nodded and I led the way out of the living room and into the kitchen-cum-diner, where I explained that this was where we usually ate.

'Something smells good,' Jill said, sniffing the air.

'Dinner, I hope,' I said. 'It's a chicken casserole. Do you like casserole?' I asked Max.

His eyes lit up, and with the most enthusiasm I'd seen since he'd arrived, he said, 'I love casserole.'

'Good.' I smiled at him. I showed them out of the kitchen, down the hall and into the front room. 'This is a sort of quiet room,' I said. 'If you want to sit quietly to read or think, or just be by yourself.' It contained a table and chairs, the computer, sound system, bookshelves and a small cabinet with a lockable drawer, where I kept important paperwork.

There wasn't much more to say about this room, so I led the way upstairs to Max's room – clean and fresh but sparse, without any personal belongings. 'It will look better once you have some of your things in here,' I said encouragingly to him.

He looked at me, puzzled. 'How will I get my things?' he asked sensibly.

'I'm going to ask your sisters to pack a bag for you and take it to the hospital tomorrow evening,' Jo explained. 'Is there anything in particular you want from home?'

Max looked thoughtful.

'Like your favourite teddy bear or toy?' Jill suggested.

'Buzz Lightyear,' Max said, referring to the toy from the movie *Toy Story*. 'He's on my bed.'

'I'll tell them,' Jo said.

'And my clothes. I haven't got any pyjamas.'

'Yes, of course,' Jo said.

'I've got pyjamas you can wear tonight,' I reassured him, although I knew the ones I'd taken out, which now sat neatly folded at the foot of his bed, would be far too small. I'd quietly change them later without a fuss.

Jo glanced out of the bedroom window and admired the view. This bedroom overlooked the rear garden, as did Adrian's room next door. I then pointed out the wardrobe and drawers to Max, where he would keep his belongings, and the pinboard on the wall for his drawings. He appeared to be a sensible child, so this would be the type of thing he might be wondering. There were already some posters on the walls and I told him we could change them or add to them. 'Perhaps some pictures of *Toy Story*?' I suggested.

He managed a small, brave smile, bless him. I appreciated there was so much for him to take in – a new home with everything different from what he was used to, and new people with different ways of doing things.

I showed them around the rest of the upstairs: Adrian's room, the toilet, Paula's room, the bathroom and finally my bedroom. 'This is where I sleep,' I told Max. 'If you wake in the night and want me, just call out and I'll be straight round. All right?'

He nodded, and we returned downstairs. Jo went briefly into the living room to fetch her bag and then joined us in the hall to say goodbye. 'His inhaler is in his school bag,' she reminded me. Then to Jill and me, 'I'll phone about the issues we discussed.'

'Thanks,' Jill said.

Jo said goodbye to Max and left. Jill, Max and I returned down the hall and Jill went into the garden to say goodbye to Adrian and Paula, while Max flopped onto the sofa. 'I'm hungry,' he said again, this time with a little groan.

'So am I,' I said. 'We'll eat as soon as Jill has gone.' It was nearly six-thirty, later than we usually ate, and I knew Adrian and Paula would be hungry too.

Jill came in from the garden. 'Well, have a good evening then,' she said to Max. He stayed on the sofa while I saw Jill to the front door. 'I'll phone you tomorrow to see what sort of night you've had,' she said. 'If you need to speak to someone tonight, phone our out-of-hours number.' I doubted I would with Max, but it was reassuring to know that twenty-four-hour support was always available from the agency if necessary.

Having said goodbye to Jill, I returned to the living room to check on Max, and as soon as he saw me he told me again that he was hungry. 'We'll have dinner now,' I said. 'While I dish it up, would you like to go into the garden and tell Adrian and Paula dinner is ready?' I could have called them myself through the open patio doors, but I find that if a child is involved in the routine of the house, they feel included and settle more quickly.

Max was happy to oblige and hauled himself off the sofa, while I went into the kitchen. Taking the oven gloves from their hook, I opened the oven door and carefully lifted out the piping-hot casserole. I set it on the work surface and began dishing it onto four plates. The children appeared and I asked them to wash their hands at the sink before dinner. I finished dishing up and returned the rest of the casserole to the oven, then went to the table and suggested to Max that he might like to sit next to Adrian. We tend to keep the same places at the meal table. 'I'm hungry, Mum,' Adrian said as they sat down, rubbing his tummy theatrically.

'So am I,' Max agreed, copying him with a rub of his tum.

I carefully carried the plates of food in from the kitchen and set them in front of each child. I added a basket containing chunks of warm baguette to the centre of the table and told them to help themselves. By the time I'd sat down with my plate Max had taken three large chunks of bread, which he propped on the side of his plate. 'There's plenty,' I said, for I wondered if he thought I might run out. I'd fostered children before who'd been so underfed at home that they grabbed and hoarded food whenever the opportunity arose, although I didn't think this was true in Max's case – it seemed to be more habit.

We all began eating and for a while all that could be heard was the chink of cutlery on china as three hungry children ate. When a child first arrives mealtimes can sometimes be awkward for them. Eating is an intimate and social occasion, with unspoken but assumed rules that can differ from household to household. I didn't even know if Max ate at a table at home; many children don't. And sitting close to people you've only just met can be embarrassing and make you feel self-conscious. I'd looked after children who felt so uncomfortable to begin with that they ate next to nothing for the first few days, and it's very worrying. Max showed no sign of being self-conscious, though, and ate confidently and heartily, mopping up the last of the gravy with another chunk of bread he took from the basket. Adrian finished at the same time and asked if there were seconds. He knew there would be.

'Yes, of course,' I said. I stood and picked up his plate. 'Max, would you like a second helping too?'

'Yes, please,' he said, and passed me his plate. Paula and I were still finishing ours.

I carried the plates to the kitchen, dished up seconds and also cut up some more bread, which I placed in the basket.

'Thank you,' Max said as I set his plate in front of him. He took some more bread, as did Adrian, and we all continued eating.

Paula is a bit of a slow eater and was still working on her first helping as both the boys came to the end of their second. Adrian sat back with a sigh of contentment and, patting his stomach, said, 'I'm stuffed.'

'Full,' I corrected.

Max was looking at me expectantly. 'Is there any more?' he asked.

'There is a little. But leave some room for the ice cream you wanted.'

'I've always got room for ice cream,' he said, with a small smile. It was a passing reference to him being overweight, but I didn't comment. I checked with Paula that she didn't want any more and then with mixed feelings spooned the last of the casserole onto Max's plate.

'Thank you,' he said. He began eating with the same urgency as he had the first serving, although I couldn't see how he could still be hungry.

Feeding one's family is laden with emotion unconnected with the food itself. As well as providing sustenance, cooking is a labour of love, and while I was pleased Max was enjoying the meal I'd made, I wondered how much of a disservice I was doing him by allowing him a third helping and all that bread, given his obesity. Wouldn't it have been kinder – and better for his long-term health – to refuse him a third helping and limit the amount of bread he'd eaten? But as this was his first meal with us I didn't think it appropriate to do so now, as it would have drawn attention to his need to diet. Similarly, when Max finished his main course and asked if it was time for the ice cream now, I said yes and dished it up. Two scoops for each child, but I didn't offer second helpings.

By the time we'd finished eating it was after seven o'clock and time for Paula's bed. I usually took the children up to bed in age-ascending order, so Paula, the youngest, would go first, then Max and Adrian. I explained to Max it was Paula's bedtime and asked him what he usually did at home in the evening before bed. I try to follow the routine the child has been used to at home as much as possible to minimize the disruption. Max said he read his book and it was in his school bag.

'Excellent,' I said. 'Adrian enjoys reading too. Perhaps you'd both like to sit in the living room and read while I take Paula up?'

Both boys fetched their school bags from the hall, sat side by side on the sofa and took out their reading books.

'What are you reading?' Adrian asked Max, interested.

'*James and the Giant Peach*,' Max said, showing him the front cover of the children's classic. It was quite advanced for the average six-year-old; Adrian, older, had read it earlier in the year.

'Are you enjoying the book?' I asked Max.

'Yes. I like Roald Dahl.'

'So do I,' Adrian said, turning to him enthusiastically. 'James's aunts, Spiker and Sponge, were horrible to him,' he added, referring to *James and the Giant Peach*. 'I'm glad he got away from them.'

Max agreed.

'Have you read *Charlie and the Chocolate Factory?*' Adrian asked.

'Not yet, but I've read *George's Marvellous Medicine*, and *The Twits*.'

'*The Twits* is so funny,' Adrian laughed. And so they began a discussion about Roald Dahl books.

They paused to say goodnight to Paula and we left them sitting on the sofa, discussing books and with the still-warm evening air drifting in through the open patio doors. I was pleased Max liked reading. I try to interest all the children I foster in books – with varying degrees of success – but Max was one of the few children who'd arrived with a passion for them. It was only later I discovered that there was another, more disturbing reason for him wanting to escape into books.

CHAPTER FIVE

RESTLESS NIGHT

While I was upstairs helping Paula get ready for bed I left her in the bathroom brushing her teeth for a few minutes and went into my bedroom to find some more pyjamas for Max. I took all the large sizes of pyjamas from the ottoman, holding them up as I went to see if they would fit him. Usually I'm quite good at judging a child's size, but in Max's case I had absolutely no idea. The ones that had 8–9 years old on the label seemed too long in the leg but not wide enough around the middle. The next size up, 10–11, seemed ridiculously big for a six-year-old, and 12–13 was gigantic. I couldn't decide, so I carried them all into Max's room for him to try on at bedtime, and removed the pair I'd previously put out.

Paula, having finished in the bathroom, was ready for a bedtime story and I went with her to her bedroom, where she chose a book from her bookshelf before climbing into bed with a yawn. I lay beside her, my arm around her shoulders and my head propped on the headboard as I read the story she'd chosen. When I'd finished she snuggled down beside me, ready for our usual cuddle and chat – part of her bedtime routine – before she went to sleep. Unsurprisingly, tonight she wanted to talk about Max.

'How long will Max stay with us?' she asked, kissing my cheek.

'I don't know yet, love. Until his mother is well enough to look after him again.'

'Does he miss his mummy?'

'I should think so, but he'll see her tomorrow at the hospital.'

'He's not crying like some children do.'

'No, he's been very brave, but I expect he's thinking lots about her and his family.'

'I'd cry if I couldn't live with you,' Paula said, snuggling closer.

'But that's not going to happen, is it?' I reminded her. 'If I had to go into hospital, Nana and Grandpa would come and look after you and Adrian. You know that.' Since my husband had left, comments and questions like this came up from time to time – from Paula and Adrian. Understandably they both felt a degree of insecurity with just one parent at home, and I always reassured them as best I could.

'Do you think Max eats too much?' Paula now asked with the candidness of a young child.

'Possibly.'

'He's very big, isn't he? I don't mean tall like big boys – his body is very round.'

'I know, but you wouldn't ever say that to him, would you?' I hoped that Adrian at his age had developed the necessary self-regulatory skills to stop him saying hurtful truths, but at Paula's age children are still highly impulsive and simply say what comes into their head without considering the consequences. Paula shook her head.

'Good. Because I'm sure Max knows he's overweight and he'd be very upset if you said anything.'

'Are you going to stop him eating so much?' she now asked.

'I might, we'll see how it goes.'

'I hope you do, then he can ride the bike.'

'OK, love,' I said, drawing the conversation to a close. 'We'll see. But in the meantime you can play other games with Max. Try to look beyond his size to the person within. I think he's a lovely boy, kind and gentle.'

'Yes, so do I,' Paula agreed. 'I promise I won't look at his big tummy but inside him.'

'Good girl.'

I kissed her goodnight and came out of her room, leaving her bedroom door slightly open so that I could hear her if she called out. Downstairs, both boys were still on the sofa, now talking about football and with their books open on their laps. I wasn't sure if they'd done much reading, but it didn't matter. They were getting along well and Max seemed relaxed. I was also pleased he hadn't needed his inhaler since he'd first arrived and his voice sounded far less husky. I hadn't heard from Jo about phoning his mother that evening, and as it was now getting late I rather assumed she wouldn't be in touch, as Caz was seeing him the following evening.

'Max, I think it's time for you to go to bed,' I said. 'What time do you normally go to bed at home?'

He shrugged. 'Any time, really. I go to my room and lie on my bed and read. Sometimes I fall asleep with my clothes on.' This didn't sound like a very good bedtime routine.

'When do you have your bath or shower?' I asked.

He shrugged again. 'When the bathroom is free. Sometimes I have a bath at the weekend.'

'So the last time you had a bath was last weekend?' It was Wednesday now.

'Maybe, or the weekend before. I can't remember.'

'OK. Don't worry. Would you like a quick bath now?'

He nodded.

I always encourage the children I foster to bath or shower every day, as good personal hygiene is obviously important, especially in the warm weather when we all sweat more. However, I'd never insist on it on their first night after the trauma of coming into care. Arriving at a stranger's house and having to take off all their clothes for a bath or shower could seem like another form of abuse for an already abused child, and so often carers don't know all the child's history. Max was happy to have a bath though, and I went upstairs with him to run it. I asked him if he usually had help with his bathing and he said he didn't, so I said I'd wait just outside the bathroom door while he had his bath and he should call if he needed me. I'd never leave a six-year-old completely unattended in the bath (or shower) in case they slipped and fell, but I always try to give the child age-appropriate privacy. I heard the water splash as he washed himself and after a few minutes I called out, 'Are you OK, Max?'

'Yes,' he returned. Then, a few moments later, 'I've finished.' It was a quick bath, but it would do for tonight.

'Good boy. Can you get out now and dry yourself?' I asked.

'Yes.'

'Then put the towel around you. I've put pyjamas in your bedroom for you to try on.'

A few minutes later he appeared cloaked in the towel and we went to his bedroom, where I told him to choose the pyjamas that fitted best while I put his school clothes in the wash so they were ready for tomorrow. Leaving him in his room trying on the pyjamas, I returned to the bathroom, gathered up his clothes and took them downstairs, where I set them to wash and dry in the machine. I looked in on Adrian in the living room, who was now reading, and I then returned upstairs. Max was still in his bedroom and I knocked on the partially open door. 'Have you got some pyjamas on?'

'Yes, but they're very long.'

The door opened and Max stood in front of me looking slightly comical with his hands and feet enveloped by the pyjamas. However, while the sleeves and legs were far too long, the set he'd chosen fitted around his middle. They were the largest pair, age 12–13 years, and another indication of just how overweight Max was. Clothes designed for a child twice his age fitted.

'Let's roll up the sleeves and legs for tonight,' I said, going into his room. 'I'll take them up properly tomorrow.'

'Mum cuts them off,' he said. He held out one arm for me to roll up and then the other. I did the same with his pyjama legs.

I could imagine it must be virtually impossible to buy clothes off the rail that would fit him, and his mother would doubtless have to adapt all his clothes. I returned to the bathroom with Max so he could brush his teeth, then I called down to Adrian that the bathroom was free. I would try to establish a better routine tomorrow that allowed time for the boys to do any homework they might have. However, I thought Adrian might have to take his with us to the hospital to do there, as we were going to be very short of time on school days. Thankfully this evening, apart from reading, which most school-age children are expected to do every day, neither Adrian nor Max had any homework.

On the first night I always ask the child I'm looking after how they like to sleep: if they like the curtains open or closed, their light on or off, and the bedroom door open or shut. These small details, which we do automatically for ourselves and our children, help the child to settle in a strange room. Max wanted his curtains slightly parted as many children do. He was happy to sleep with the light off and said he had his door closed at home so he didn't get woken by the noise his sisters made.

'It's quiet at night in our house,' I reassured him. 'Adrian and Paula will be asleep too, and when I come up to bed I'm very quiet, so I won't wake you.'

'I wish I had Buzz,' Max said as he climbed into bed, referring to his favourite toy.

'Jo is going to ask your sisters to pack it, so you should have it tomorrow tonight,' I reminded him. Then I had a thought. 'Just a moment. Stay there.'

I left his room and went round the landing and knocked on the bathroom door. 'Adrian, could Max borrow your Buzz Lightyear? Just for tonight.' Like many children, he had a collection of *Toy Story* toys.

'Yes,' he called. 'It's in the cupboard in my room.'

'Thank you.'

I went into Adrian's room and to the small built-in cupboard, which contained many of his toys. Buzz sat next to Woody on one of the shelves and I carefully lifted him down. I carried him into Max's room and his eyes lit up. 'Buzz!'

'Adrian said you can borrow his for tonight. Where would you like him to sit?'

'Just here,' Max said, patting a place on the bed beside him.

I positioned the toy as Max wanted and then asked him if he needed anything else. He shook his head.

'Goodnight then, love. Sleep well. Would you like a good-night kiss?' I always ask the child – for while a kiss is a sign of affection, it's also an invasion of their personal space and can make them feel uncomfortable – apart from babies and toddlers, whom I kiss and cuddle spontaneously and often.

'Don't mind,' Max said.

'Does your mum kiss you goodnight?' I asked.

'No. She watches television when I'm in bed.'

'OK. Night, love.' I kissed his forehead, and reminding him again to call me if he needed me in the night, I came out, drawing his door to behind me.

Adrian had finished in the bathroom now and was in bed, waiting for me to say goodnight. I lay beside him and we had our usual hug and chat, which tonight was mainly about school and the long summer holidays that would start at the end of the month. A quarter of an hour later I kissed him goodnight and left him to go to sleep. I checked on Max and Paula, who were both fast asleep, and went downstairs where I tidied up. Then, with a cup of tea and my fostering folder, I sat on the sofa in the living room and began writing up my log notes. Foster carers are required to keep a daily record of the child or children they are looking after, which includes appointments, the child's health and wellbeing, education, significant events and any disclosures the child may make about their past. When the child leaves this record is placed on file at the social services. As I worked the phone suddenly rang and I quickly snatched it up, hoping it hadn't woken the children. It was nine forty-five, rather late for a friend to be phoning for a chat, as most of my friends had young children.

'It's Caz, Max's mother,' she said, clearly annoyed. 'I thought Max was supposed to phone me.'

'I'm sorry. I was under the impression Jo was going to phone me with the arrangements after she'd spoken to you.'

'And she didn't?'

'No. I expect something came up and it slipped her mind.' I heard her tut. 'Max is fine,' I reassured her. 'He ate a good dinner, had a bath and is now in bed asleep.'

'So I can't speak to him if he's asleep.'

'I'd rather not wake him, if you don't mind. I'm sorry. It was getting late and with school tomorrow I thought he should go to bed.' In fairness to Caz, she had a right to be annoyed; she'd been expecting Max to phone her and due to a breakdown in communication, he hadn't. I was now expecting a rant, but she said, 'OK. Tell him I phoned. Goodbye.' And the line went dead.

A little unsettled and concerned that we hadn't got off to the best start – again – I picked up my pen and finished writing my log notes. Then I read the essential information forms, noting where Max's school was. A little before ten-thirty I returned the folder to the locked drawer in the front room, put Toscha to bed and went up myself. I checked on the children, who were all asleep, and then washed and changed and got into bed, leaving my bedroom door open so I could hear the children if they woke.

I never sleep well when there is a new child in the house. I'm half listening out in case they wake, frightened, not knowing where they are and needing reassurance. With Max there was the added worry that he might need his inhaler in the night. He hadn't needed it all evening so I was hopeful he'd have a good night. I'm a light sleeper and would hear him if he was restless. His inhaler was in his school bag in the hall and I could easily pop down and get it if it was needed. Jo was going to find out more about Max's condition and the directions his mother had been given regarding when the inhaler was to be used. If his mother had stayed on the line a little longer and had been less hostile, I could have discussed it with her. In the meantime I would use my judgement and common sense. All foster carers have first-aid training and I'd fostered children before who'd arrived with inhalers.

During the night I was repeatedly woken by Max, not because he was frightened or needed his inhaler, but because of his snoring. I'd never heard a child snore so loudly. In the still of the night, with the bedroom doors open, it echoed along the landing, creating a rhythm of its own. Beginning with some snorts and grunts, it rose with each breath to a crescendo, and then there was a short silence before it began again. I was so concerned he would wake Adrian and Paula that I closed their bedroom doors. Each time I went into Max's room he was flat on his back, fast asleep, mouth open and snoring heavily through his nose, although his chest sounded clear. He wasn't too hot and the room was well ventilated, so there was nothing I could do. If I tried to move him onto his side, which might have helped, I ran the risk of waking him with a start. I knew that snoring could be linked to a number of medical conditions and I would raise it with Jo when we next spoke.

At six o'clock, with very little sleep, I was out of bed earlier than usual to begin our new school routine. I showered and dressed, brewed coffee, fed Toscha and let her out for a run. Then at seven o'clock I returned upstairs to wake the children.

'Did you hear Max snoring?' Adrian asked me as soon as he was awake. His room was right next door to Max's.

'Yes. I hoped you hadn't been disturbed,' I said, concerned.

'It's OK. I wondered what it was to begin with, but when I realized it was Max snoring I went back to sleep.'

'Good.'

Paula didn't appear to have heard anything, and when I asked Max if he'd slept well, he said, 'Yes. It's quiet in this house, like you said.' Not for me, I thought.

'Do you know you snore?' I asked him lightly as I placed his freshly laundered clothes on his bed.

'Yes. My sisters say they need earplugs.'

I smiled and left it at that. There was nothing Max could do about his snoring, and I didn't want him to feel embarrassed by it. I asked him if he needed any help dressing, although I was pretty sure he didn't, as he seemed to have good self-care skills. However, children can panic in an unfamiliar setting if they are asked to do something they are not capable of. It's a horrible feeling and one I can remember from being a small child at school. I'd been asked by my teacher to deliver a message to a teacher in another classroom. This was a responsibility coveted by the class and I felt proud to have been chosen. But once outside the classroom I realized I didn't know where the other teacher's room was and I panicked. Instead of going back into the classroom and asking where I had to go (and feeling a bit of a fool), I began wandering around the two-storey building, hoping I would stumble across the correct classroom. I didn't, and I must have been gone for a long time, for eventually two other children from my class were sent to find me, and they then helped me deliver the message. Of course I felt silly and self-conscious when I

44

returned to the classroom, as everyone knew I'd got lost. With this in mind, I never assume a child can do something or knows something, even if it is obvious, until I am certain they are up to the task. We all acquire skills at different rates and it's crushing to have one's lack of knowledge highlighted through failure.

As it was, Max confirmed he didn't need help dressing, so I told him to come down to breakfast as soon as he was ready. That he was in the habit of having two breakfasts – one at home and then another at school – was of concern to me, but I wasn't about to start changing his routine straight away. Of further concern was the amount of sugar Max had on his cereal. Slightly disappointed that I didn't have chocolate pops, as he usually had at home, he chose wheat flakes, drowned them in milk and then began ladling on the sugar, heaped teaspoon after heaped teaspoon. Adrian and Paula watched, wide-eyed.

'I think that's enough sugar now, love,' I said after the fourth or fifth teaspoonful, and sliding the sugar out of reach.

Max grinned. 'My mum says I've got a sweet tooth.'

You won't have any teeth at all if you eat that much sugar, I thought, but didn't say.

Adrian and Paula had a bowl of wheat flakes too, with half a teaspoonful of sugar on each.

'Do you have another breakfast at school?' Max asked Adrian as we ate.

'No,' Adrian replied. 'We take a piece of fruit and a drink to have at morning break, and then at lunch I have school dinner.'

'Do you have to take in a piece of fruit?' I asked Max. I knew that many primary schools did this now.

'Some kids do, but I don't,' he said. 'I hate fruit.'

'What? All of it?' I asked.

'Yes.'

'What about bananas?' Adrian asked.

Max shook his head. 'Grapes are OK sometimes, but that's all,' he said. I could guess why he liked grapes – they're often very sweet.

'What's your favourite food?' Adrian asked.

Max thought for a moment. 'Chocolate cake with choco-late ice cream,' he said, smacking his lips. 'Yummy.'

'That's mine too,' Adrian agreed, although I couldn't remember him ever having both in the same dish.

'I like chocolate cake and ice cream,' Paula said, not want-ing to be left out of the conversation.

'What food do you hate the most?' Adrian now asked Max.

'Cabbage, carrots, broccoli, cauliflower,' Max reeled off. 'And tomatoes and the green stuff they give us at school. I leave it. What food do you hate?'

'Brussels,' Adrian said without hesitation.

And so the discussion about food continued as we ate and it was very insightful. By the end of breakfast I knew that Max actively avoided all vegetables and fruit apart from grapes, loved all things sweet, and that at home they lived off fast food and takeaways because his mother couldn't stand for long on her bad legs to cook, and his dad said cooking was women's work.

'Don't your sisters cook?' I asked casually as I cleared away the dishes.

'No,' Max said, leaving the table. 'Dad says they're too fucking lazy.'

Adrian paused and looked at me, aware this wasn't a word we used.

'I think I get the picture,' I said to Max. 'I'm so pleased *you* don't swear.'

'I get clouted at home if I do,' he said. 'But my dad can swear.'

'That's the problem with grown-ups,' Adrian commiserated. 'They can do things children can't, like stay up late and drive cars.'

'I know,' Max agreed. And the two boys went upstairs to brush their teeth and get ready for school, continuing their discussion on the numerous advantages of being an adult compared to being a child.

CHAPTER SIX

HOSTILE

I pulled up outside Max's school at 8.15 a.m. and parked in the road. I always introduce myself at reception on the first day, check that the school has my contact details and if possible arrange to meet with the child's form teacher. Not wishing to leave Adrian and Paula alone in the car, I brought them in with me. I went up to reception, where I gave the school secretary my name and said I was Max's foster carer.

'Really?' she said. 'I haven't been given your details.' Which was often the case. She suggested Max went through to join breakfast club while I completed the paperwork, as breakfast finished at 8.30. I told Max I'd collect him from after-school club and wished him a good day, and then the three of us said goodbye to him. With his school bag over his shoulder and dressed in just trousers and shirt, as the weather was still good, he waddled off down the corridor towards the dining room.

Adrian and Paula now sat on the chairs in the reception area, looking at the children's artwork displayed on the walls, while I filled in the forms with my contact details. Adrian and Paula had come in with me before when I'd taken a new child to school, so they knew they had to sit quietly while I completed the necessary paperwork. Once finished I handed the forms back to the receptionist and asked her where I should collect Max from the after-school club.

'It's held in the hall,' she said, pointing towards the corridor behind me. I then asked if I could make an appointment to see Mrs Marshall, Max's teacher.

'Now? I think she's busy.'

'No, I have to take my children to school. Can we make it another time?'

'I'll ask her when she's free and either she or I will phone you.'

'Thank you.'

Adrian, Paula and I returned to the car. I retraced the route, passed the end of my road and drove on to Adrian's school. Paula's nursery was on the same site and she attended five mornings a week. Having seen them both in, I returned home. I'd only been in a few minutes when the telephone began to ring. It was Jo and I could tell immediately she was stressed, and it was only 9.30 a.m.

'You didn't phone Max's mother last night,' she said. 'She's been on the phone and she's very upset.' My heart sank.

'I'm sorry. I did apologize to her. I must have misunderstood the arrangements. I was waiting to hear from you. I hadn't realized we were supposed to phone her.'

'I thought you didn't want her to phone you,' Jo said, misinterpreting. 'Well, never mind. As long as it doesn't happen again. You know what time you have to take Max to the hospital tonight?'

'Yes. Five-thirty.'

'His sisters will pack his bag and take it with them. I told them to bring his toy. Caz said she doesn't want you waiting on the ward, so you can go and do something and then return to collect Max around seven.'

'All right.'

'Don't be late, will you? She's not happy with you or me right now.'

'I won't.'

'Caz has given permission for Max to have a medical, so I'll set it in motion. You should receive an appointment letter in the post in a couple of weeks.'

'OK.'

'I asked Caz about allergies and she said she thought Max might have some but didn't know what they were. Sometimes he comes out in a rash, so just keep an eye on him.'

'Yes, I will.'

'She said to tell you to make sure he has his inhaler with him at school for his asthma.'

'Yes. It's in his school bag. He didn't need it again last night. It's blue – a reliever inhaler – so I'm assuming he just has it when he needs it.'

'I'll need to set up a review if he's with you for more than a few weeks,' Jo continued in a rush. 'I'll let you know. As I thought, Max has seen the dentist recently. He had to have some teeth out. Caz said he hasn't been to an optician but there's nothing wrong with his eyesight and he doesn't wear glasses. The paediatrician will give him an eyesight test as part of his medical, so if there are any concerns he can see an optician after.'

'All right,' I said. 'So I don't need to make an appointment for him to see either a dentist or an optician?' I wanted to clarify this to avoid any more misunderstandings. When a child comes into care under a court order the foster carer usually arranges both check-ups straight away and in time for their first review.

'Not at present,' Jo confirmed. 'So what sort of night did he have? I can't be long, as I'm due in a meeting now.'

'Max slept well, although he snores very loudly. It could be connected to his asthma, although his chest sounded clear. Has Caz mentioned it? There may be other reasons for it.'

'Like what? She hasn't said anything.'

'Enlarged tonsils and adenoids can cause snoring in children.'

'I'm sure she would have said when I asked her about Max's health, but I'll ask her when I see her. And you can raise it with the paediatrician when he has his medical.'

'Yes.'

'I think that's everything.'

'I found some pyjamas for Max to wear last night, but they were for age twelve to thirteen,' I said.

'He should have his own things by tonight,' Jo replied, missing the point. 'Make sure you're at the hospital for five-thirty. Speak soon.' And with a brief goodbye she was gone.

Twenty minutes later Jill telephoned to ask how Max's first night had been. I told her, and then about Caz's and Jo's phone calls and the misunderstanding over telephone contact. It's important for a foster carer to keep their support social worker up to date even on relatively minor issues, as they have a habit of escalating, and a missed contact – even phone contact – was certainly not a minor issue.

'Well, you apologized,' Jill said. 'Max is seeing his mother tonight, so hopefully that will make up for it. To be honest, my understanding was the same as yours: that Jo was going to speak to his mother first and then phone you.'

'Thank you, Jill,' I said, and felt slightly exonerated. I found Jill very easy to talk to and, as an experienced social worker, greatly valued her opinion and advice. 'On another matter, I am concerned about Max's weight,' I said. 'I haven't weighed him but you've seen him – he is badly overweight. Last night the only pyjamas that would fit him were for age twelve to thirteen. They were too long in the arms and legs but fitted around his middle.'

'Yes, he's certainly a big boy. What has Jo said?'

'Nothing. I appreciate he may not be with me for very long, but I feel I should do something to help him. His mother knows he has a sweet tooth, so I was thinking of limiting the sweet things he eats. And trying to get him to eat some fruit and vegetables, which he tells me he hates. I think it would be wrong of me to do nothing while he's with me.'

'I can't see any harm in limiting his sweet foods as long as you do it subtly, which I am sure you will do,' Jill said. 'The whole area of obesity is a minefield, not just in respect of childhood obesity but adults too. In one camp there is the "big is beautiful" and "it's the person I am" argument, while all the medical evidence is now pointing to obesity doing as much damage to our health as smoking. We had some foster carers a couple of years ago who were both badly over-weight,' she continued. 'They kept piling on the pounds until it was mentioned at their annual review in the context of it not setting a good example to the children they fostered. They took offence and left the agency. Although I heard later that when they applied to foster for the local authority they took the same view and refused them. I know you need a lot of willpower to lose weight, but as professionals working with children we have a duty to set an example by eating healthily and not smoking. But obviously don't make an issue of it.'

'I won't. Thank you.' I felt Jill spoke a lot of good sense.

'And Max went into school happily this morning?' she now asked.

'Yes. He likes school and reading. He seems to be taking being in care in his stride. He's a sweet child.'

'He's very likeable, rather a character. And you're OK to take him to the hospital tonight?'

'Yes. Jo has confirmed I can wait in the café.'

'Good. It will be nice for you to finally meet his mother. It should help your relationship with her.'

'I do hope so.'

'I'll be in touch then. You know where we are if you need us.'

'Thank you.'

We said goodbye and within five minutes the phone had rung again. This time it was the secretary from Max's school to say that Mrs Marshall could see me the following day at the start of her lunch break at 12.15 p.m. I thanked her, confirmed I'd be there and made a mental note to ask a friend to collect Paula from nursery, which ended at noon.

The afternoon disappeared. After Paula and I had eaten lunch, she amused herself while I cleared up and then prepared dinner. Although the logistics of the afternoon school run – collecting Adrian and then Max, fitting in dinner and then going to the hospital for contact – were manageable, I knew there wouldn't be a minute to spare. At 3.30 Paula and I were in the playground again to collect Adrian. Max didn't have to be collected until around 4.15, so we had time to pop home for a quick drink and to freshen up before leaving again.

Adrian and Paula came with me into the school and to the hall where Max's after-school club was held. He saw us as we entered and immediately stood and came over. I explained to the person in charge who I was and showed her my ID, which all foster carers now carry. She'd been informed that I would be collecting Max and, thanking her, we left.

On the way home in the car I asked Max if he'd had a good day as I always ask the children at the end of school. Max said he had, adding that he liked school and school dinners, particularly the sticky toffee pudding and custard they'd had today, of which he'd had second helpings.

Once home, the children washed while I put the finishing touches to dinner. There was just enough time for us to eat before we had to leave again at five o'clock to go to the hospital. I was pretty paranoid about being late after all the warnings from Jo and had one eye on the clock the whole time, but despite meeting traffic in the town we arrived at the hospital with ten minutes to spare. I knew the name of the ward and Max knew where it was from his previous visits. Using the handrail, Max hauled himself up the two flights of stairs and we went into the ward.

It was a typical National Health Service six-bed ward, with three beds on each side, separated by a bedside cabinet, chair and curtains, none of which were closed at present. Everyone had visitors, and even if one group of visitors hadn't looked over as we walked in I still would have guessed which was Caz's bed. At the far end of the ward on the left, three teenage girls were grouped around a bed, one sitting in the chair and the other two leaning against the bed. All were badly overweight.

'Hi, Max,' one of the girls called. 'Come here.'

He waddled down the ward and I told Adrian and Paula to wait just inside the door while I said hello to Max's family. They knew we were going to go to the café afterwards.

I went up to the bed as Max was giving his mother a kiss on her offered cheek. His sisters stared at me, looking me up and down, curious as to who was looking after their brother. I smiled. 'Hello, I'm Cathy. Nice to meet you all.' Then to Caz, 'How are you?'

She was propped on three pillows, the covers raised off her legs and feet by a curved blanket support. She completely ignored me and made a point of concentrating on offering Max a sweet from one of the many packets open on the bed. I'd experienced parents of children I'd fostered blanking me, or even being rude and aggressive, because they were angry at having their children taken into care. Clearly Caz was still angry with me. Apparently, so too were her daughters.

'Mum doesn't want to talk to you,' the girl leaning against the right side of the bed said to me.

The girl on the other side nodded. 'You should go,' she said rudely.

I looked at Caz, who kept her gaze down and was helping Max choose another sweet. 'I'll come back at seven o'clock then,' I said positively. 'I'll be in the café and play area if you need me.'

'Why should we need you?' the girl to the right said.

'In case Max wants to leave early,' I replied politely.

'He won't,' Caz said, still not looking at me.

I nodded, forced a smile and walked away to the sound of them whispering and laughing, probably about me.

Hiding my discomposure, I went to Adrian and Paula and we left the ward. I was hurt by Caz and her daughters' open hostility and rudeness. It wouldn't help Max either, witnessing that. Children in care often struggle with divided loyalties: wanting to like and get on with their foster family, while loving their own family. It can be very confusing and it helps the child enormously if they see everyone getting along. But clearly that wasn't going to happen yet.

We went up another flight of stairs to the play area and café, which were adjacent to each other. Children of various ages were already there. Adrian and Paula went over to play, while I sat at one of the tables and watched them, then after a while they came over and I bought us all a drink. I wondered if Max was thirsty, but I didn't think going back to the ward to ask if he wanted a drink would be welcomed by his mother right now. Adrian set about doing his homework while I read Paula a story, then she returned to play with another similar-aged child in the play area.

So the time gradually passed. Adrian completed his homework and Paula was happy to play. Just before seven o'clock I said it was time to go and we packed away. Paula called goodbye to the new friend she'd made and we returned to the ward. Again I told Adrian and Paula to wait just inside the door while I went over to Caz. There was only one of her daughters there now, the youngest, sitting in the chair by the bed and yawning while absently flicking through a glossy teenage magazine. She looked bored stiff. Max was leaning against the bed but straightened when he saw me. 'Are we going?' he asked brightly.

'Yes. It's seven o'clock. Have you had a nice time?'

'Of course he's had a nice time,' Caz snapped. I hadn't intended any harm by the comment. I always ask a child if they've had a nice time if they've been somewhere.

'Good. How are you doing?' I tried again with Caz.

'She's had her toes off,' her daughter said, stifling another yawn.

'And it bleedin' hurts,' Caz said forcefully to her.

'I'm sure it does,' I sympathized. I would have liked to engage Caz in a proper conversation, but clearly that wasn't going to happen, and Max seemed ready to leave.

'My bag is under the bed,' he said, struggling to bend down to retrieve it. I helped him pull the large zipper holdall from beneath the bed. 'They remembered Buzz, so Adrian can have his back,' he added.

'Who's Adrian?' Caz said, suddenly turning to me.

'My son. He's waiting over there by the door with my daughter.' She looked over and then returned her attention to her daughter. 'Any good celeb gossip in there?' she asked her, referring to the magazine.

'Nah,' she said, flicking the page and just looking at the pictures.

'We'll be off then,' I said. 'See you tomorrow.'

Caz turned to Max. 'Give us a kiss then.' She offered her cheek and he dutifully kissed it. 'And your sister.' His sister didn't move, so Max squeezed around the bed to where she sat and she lowered her cheek, just enough for him to kiss it, while keeping her gaze on the magazine.

'Goodbye,' I said to them both, raising another smile. 'Take care.'

But they kept their eyes down and Caz reached for the bag of sweets.

I picked up the holdall and we crossed to where Adrian and Paula were waiting and left. Some children become very distressed after separating from their parents at the end of contact, but Max seemed to deal with it in his usual pragmatic, matter-of-fact manner. He plodded along the corridor, then, taking the handrail, carefully manoeuvred himself down the stairs. By the time we were outside he was telling me he was hungry and asking if there would be time to have a snack before bed. I said there would be. We'd had an early dinner so it was reasonable for us to have a drink and a snack before bed. I asked Max if he'd been thirsty while he'd been on the ward, as he could take a bottle of water in with him next time. He said it was OK, as his sister had got him a bottle of cola. Then as I drove he asked if he could read in bed as he did at home.

'Yes, of course, love. Once you've had your bath and are in your pyjamas. I'm pleased you like reading, it's a nice way to end the day.'

It was 7.30 p.m. when we arrived home and the air was still warm, so the children ate the cheese on toast and cherry tomatoes I made for them sitting on the patio, while I took Max's bag upstairs to unpack. All children in care feel more at home once they have some of their belongings around them, and I always make it a priority to unpack. It would also mean that Max would have fresh clothes for tomorrow without me running the washer-dryer tonight. I set the bag on the floor and unzipped it. I found Buzz and sat him on the bed where Max liked him and returned Adrian's Buzz to his room. I began unpacking Max's clothes, folding and hanging them in the drawers and wardrobe. As I did I noticed that all the labels showed they were for age 12 or older, as the pyjamas he'd worn the night before had, and of course they'd all been shortened in the arms and legs. However, while his school uniform had been neatly turned up and hemmed, as had the one he'd arrived in, his casual clothes were either rolled up or fastened with a safety pin. His pyjamas had been cut to length and were now fraying badly at the raw edges. I wondered why Caz hadn't bothered to take up all his clothes properly, as it looked so much better and stopped the hem from fraying. There wasn't much in the holdall, and I was aware that some parents of children in care purposely didn't send many of their child's belongings to the foster carer, in the hope that the child would soon be home. Having unpacked Max's bag, I stowed it on top of his wardrobe. I went downstairs to start bringing the children up to bed and for a moment I thought Max had eaten the cherry tomatoes I'd put on his plate, but then Adrian said, 'Max didn't want his tomatoes, so I had them.'

'OK, love, but that won't do Max any good, will it?' I said lightly.

'I hate tomatoes,' Max said.

'They may not like you either,' Adrian quipped, and both boys laughed.

I took Paula up to bed first, then Max and Adrian, and by a quarter to nine all three children were in bed. Paula was fast asleep and the boys were reading. Downstairs I took the opportunity to check a few details in the essential information forms, the first being the names of Max's sisters. If I was going to meet them every evening, it would help to know their names and give me a better chance of establishing a relationship with them. I flicked through the sheets and found the page I wanted. They were called Kelly, Paris and Summer, aged seventeen, fifteen and thirteen respectively. Then I turned the page to the section that covered the reason Max was in care: he'd been left alone in the house while his mother was in hospital having her toes amputated. She had type 2 diabetes, and the primary cause of this condition was obesity. I struggled to understand why, having suffered so much, Caz appeared to be inflicting the same fate on her children, for clearly if something didn't change Kelly, Paris, Summer and Max were all going to suffer as their mother was.

CHAPTER SEVEN

JOINING IN

M ax was already snoring loudly when I went up to bed, so I shut all the children's bedroom doors, including his. Usually – unless a child specifically asks to have their door completely closed – I leave it ajar so I can hear them in the night if they are out of bed or upset, but I didn't want Adrian being woken up again, and Max had slept well the night before. Knowing him a little better now, I felt sure he would call out if he needed me. I left my door open though, and Max's snoring rumbled on in the distance all night, like a storm advancing and retreating. I would mention the snoring to the paediatrician when I took him for his medical.

The following morning we fell into our school routine and all three children were pleased it was Friday. Over breakfast (when I limited Max to one spoonful of sugar on his cereal) they talked about making a camp in the garden at the weekend. I thought this was a good idea, as it was a game Max could easily join in with. The weather was settled so I suggested we put up the tent on Saturday morning. It was a small one that the children sometimes used for playing.

'Why not tonight?' Adrian asked excitedly. Then remembering, 'Oh yes, there won't be time. We have to go to the hospital.'

'I don't mind if we don't go,' Max said, also delighted at the prospect of playing in a tent.

'Your mother will mind,' I said. 'We can put up the tent first thing on Saturday morning, even before breakfast. And you'll have all weekend to play in it.'

Max nodded, then looked thoughtful. 'I think I'd rather have my breakfast first,' he said.

'OK, love,' I smiled.

Sometimes I saw my parents at the weekend, but I'd purposely kept this weekend free to allow Max time to settle in. And, of course, we'd still be visiting the hospital on Saturday and Sunday from five-thirty till seven o'clock, but it wouldn't be such a rush without school.

I'd arranged for Paula to be collected from nursery by a friend of mine who had a similar-aged child at the same nursery so that I could meet Mrs Marshall; we'd helped each other out in the past. Paula was looking forward to going to her friend's house to play and I anticipated collecting her around one o'clock. I told Max I would be going to his school to meet his teacher and to hear how well he was doing in case he saw me in the building and worried about why I was there.

At 11.30 a.m., having prepared the dinner for that evening, I changed out of my jeans and T-shirt and into a pair of smarter cotton summer trousers and a short-sleeved blouse, then drove to Max's school, arriving at 12.10 p.m. The receptionist remembered why I was there and asked me to sign the visitor's book and then wait in reception for Mrs Marshall. At exactly 12.15 a lady approached with a friendly, 'Hello, Cathy Glass?'

'Yes.' I stood.

'Daisy Marshall. Lovely to meet you.'

'And you.' We shook hands. Dressed practically in a pleated blue summer dress, and with short, neatly layered grey hair, I guessed her to be in her late fifties.

'Let's go to my classroom to talk,' she said. 'There's no one in there.'

'Thank you for making the time to see me,' I said as we went. 'I know how busy you must be.'

'Not at all. I'm pleased you've come into school. I like to meet the foster carer as soon as possible if a child moves home. We don't have many children in care – last year one of our older children lived with a foster carer, but an aunt has him now.' With 70,000 children in care in the UK, most schools have experience of pupils living with a foster carer. 'How is Max settling in?' she asked.

'Very well indeed.'

'He's a lovely boy, I've got a lot of time for him.' Mrs Marshall opened the door to her classroom and we went in.

'You've been busy,' I said admiringly. The classroom was festooned with the children's work. Every wall was covered with paintings, drawings, pie charts, essays, poems and so on. Handmade bunting hung from the ceiling showing the different flags from around the world, and a magnificent model of a Roman village stood in one corner. There was also a nature table, the like of which I hadn't seen since my own school days.

'Yes, the children keep me on my toes, but I wouldn't have it any other way,' she said with a smile. 'Take a seat.' She drew out two of the children's chairs from beneath a table and we sat either side.

I'd taken an immediate liking to Mrs Marshall; she came across as a kind and caring person as well as a dedicated teacher. She was straightforward in her manner and I sensed she could be firm with her class when necessary.

'Max is a lovely child and a pleasure to teach,' she began. 'He's interested in learning and will join in and ask pertinent questions in class discussion. He's well above average in his learning, especially literacy. He loves reading. It's a form of escapism for him, as indeed it is for many people. Although now, sadly, watching television has largely replaced reading in many homes.' I nodded. 'However, I do feel sad when I see him sitting all by himself in the playground with a book instead of joining in with the other children. Of course, Max can't run and play like others his age because of the thing we're not allowed to talk about.'

I held her gaze. 'His weight?' I asked quietly.

'Exactly. It's a taboo subject with his mother, and apparently it's not politically correct to raise it with his social worker, although obviously she must be aware of the problem. Max struggles. If he had a learning disability, he'd receive all the help he needs, but obesity isn't being properly acknowledged and dealt with.'

'I know it limits what he can do,' I agreed. 'How does he manage in PE lessons?'

'He changes into his kit and joins in as best he can. He would rather sit and read a book, but it's important he has some exercise, just as it is for all the children. I know he feels self-conscious and I never suggest he tries something of which he is not capable. We have another obese child in the class, although she's not as overweight as Max, and she's on a diet and losing weight. Her mother wants her to exercise more, but I'm always sensitive to her and Max's limitations. By the way, Max's PE kit could do with a wash. I'll remind him to take it home with him tonight.'

'Yes, please do. I usually take the children's PE kits home every week to wash them. He hasn't come with a spare.'

'They can be bought here from reception.'

'I'll get an extra set on the way out.'

'I'll leave you to shorten it this time, save me a job,' Mrs Marshall said with a smile. I looked at her questioningly. 'You've probably noticed how the clothes that fit Max are for much older children. His mother rolls up the sleeves and trouser legs to make them fit, or fastens them with a safety pin. It's not nice for Max. The trousers unroll and he trips over them. Other kids notice. So I've been turning up his school uniform.'

'That's very kind of you, and also explains something,' I said. 'When I unpacked his bag last night I wondered why his school uniform was neatly turned and hemmed but his other clothes weren't.'

'It helps his mother, although I'm not sure she's noticed. The poor woman has so many health issues of her own to deal with. Have you met her?'

'Yes, briefly last night when I took Max to the hospital to see her.'

'She was supposed to be out of hospital by now, but I understand her foot is taking longer to heal than anticipated.'

'Yes. The care plan is that Max will stay with me until she is home and sufficiently recovered to look after him.' She nodded. 'Max has an inhaler, but doesn't seem to need it much,' I said. 'Does he have asthma?'

'I don't think so,' Mrs Marshall said. 'Max gets out of breath after exertion, but I think that's because of his weight. His mother has been committed to him having an inhaler for a long time and it seems the doctor has finally agreed. Many children in the school have inhalers now. Personally I think they're over-prescribed. One of my children had asthma – he still does – so I know the signs and symptoms. Max has used his inhaler once since he got it and that was after his sister, Summer, made him rush in, as she was going to be late for her school. He was out of breath but more panting rather than wheezing, which is what you hear when a child has asthma. But obviously I'm no doctor and we have to let him use it if necessary.'

'He's used it once with me, when he first arrived,' I said. 'He'll be having a medical before too long, so I'll raise it with the paediatrician.'

'I'd be interested to know what they say. And also what is said about his weight and going on a diet. Caz says it's their genes, and it's true they are all chronically overweight apart from the father. But when you hear what they eat, coupled with an inactive lifestyle, it's hardly surprising. As part of our "staying healthy" project in school all the children kept a food diary for a week and it was quite an eye-opener.'

'I'm limiting the amount of sweet foods Max has,' I said.

'Good. But we can't do that here in school unless we have the parent's permission and the child is following a special diet. We have a child with a nut allergy, another who has gluten intolerance, and the girl I mentioned earlier in the class who is trying to lose weight has a diet plan. The kitchen staff are aware of what these children can and can't have, but they can't stop a child having a second helping of pudding unless

they're told to do so. And the puddings here are delicious.'
She licked her lips.

'So I understand,' I said with a smile. 'Max said it was
sticky toffee pudding yesterday.'

'It was tasty.' She paused thoughtfully. 'I wish I could do
more for Max. He's bright and has huge potential but isn't
given the support he could be at home. There are no books in
his house and reading isn't encouraged, so he borrows books
from the school library and reads them in his bedroom. He
has a lot to contend with. He'd love a proper relationship
with his father, but he has little time for him and refers to
him as "Mistake". There's a gap of seven years between
Summer and Max, and according to Caz, Max *was* a mistake.
But it's not fair to make the child aware of it, and in some
ways he is very different to them.' Mrs Marshall paused and
a smile crossed her face. 'He reminds me of Matilda in the
Roald Dahl children's story. Do you know it?' I nodded.
'Matilda is bright and loves reading and learning just like
Max, but her parents don't and are so wound up in their own
lives that they don't recognize her worth. Eventually she is
saved by her teacher, Miss Honey. Perhaps you will be Max's
Miss Honey?'

I returned her smile. 'I will certainly do my best while he is
with me.'

'I know you will. And if Max ever mentions being bullied
let me know straight away, please. We have a strict anti-
bullying policy in this school and we keep a close eye on our
most vulnerable children, but we can't monitor them every
second, especially in the school playground. I have a quiet
chat with Max every so often, but I'm not sure he would tell
me if someone was being unkind to him.'

'I'll keep a lookout for it,' I said. 'Thank you for all you are doing for Max.'

'It's a pleasure. Pop in any time if you have any concerns. Academically, Max is doing very well.'

We said goodbye and I left the classroom and went to reception, where I bought a spare PE T-shirt and shorts for Max – size age 12. I returned to my car and collected Paula from my friend's house. She'd given Paula lunch, so, thanking her, I then took the opportunity while I had the time to pop into town to buy Max the *Toy Story* posters I'd promised him for his bedroom wall. I also bought a poster each for Adrian and Paula so they wouldn't feel left out, although they already had plenty on their bedroom walls, built up over the years. From town I drove straight to Adrian's school, collected him, then we returned home briefly for a drink before leaving again to collect Max.

Max came out of school carrying his PE kit for washing and a school bag weighed down with books. 'That looks heavy,' I said, taking the bag from him to carry.

'Mrs Marshall always gives me extra books to read over the weekend so I don't run out,' he said.

'Great. Although you are going to spend some time playing as well. We're going to put up the tent,' I reminded him. Having heard what Mrs Marshall had said about Max's social isolation and using books as a means of escape, both at home and in the playground, I thought it was even more important that he spent some time playing and interacting with Adrian and Paula. Reading is a lovely pastime, but children need to play with other children to develop their social skills, and hopefully have fun.

Once home I showed Max the posters I'd bought and he

was delighted with them. Adrian and Paula liked theirs too. I said I'd put them up later after we returned from the hospital, as there wasn't time before. I served the meal I'd previously prepared and as soon as we'd finished we set off for the hospital and arrived just before 5.30 p.m. As with the evening before, I left Adrian and Paula to wait just inside the ward while I saw Max to his mother. Had Caz and her daughters been more friendly I would have introduced Adrian and Paula to them. Parents of children in care often like to meet the carer's family, but Caz and her daughters didn't want anything to do with me, so I doubted they'd be interested in meeting my family. Caz was propped on the pillows as she had been the night before and her daughters were draped around her bed, popping sweets from the various bags open on the bed. They all looked bored stiff.

'Hello,' I said brightly as Max joined the throng.

'Kiss,' Caz said, pointing to her cheek. He went up and kissed her cheek, then, helping himself to a sweet, joined his sisters in lolling against the bed. I wondered what he would find to do for an hour and a half apart from eat sweets, and it crossed my mind that perhaps he should bring in a book to read. It was a long time for a young child to spend on a hospital ward, even if it was with his family.

No one had responded to my hello so I said a general, 'Have a nice time, see you later.'

'Bye, Cathy,' Max said. I smiled and left.

Following the same routine as the evening before, Adrian, Paula and I went up to the café and children's play area, where Adrian completed some of his homework – the rest could be done over the weekend – and I read to Paula, and then they both spent some time playing. There was another boy Adrian's age there and they had a few games of draughts. At seven o'clock we packed away and returned to the ward. Again, Caz's youngest daughter, Summer, was the only one still there, sitting in the chair, staring into space and twiddling her hair. For whatever reason, clearly the older two girls could go but Summer had to stay.

I smiled politely at them both, remembered not to ask Max if he'd had a nice time and said, 'OK? Ready to go then?'

'Bye, Mum,' Max said. 'See you tomorrow.' Kissing her cheek, he left her bed.

'See you tomorrow,' I said. Caz nodded and Summer just stared at me.

The ward was hot and stuffy and Max yawned repeatedly on the way out of the building, but once outside in the fresh air he perked up. 'Have we got time to put up my posters tonight?' he asked.

'Yes.'

'And tomorrow we're going to play in the tent?'

'We are.'

'I'm hungry. Can I have a snack when we get home?'

'Yes.'

And his face lit up at the prospect of eating, the thought of food giving him as much – if not more – pleasure as his posters or playing in a tent, which I thought, for a child of his age, was sad.

That night, as Max climbed into bed, with the *Toy Story* posters on his bedroom walls and Buzz Lightyear sitting on the bed, he said wistfully, 'I wish I was Andy, then all the toys could be my friends.' For anyone who doesn't know the film *Toy Story*, it is a computer-animated adventure story where the toys owned by six-year-old Andy come to life and have amazing adventures.

'It's a nice idea,' I said.

He nodded. 'I don't really have friends at school.'

'I'm sure you do,' I said, sitting on the edge of the bed. 'Mrs Marshall said what a lovely boy you are.' I'd already told Max in the car coming home from school that she'd said he was doing very well in lessons.

'If my toys were alive, I could play games with them. I don't play with anyone at school.'

'Why is that?' I asked gently. I was pretty sure I knew the reason, as Mrs Marshall had, but I wanted to hear what Max had to say.

'The kids play running games and I can't keep up with them,' he explained. 'They don't want me to play with them, really.'

'How do you know that?' I asked, inching the conversation towards the possibility of Max being bullied. 'Do they say something?'

He shrugged. 'Not really. They're not allowed to. It's the way they look at each other. I can tell from their faces they don't want me in their team.'

'I understand,' I said. It wasn't overt bullying but the result was the same, and clearly you can't force children to play with a particular child. In PE Mrs Marshall was in control and included and encouraged Max to participate, as she did the other overweight child in the class. The playground was very different and a free-for-all.

'I can't run like they can,' Max added quietly, picking up Buzz Lightyear for comfort. 'I'm very slow and I can't keep up. I get hot and out of breath and go red in the face.'

I nodded sympathetically. 'But perhaps you could join in with their games in a way that doesn't involve you running fast.'

'Like what?' he asked. 'All their games involve running.' Which was probably true, as children of this age are usually very active, especially after having to sit quietly during lessons.

'Well, let me see,' I said, thinking. 'What about this for an idea? If they play football you could offer to be the goalkeeper, or the linesman, or referee. You wouldn't need to run much in those positions.'

'That's true,' he said, 'but they play a lot of tag and other chasing games like stuck in the mud and shipwrecked.'

'OK. So you could be "home" or the "safe place"?' This was the person or place the child being chased could go to so they couldn't be caught.

Max looked thoughtful. 'That might work.'

'Have a think about it and I'm sure you can come up with ways of joining in. You read a lot of books and have a good imagination.' He nodded. Max hadn't mentioned his actual weight as being the problem. He hadn't said, 'I'm fat and I can't run fast enough.' His concern had been about joining in and I thought it best to deal with that issue. If he began talking about his weight and the need to lose some then I would do all I could to help him. But of course losing the weight would be a long-term goal and would require encouragement, willpower and the full commitment of his mother.

CHAPTER EIGHT

TEARS

On Saturday morning, when I went into Max's bedroom to see if he was awake, I found him sitting up in bed reading, which he told me he did at home at the weekends. Then he said that on Saturdays and Sundays and during the school holidays he had two breakfasts at home to make up for the one he didn't have at school, and would he be doing the same with me. I explained that we usually had breakfast and then a mid-morning snack, which he accepted, but it soon became clear that this wasn't enough for Max. Not only was he used to having two breakfasts, he also ate constantly throughout the day, given the opportunity. I sensed that eating had become a habit for him – a pastime – rather than resulting from any pressing need to satiate hunger, which is what usually drives healthy eating. Max told me that at home he and his sisters helped themselves to biscuits, packets of crisps, chocolate bars and drinks of cola and lemonade whenever they wanted to. He said he ate these snacks in his bedroom, where he appeared to spend most of his time, as the television was always on in the living room with programmes about celebrities that his sisters liked. Of course, Max could have some snack foods with me, but in moderation, and I hoped to replace some of them with healthier alternatives.

After breakfast, when the children were washed and dressed, we took the tent from the shed, laid it on the lawn and everyone helped to erect it. This was an activity Max could fully join in with and it was lovely to see him so involved, trying to decide which tent pole fitted where (as indeed we all were, for we can never remember from the last time), then helping to hammer in the stakes. In this activity at least he was on an equal footing with everyone else and size didn't prevent him from participating. Even so, the exertion of assembling the tent and hammering in the stakes caused him to go red in the face and break out in a hot sweat, which it wouldn't have done to a slimmer, healthier child.

Once the tent was up Max asked if it was time for the mid-morning snack and I agreed it was. I went indoors to make the snack and pour drinks while the children fetched some toys they needed for the imaginary game they were planning to play in the tent. When I returned, carrying the tray, the door to the tent was zipped shut and I had to give the password before it was opened. Adrian took the tray and explained I was now the enemy alien and I had to leave the area immediately or I would be zapped. Max, meanwhile, having given it some thought, asked if this snack was his second breakfast or would he have a snack as well later. I said it was a mid-morning snack and the next meal would be lunch – obvious to us, but Max's routine at home had been very different to ours. I then quickly left the area to avoid being zapped.

While the children played I decided to take the opportunity to turn up Max's new PE shorts, and also his casual trousers from home. I worked in the living room, where I could keep an eye on the children. Having eaten their snack, they were in and out of the tent, playing. The PE shorts I'd bought were for age twelve and would have come halfway down Max's shins rather than his thighs, so I used the pair Mrs Marshall had turned up as a guide. I cut off some of the length and then turned and hemmed the edge. I didn't cut off the excess from Max's casual clothes that had come from home though; I just turned them up with neat hemming stitches. Foster carers have to be very careful in respect of the child's possessions that the parents have bought. All these are the property of the parent and have to be returned to them intact, whether the child goes home or not, even those the child has outgrown or worn out. Had I cut the extra off the trousers, I could have been accused of damaging them. As it was, Caz could let them down again and restore them to how they were if she wished.

Once I'd turned up the clothes I pressed them with a hot iron and damp cloth and returned them to Max's wardrobe. Downstairs again I stood on the patio, watching the children play for a while. Toscha had gone into the tent (of her own accord) and the children were now hunting the jungle for other ferocious lions and tigers. Adrian was leading the hunting party and Max and Paula were following, Paula having slowed her pace so Max could comfortably keep up. Presently I went over and asked them if they'd like a packed lunch in the tent rather than coming inside to eat. There was a resounding yes, so I suggested they use the bathroom and wash their hands ready. I returned indoors and made up three packed lunch boxes, containing sandwiches, a packet of crisps, a piece of fruit, a yoghurt and a drink. I took the packed lunches to the tent where the door was now open to let in more air, as it was hot inside, then I ate my sandwiches on the patio, enjoying the lovely weather. Once finished the children brought their rubbish to me, but then no more than thirty minutes later Max came to me and asked if it was time for a snack yet. I thought he couldn't really be hungry, so I explained we'd have a snack mid-afternoon and then dinner at five o'clock before we left for the hospital.

Fifteen minutes later Max asked me again if it was time for a snack, and then I overheard him ask Adrian if he wanted a biscuit, meaning he wanted one. 'Not fussed,' Adrian said, too busy playing. Max's thoughts even when playing weren't far from food, which I supposed was a result of his habit of snacking all day. Halfway through the afternoon I gave them all ice cream and fruit in a bowl, and I also made sure they had plenty of water to drink all day, as it was hot. They'd had juice with their lunch and Max seemed happy to have water.

At 4.30 p.m. I said we needed to start packing away, ready to have dinner and go to the hospital, and I asked them to bring in their toys – the tent could stay up. They'd spent all day playing nicely together and I was pleased.

I always like the children I foster to look smart for contact, so after we'd eaten I set out a fresh set of clothes for Max on his bed and he changed into them. We then left for the hospital and in the car I heard Max say to Adrian that he really liked playing in the tent and could we do it again tomorrow.

'Yes,' I said. 'Also, I was thinking, we could go to our local park for a while. It's got swings and other play apparatus, and a duck pond.'

'Great!' Max said excitedly. 'I haven't been to a park in ages. Mum can't take me.'

'Because she's been poorly,' I said, although I wondered why one of his sisters or his father couldn't have taken him to a park for a while.

We arrived on the ward on time to find Caz and her daughters arguing. It became immediately apparent what it was about. It was Saturday evening and the older two girls, Kelly and Paris, were leaving earlier than usual to go out, while Summer had to stay behind with her mother.

'It's not fair,' Summer moaned. 'I'll miss my favourite television programme again.'

'I'm not sitting here all alone like a wally on a Saturday night,' Caz said, clearly put out.

'So *they* can stay with you,' Summer said, jutting out her chin and referring to her older sisters. 'It's always me that has to stay. It's not fair.'

'Because you haven't got anything better to do,' Kelly said, which clearly didn't help the situation.

But I could appreciate that sitting on a hospital ward night after night wasn't much fun for Summer, especially on a Saturday when her sisters were going out, although I'm sure all the girls loved their mother. I took the opportunity of a gap in the exchanges to say hello, which was ignored. Max made his way to his mother, squeezing past Kelly to get to her. 'See you later then,' I said. 'Have a nice time.' And I left.

Upstairs in the café Adrian finished off his weekend homework so he wouldn't have to do it tomorrow, then he and Paula played for a while; there were only a couple of toddlers in the play area that night. I bought us a drink and then Adrian read his book while I read a story to Paula. Every so often Adrian glanced at the wall clock. 'Not much longer,' I said. I felt sure that Adrian, like Summer, would rather have been at home, probably still playing in the garden on a fine summer evening, than waiting here.

When we returned to the ward Summer was in the chair beside the bed as usual. Caz was propped up on her pillows and both were staring into space, having run out of conversation and sweets. Max looked pleased to see us and, giving his mother a quick peck on her cheek, made his way to my side. 'Hopefully you'll be able to go home before too long,' I said to Caz, appreciating how boring it must be for her to have to stay in hospital.

'Hopefully,' she agreed. It was the nearest we'd had to a conversation.

'Can I go now? Max is,' Summer asked her mother. 'I've got an hour's bus ride.'

'If you want,' Caz said with a dismissive shrug. 'You're no good when you've got a face on you. And don't talk to strangers.' Summer rolled her eyes.

'Would it help if I gave Summer a lift home?' I asked Caz. 'It's not far out of my way.'

'Yes,' Summer said, her face immediately losing some of its grumpiness. 'Then I'll be able to watch *Whose Date Is It?*'

'It's up to your mother,' I said.

Caz nodded. 'Save me giving her the bus fare.' Summer stood and began to walk away from the bed. 'Haven't you forgotten something?' Caz said. Summer returned and kissed her mother's cheek.

'Bye,' I said. 'See you tomorrow.'

Caz nodded.

Outside the ward it soon became clear that Summer had a bit of a dilemma. Should she remain loyal to her mother and continue to be hostile towards me, which would be a little awkward as I was giving her a lift home, or was it OK to talk to me? She began by making a point of talking to Max with her back to me and then, once in the car, settled in the passenger seat beside me, she turned and gazed out of her side window.

'I don't know your exact address,' I said as I drove, 'so when we get closer, can you direct me to your home?'

'Yes,' she said, and then added, 'Thanks.'

'You're welcome. I watch that programme *Whose Date Is It?* sometimes,' I said, trying to make conversation.

'I see it every week,' Summer said, glancing at me. 'I always guess who is the best match and gets to go on the date.'

'Really? I'm usually way out.'

'Last week I knew it would be that guy with the blond hair …' she said animatedly, and with the ice now broken she began chatting easily about the programme and conversation flowed. We talked about other television programmes she liked too, and then I remarked that it must be difficult at home with her mother in hospital, and they must miss her.

'Yeah, we do,' Summer admitted. 'And Max. Even though he spends most of his time in his room with his head in a book, you just know he's there and it's strange without him.'

'It's strange without you too,' Max's voice came from the back seat.

Summer turned. 'Big ears,' she said affectionately to him. 'Anyway, Mum should be home soon.' She returned her gaze to the front.

'That's good.'

'She said they're making her get out of bed and walk more. She doesn't like it, but the nurse said she has to walk to get ready for going home.'

I nodded. 'I'm sure she'll be pleased to get home.'

'Dad doesn't think so. He says she likes lying in bed all day with nothing to do but eat and sleep.'

It was the first mention I'd heard of their father.

'Does your dad visit her much?' I asked. I hadn't seen him.

'He's been once,' Summer said. 'He says he can't stand the smell of hospitals. Kelly told him he should go, but I think he might be right that Mum likes it there. It's better than being moaned at by him all day.'

'Your dad moans at your mum?' I asked.

'Yeah, and me and Kelly. Max keeps out of his way. Paris is his favourite. He likes her and buys her loads of stuff. But we all got a bollocking when we left Max alone and he had to go into care.'

'I can imagine,' I said.

'I'm leaving home as soon as I can,' Summer continued. 'My mate and me are going to be hairdressers and live in London so we can do the celebrities' hair. They have it done lots, some of them every day.'

'Do they?'

'Yeah. Before every photo shoot.'

I smiled. Many teenagers have dreams of living in the city and mixing with celebrities, although I was sorry to hear that Summer felt her father favoured one of her sisters more than the others. Parents shouldn't have favourites; they should love, respect and care for their children equally. If a child grows up feeling second best, it can undermine their confidence for life.

We were now approaching the area where Summer lived and I asked her for directions. A few left and right turns later I pulled onto the estate and then stopped outside her house –

about a ten-minute drive from where I lived. She thanked me for the lift and then, turning in her seat, said goodbye to Max. 'What are the names of your kids?' she asked me.

'Adrian and Paula.'

'Goodbye, Adrian and Paula,' she said.

'Goodbye,' they returned.

'See you tomorrow,' I said to her as she got out.

I waited until she'd let herself in through the front door before I pulled away. I knew it had been positive for Max to have seen Summer getting along with me, and sure enough, a few minutes later, he said, 'You like my sister, don't you?'

'Yes,' I said, glancing at him in the interior mirror. 'And I like you too.'

He grinned back at me.

Once home we followed our usual evening routine of a snack and a drink, and then bath and bed. Once the children were in bed I wrote up my log notes, including that I'd given Summer a lift home from the hospital. I wondered at Summer's comments about her mother preferring to be in hospital rather than at home and being nagged at by her husband. It didn't sound like a very happy home to me, but Jo had said the social services had been involved with the family for some time, so I assumed she was aware of this.

The children slept well, undisturbed by Max's snoring, which I heard from time to time even though his bedroom door was closed. The following day, Sunday, I decided to take the children to the park in the morning before it became too hot, so after breakfast I packed bottles of water and Max's inhaler in case he needed it. I didn't suggest we take the bikes to the park as I often did with Adrian and Paula, as it would have highlighted Max's inability to ride a bike of any size. If he was still with us during the long summer holidays then I would take the bikes sometimes, as it would be unfair to deprive Adrian and Paula of riding all summer. As we set out Max asked why we weren't using the car to go to the park and I explained that it was only a short walk. Mindful of the strain that walking put on him I kept the place very slow. Even so, he was red in the face and sweating by the time we arrived at the park. He sat next to me on a bench for a while as Adrian and Paula played, although he didn't need his inhaler.

Max watched the children play on the apparatus for some time and eventually summoned the courage to go to the swings when one became free. I saw him tentatively sit on it, but then it became obvious that he didn't know what to do to get the swing going. I went over and explained and then showed him, but he struggled. He was pretty uncoordinated, so I pushed him for a while. Used to pushing little children and those of average weight, I was served another reminder of just how heavy Max was, although obviously I didn't show it. After he left the swing he walked around the play area for a while, looking at but not trying any of the other activities. Normally when I fostered a child who was timid or reluctant to try new things I encouraged them, but I appreciated that Max's reluctance was probably due to his size – he knew he would struggle to use the apparatus and I didn't want to suggest something that could make him look ridiculous in front of others. I was aware, as Max must have been, that other children were looking at him. His arms bulged from his short-sleeve T-shirt and the rolls of fat beneath his clothes were obvious. Although I'd turned up his trousers so he wouldn't trip over them, he was so thick around the waist that he was nearly as wide as he was tall. I hesitate to use the phrase but he was like a little barrel, and other children noticed and stared. Presently I suggested we went to see the ducks and we left the play area.

Max enjoyed seeing the ducks and spotting the goldfish that swam to the surface every so often in search of food. The kiosk selling drinks and ice creams was visible from the pond and he pointed it out. When we'd finished at the pond we went over and I bought them all an ice cream, but not the cola drink Max also wanted, as we had bottles of water with us. Licking the ice creams, we began a slow walk home with Max melting as fast as his ice cream. Once home the children sat in the cool of the living room to recover, then went into the tent, where they spent most of the afternoon doing puzzles and crayoning (and Adrian also taught Max a simple card game), only coming out for lunch and then dinner. With school the following day and rain forecast, I packed away the tent before we left for the hospital, and whereas when we'd erected the tent I'd had lots of helpers, now it was left to Paula and me to put it away. But it didn't take long – it was much easier to disassemble than assemble – and five minutes later it was packed away and in the shed, ready for next time.

That evening, when we arrived at the hospital, Max's sisters were all there and Summer threw us a small smile, so she at least was less frosty. I made a stab at conversation with Caz, Paris and Kelly but it was ignored. When we returned to collect Max only Summer was there and I asked Caz if she would like me to give her a lift home again.

'No. She's staying until eight,' she said. Which was the end of visiting time.

Summer pulled a face at her mother, but it wasn't for me to interfere.

Once home we fell into our evening routine and with school the next day I set out Adrian's and Max's uniforms, ready for the following morning. Max appeared very quiet and pensive as he got ready for bed and I asked him if he was all right. He gave a small nod. I wasn't convinced. 'Max, is there anything bothering you?' I asked as he climbed into bed. He nodded again. 'Can you tell me what it is?'

He hesitated. 'You won't be angry, will you?'

'No.' But my heart was already thumping loudly. What on earth could Max have done? 'What is it, love?' I coaxed. 'What's bothering you?'

He slid his hand under his pillow and pulled out a crumpled sheet of paper. 'I was supposed to give you this, but I hid it.'

I frowned, puzzled, as I unfolded the paper. It was a standard printed letter from his school, sent to all parents and beginning, *Dear Parent or Guardian*. This one was about the arrangements for the school's annual sports day, due to take place on the coming Friday.

'OK,' I said, glancing up. 'I'll make a note of the time I have to be there.' Parents and carers of the children were invited to watch, and I assumed that as his mother wouldn't be able to attend then I would go instead, although I'd mention it to Caz when I next saw her.

'No, you don't understand. I can't go,' Max said anxiously.

'Why not?'

'Look at me. I can't take part in sports day.' And he burst into tears.

CHAPTER NINE

ACT OF DEFIANCE

As I held and comforted Max I could picture only too clearly the embarrassment school sports day would cause him. It was supposed to be fun, when all the school came together to show off their fitness and agility skills in healthy competition – although I didn't remember my school sports days with relish. I wasn't overweight, but neither was I very good at sport, and regardless of how hard I tried, I always came near the end in a race – not last, but well back from the leaders. In high jump and long jump my legs didn't seem able to generate the necessary spring to propel me high enough or far enough, and I remember how self-conscious I felt in the qualifying heats when I tried and failed, with the rest of my class watching. Then there was the relay race, in which we all had to participate, but I could never run as fast as the person passing the baton to me or to whom I passed it, so I always felt I'd let down the team. The fun races at the end were OK – the egg and spoon race, sack race and three-legged race, but they were just for fun and held little in the way of true competition or achievement. Looking back, my performance was probably average for my age, but it didn't feel like that at the time, so I had every sympathy for

Max, whose obesity put him at such a disadvantage in most physical activities.

'Come on, love,' I said, passing him a tissue. 'Dry your eyes. We'll sort something out.'

'Can I stay at home, please, and pretend I'm ill, like I did last year?'

I helped him wipe his eyes. 'If that's the only way, but first I want to speak to your teacher and see what she has to say.' Given how sensitive Mrs Marshall was to Max's limitations, tailoring his involvement in PE lessons, I wanted to discuss it with her first.

Eventually Max's tears subsided and I put my arm around him and gave him a hug. With more reassurance that he wasn't to worry about sports day and no one would force him to participate, he lay down, ready for sleep.

'I wish I wasn't so big,' he said wistfully. 'It's because I eat too much, isn't it?'

'It's the most likely reason, yes. We get energy from the food we eat and what we don't need is stored in our body as fat.'

'So how do you get smaller?' he asked. Cleary the subject hadn't been discussed at home.

'By eating a little less each day, especially sweet things. And exercise, like walking rather than going in the car, which you are doing here with me.'

'Why don't my sisters and mum do that?'

'I don't know, love.'

'My dad says he likes big women.'

'Does he?'

'Shall I try to eat less sweet things so I can run in sports day?'

'Yes, but it takes quite a long time. You won't suddenly see a change. It takes many months to lose weight, sometimes years. But please don't worry about sports day. I'll sort something out.' And so the conversation ended as it had begun, with me trying to allay Max's fears about sports day.

I sat with him a while longer to make sure he was ready to go to sleep and wouldn't lie there worrying. It was late and we had school in the morning, so I didn't suggest he read for a while. When I was satisfied he was slowly drifting off to sleep I kissed his forehead, said goodnight and came out.

Paula was already in bed asleep and Adrian, aware that I was spending longer than usual with Max, had come up and got ready for bed and was now in bed waiting for me to say goodnight. Adrian's school had already had their annual sports day, and because Adrian was reasonably fit and athletic he'd met the day with excitement – a challenge – not dread. And he'd done very well.

When I wrote up my log notes that night I included Max's anxiety about his school's sports day and the discussion we'd had about losing weight. As well as containing appointments and charting the child's day-to-day progress, the log can act as an aide-mémoire. It's easy to forget what happened or was said on a particular day months later, and I'd learnt from experience to be conscientious in my record keeping. I'd once been asked to check my log notes in respect of a child who'd left me nine months previously, when a child protection matter arose and the case went to court. So regardless of how tired I was, I always updated my log before I went to bed, while the events of the day were still fresh in my mind. Jill checks them each month as part of her statutory visit.

* * *

There wasn't time to try to see Mrs Marshall when I took Max to breakfast club the following morning, as I had to take Adrian and Paula to school and nursery straight after. Once home, I telephoned Max's school secretary and said I'd like to arrange to speak to Mrs Marshall and asked when it would be a good time for me to phone. I didn't think this necessitated us meeting, as it was something that could be discussed over the phone. The secretary said she'd speak to Mrs Marshall and let me know. Then, at eleven o'clock, the phone rang and it was Mrs Marshall, taking the opportunity to call while the children were in the playground on mid-morning break.

'Thank you so much for phoning,' I said. Aware that her time would be short I came straight to the point. 'Max was very upset last night because of sports day. He tells me he was so worried last year that he took the day off school. He wants to do the same this year, but I said I'd speak to you.'

'Oh dear, the poor child,' she sympathized. 'He should have told me rather than worrying.'

'Exactly, but he thinks if he goes into school on Friday he will be made to participate.'

'It's true we like all the children to join in, but our sports day, like in many other primary schools, is different now from what you and I remember. The children compete as teams, not individually, so there is no pressure.'

'How does that work?' I asked. Adrian's school sports day was traditional and similar to the ones I remembered.

'They compete in their house teams,' Mrs Marshall explained. 'The children are divided into their four house teams and each team consists of all ages of children, from Reception to Year 6. The teams then rotate around fun activities; for example, an obstacle course, shuttle run, hockey dribble, beat the goalie and so on. They collect points for their house. They have regular breaks when they have a drink of water, and each activity only lasts about five minutes. At the end all the children receive a sticker and the trophy is presented to the house with highest number of points.'

'I see,' I said. 'So Max would be in a team with older and younger children, and always competing as part of the team?'

'Yes. There's no pressure on any individual child, and some children do sit out from time to time. Some need to use an asthma pump and some just need a rest. I'll talk to Max and explain again what happens. I'm surprised this wasn't made clear to him last year, but perhaps his teacher wasn't aware how anxious he was about sports day.'

'It took a while before he would tell me. Thank you so much. I didn't want him to just stay at home.'

'No, he needs to join in as much as possible. How was he at the weekend?'

'Good. He played with my children during the day and then I took him to see his mother in the evening. His sisters were there.'

'He told me he'd been playing in the tent with Adrian and Paula. Let me know if he has any other worries, won't you? And I'll look forward to seeing you at sports day.'

I thanked her again and we said goodbye.

I was very pleased I'd spoken to Mrs Marshall. I felt considerably relieved, as I hoped Max would, and easier about him participating in sports day, although of course even team events could hold some anxiety for him. But I agreed with Mrs Marshall that he should join in, and I'd do all I could to reassure him, as I knew she would. Feeling the week had got off to a good start, when the phone rang again a few minutes later I answered it with a bright 'Good morning'.

'Cathy, it's Jo, Max's social worker,' she said, her voice tight and flat, so I knew straight away it wasn't good news. 'Max's mother telephoned me first thing this morning with a list of complaints about his care.' My heart sank. I always try to do my best for the children I look after and it was soul-destroying to receive one complaint, let alone a list. 'I told her I'd speak to you straight away.'

'Oh dear. What am I supposed to have done?' I asked.

'Firstly, and most worryingly, she says you're not feeding Max properly. She says he's always hungry and that you won't give him second helpings. She said you refuse to let him have any biscuits, cakes and sweets and keep putting stuff on his plate that he doesn't like. He's told her there are no fizzy drinks in your house so he has to drink water, which he doesn't like. She also says you're too stingy to use your car so you make him walk everywhere. He hates walking. Then there's the matter of his clothes – she says you've ruined them. There's other stuff, but those are the main ones.' I heard her let out a sigh of exasperation.

As well as being hurt, I was now annoyed – not with Max, for I doubted he'd complained; it wasn't in his nature. I thought that Caz (and possibly her daughters), still angry at having Max in care and wanting to make my life difficult, had seized on comments Max might have made, exaggerating and twisting them to put me in a bad light.

'Jo, the last point first,' I said as calmly as I could. 'I'm assuming Caz is referring to the fact that I've taken up Max's trousers.'

'I think that's what she said.'

'Because of Max's size, he needs clothes that are made for

much older children and they are far too long in the arms and legs. His teacher has been turning up his school uniform, but his casual clothes have just been rolled up until now, so I turned them up and hemmed them. There's no damage done. They can be let down again when he grows. I thought it would help Caz, and Max appreciated not tripping over the trouser legs when they unrolled.'

'That's all you've done to his clothes?'

'Yes. Well, I've been washing them, but I assume that's all right?' I added a touch sarcastically.

'Perhaps don't alter any more of his clothes that come from home,' Jo said.

'And let him trip over them?'

'Or you buy him some casual clothes. Then if you turn them up it won't cause the same problem. It's just the stuff she's bought she's sensitive about.'

'OK,' I agreed. 'Now, the matter of what I've been giving him to eat – or not giving him. Max is badly overweight and ...'

'You can't say that!' Jo interrupted.

'But he is.'

'You haven't told him, have you?'

'He already knows. He asked me how he could get smaller.'

'What did you say?'

'By eating a little less and exercising more.'

'So that's where that has come from,' Jo said, obviously referring to something else Caz had said. 'Give him what he wants to eat.'

'Jo, the child is obese. He'd eat all day long if I let him. If something isn't done soon, he'll end up with the same health problems his mother has.' Why it was necessary for me to point this out to his social worker I didn't know.

'It's not for you to say that,' Jo said. 'Leave it to his mother to sort out.'

Clearly Caz hadn't 'sorted it out' and from what I'd seen of her and her daughters, they all needed as much help as Max. I wasn't being sizeist, but I was genuinely concerned for Max's health.

'Jo, I give Max second helpings of the main course but not pudding,' I continued, addressing the complaints Caz had made. 'Likewise with ice cream, cakes, biscuits and chocolate. He has one, the same as Adrian and Paula, but he'd eat sweet things non-stop if I let him. I assume the stuff Caz says I put on his plate that he doesn't like is fruit and vegetables. He's eaten some without a problem and what he doesn't like he leaves. I don't force him to eat anything, but I do encourage healthy eating. And it's true I only usually have fizzy drinks in the house for special occasions, but Max has been having juice as well as water. He's already had teeth out – he doesn't want to be losing any more – and he only has water at school.'

'Perhaps buy some cola to keep him happy.'

'OK, if that's what you want,' I said, struggling to keep my voice even.

'So what's all this about making him walk because you don't want to use your car?'

'That's ridiculous. On Sunday we walked to our local park. He's been in the car on all other trips.'

'How far is the park? Caz said walking is bad for Max's asthma. Did you take his inhaler with you?'

'Yes, of course, I take it everywhere, but he didn't need it. The only time he's used it was when he first arrived with you. The park is about a ten-minute walk.'

'I'll tell Caz, but in future can you take him in the car if you go to the park so she doesn't worry?'

'Not to that park,' I said. 'There are only a few car-parking places.'

'So take him to a park where there are more parking places.' I sighed, and so too did Jo. She was stressed and doing everything she could to appease Caz, but it made a nonsense of what I was trying to do to help Max have a healthier life-style. 'You've got a big back garden,' she continued. 'He can play in there, it's just as good. And the other thing I have to mention is, can you buy him a bag of sweets to take to the hospital to share with his mother and sister? Apparently they all take in a bag and share them. Max hasn't been able to join in.'

'But he's been eating their sweets,' I said.

'He wants to take in a bag of his own. Sharing sweets is like a little family ritual. He's feeling left out.'

'OK, if that's what you want, but eating that number of sweets every evening goes against my instincts to help Max.'

'It will make Caz happy,' Jo said, as if that was the sole objective. 'I'll phone her and reassure her that in future you will keep to what Max is used to.'

'And ignore the fact that obesity is ruining his childhood?'

'That's a bit dramatic.'

'Is it? The poor child was in tears last night because of his size. He didn't want to go to school on Friday because it's sports day.'

'I didn't like sports day either, I never won anything,' Jo said, missing the point.

'But this wasn't about winning or losing, it was about not wanting to participate because of his size.'

'What did you say?'

'That I'd speak to his teacher, which I have done just now. They like all the children to join in, but she's reassured me that Max won't have to do anything beyond him or compete by himself. They are all in house teams. She's going to have a chat with him.'

'Mrs Marshall is very good,' Jo said. It was about the only thing we agreed on. 'But please don't say anything to Caz about his size. It will upset her.'

'Of course I won't. She hardly speaks to me.'

'I need to go now and phone Caz. I'm tied up for the rest of the day. And by the way, I've had notice of Max's medical. It's this Thursday. There's a letter in the post to you.'

'All right, thank you.'

We said goodbye and I hung up.

Jo had clearly been very stressed and short of time, as many social workers are. She'd focused on placating Caz, rather than looking at the wider picture. She hadn't even asked how Max was settling in and what sort of weekend he'd had as I'd expect the social worker to do. I didn't agree with the way Jo was handling this – keeping Max's mother happy at the expense of Max's health – but as the foster carer I had to do as I was told by the child's social worker. That is the bottom line, whether we agree with it or not.

On my way to collect Paula from nursery I stopped off at our local shop, where I bought a bag of mixed sweets for Max to take with him to the hospital that night. In a small act of defiance I also bought a bag of grapes. If I was being forced to contribute to Max's family's poor eating, I would also offer a healthy option. If they didn't want the grapes, I'd bring them home again.

CHAPTER TEN

AN ALLY

That afternoon Jill phoned to ask how the weekend had gone and I updated her, including that I had seen Max's teacher on Friday, the hospital visits, Max playing in the tent, our trip to the park, Max's concerns about sports day, and Jo's call and the complaints from Caz. Had Jill not telephoned me I would have phoned her before the end of the day. Jill tutted when I told her of Jo's response to the complaints, although I knew she was too professional to criticize another social worker.

'At least Jo is dealing with the complaints, so they are unlikely to go any further,' Jill pointed out. 'I suppose she feels that as Max will only be with you for a short while, there's no point in making big changes. It would be different if he was with you long term.'

'Yes, I understand.'

'But generally Max is settling in well?' she asked.

'Yes. Which was why I was surprised to receive these complaints.'

'I doubt they've come from Max, but obviously don't question him.'

'No, I wouldn't.'

'You dealt with the matter of sports day well,' Jill added. She always found something positive to say. 'I'm sure he'll feel he can go and participate once his teacher has spoken to him.'

'Yes, I hope so.'

'Has Caz got a discharge date yet?'

'Not as far as I know, although when I gave Summer a lift home she said her mother was having to walk more in preparation for going home.'

'I'll ask Jo next time I speak to her, and well done. Thanks for all you are doing for Max. It's much appreciated.' And those few words of thanks were enough to lift my spirits and renew my confidence, allowing me to move forward and once again concentrate on doing my best for Max while he was with us, which is what fostering is all about.

That afternoon, when I collected Adrian from school, he handed me a letter that informed all parents that the children needed to stay late on Friday, as it was a full dress rehearsal for the school's end-of-year show. Adrian was excited to be in the production – based on *Joseph and the Amazing Technicolor Dreamcoat* – as were all the children. Adrian's costume – an ancient Egyptian – was already in school, hanging on his peg, having been checked and okayed by his teacher. That Adrian had to stay late on Friday would help me, as Max's sports day was the same afternoon and wasn't due to finish until four o'clock. Paula and I would be watching, so it meant I would now have enough time to leave there and meet Adrian when his rehearsal finished.

When I collected Max from after-school club that afternoon I quietly asked him if Mrs Marshall had spoken to him about sports day. He nodded. 'How do you feel about going now?' I asked.

'I think it will be a challenge, but one I can overcome,' he said proudly.

'Well done,' I said, patting him on the shoulder. And well done, Mrs Marshall, I thought, for clearly these were her words and they seemed to have done the trick.

Before we left for the hospital that evening I handed Max the bag of sweets I'd bought. 'Wow!' he said, his eyes lighting up, as did Adrian's and Paula's.

'They are for you to share with your mother and sisters,' I said to Max. 'And you two can have something in the café,' I told Adrian and Paula so they wouldn't feel left out.

'Thank you. That is kind,' Max said, looking at the bag and genuinely surprised.

Judging from his reaction, I thought (as Jill had done) that the request to bring in sweets hadn't come from him but his mother. Caz could easily have asked me. Indeed, much of what she'd complained about to Jo she could have mentioned to me, rather than making an issue of it. I hoped that before long she would drop her hostility and start to try to interact with me – for Max's sake. But when we arrived at the hospital that evening I realized it wasn't going to be any time soon. Empowered by the complaints she'd made to Jo and having them acted on, she was ready with more. Upright on her pillows, surrounded by her entourage and clutching the bag of sweets Max had given to her, she glared at me. 'You need to bring his inhaler in with him. It's irresponsible not to. He's got asthma.'

'Absolutely,' I agreed. 'I take it everywhere with us.' Opening my bag I took out the inhaler and placed it on the bed beside her. 'I'll leave it with you for safekeeping. And here's a few grapes I thought you might all enjoy.' I set the bag beside the inhaler.

'Oh, I love grapes,' Kelly said, immediately dipping her hand into the bag. Caz scowled at her as if she was letting down their side.

'They've been washed,' I said. 'I'll see you later. Have a nice evening.' I turned and left. It was quiet as I walked away, no laughing, although I could feel Caz looking daggers at me.

Upstairs in the café Adrian and Paula chose a chocolate biscuit each to have with their drinks and we settled at our usual table, close to the play area.

'Why doesn't Max's mother like you?' Adrian asked. I guessed he'd read her body language, for I doubted he or Paula could have heard what she'd said from where they'd been waiting by the ward door.

'She's angry because Max had to go into care.'

'But it's not your fault,' Adrian said, with a shrug.

'I know. Don't worry, I'm sure things will improve. Max is happy, so that's the main thing.'

'Do his sisters like us?' Paula asked.

'I'm sure they do,' I replied.

She shrugged just as Adrian had done.

'Copycat,' he said.

'You're a copycat,' Paula retaliated.

'There you are, you've don't it again. Copycat.' He grinned provocatively.

'No, I'm not.'

'Yes, you are.'

'Enough,' I said. 'Adrian, have you brought your home-work with you to do?'

'We haven't got any.' Homework was tailing off with the end of term approaching.

'OK, so find something to do.'

With a small sigh he took his book from his bag. 'I'll read for a bit, but it's boring here. I could be at home in the garden.'

'I know. It shouldn't be for much longer,' I sympathized. I felt it too. Although we kept ourselves occupied, all our evenings had vanished, taken up with the hospital visiting when there were so many more productive things we could be doing.

When we returned to the ward Adrian and Paula waited in their usual place by the door while I went over to Caz's bed. All four bags of sweets were empty and so too was the bag of grapes, the empty bags and sweet wrappers scattered across the bed. I resisted the temptation to start clearing them up.

'Did Max ask you about sports day?' I said to Caz.

'Yes, but clearly I won't be going,' she rebuffed.

'But I wondered if the girls or Max's father might like to go. Anyway, he's told you the details – Friday at one o'clock.'

Ignoring me, she pointedly turned her head and began talking to her daughters. Max seemed to accept her behaviour as normal, and again I was reminded of Mrs Marshall's comparison with Roald Dahl's Matilda. Max was so different to his family.

From that evening on, as well as buying Max sweets to take into hospital I also bought some fruit, washing it first: grapes, strawberries, blueberries, tangerines and apples, which I sliced. No one said thank you, but according to Max they all enjoyed them, including his mother. I felt my small olive branch of friendship had been partially accepted.

* * *

The letter advising me of the appointment for Max's medical arrived the following morning. It had been arranged for 2 p.m. on Thursday at the local health centre. I didn't think it was appropriate to take Paula, and Adrian might need collecting from school if it overran, so I telephoned my parents and asked them if they were free to help. Mum said they were and they'd be delighted to come. I suggested they stay for dinner and Mum said she'd make a pudding and bring it with her. They lived about an hour's drive away and had helped me out before. Indeed, since my husband had left they'd been a great support and my father was a fine male role model for Adrian, who missed his father more than he admitted. I mentioned to Mum that Max was considerably overweight so that she and Dad were prepared. This would be the first time they met him, and while they'd never comment, they may have had to hide their surprise or shock, and children pick up non-verbal signs just as adults do. Similarly, when I fostered a child with very challenging behaviour I always warned my parents in advance so they were prepared. Fostering involves the whole family, which often includes grandparents, aunts and uncles. While I would never divulge confidential information to them, some things they need to know so that family get-togethers run smoothly and are pleasant for everyone.

Jo's instructions to give Max whatever he wanted to eat had created a double standard for me. I encouraged Adrian and Paula (and all the other children I'd fostered) to eat healthily and I wasn't about to change that. Neither was I going to restock my cupboards with bottles of fizzy drinks, packets of biscuits, cakes, bags of sweets and so on, but I recognized I had to make some concessions. I still intended to offer Max the healthy option by, for example, putting vegetables on his plate, which he could leave if he didn't want them, as he had been doing. We'd drink water with our meals, although I did say that as Nana and Grandpa were coming to dinner on Thursday it was a special occasion, so I'd buy some fizzy drinks. I asked the children what they'd like. Max chose cola and Adrian and Paula lemonade. I felt this was a reasonable compromise and one evening of fizzy drinks wasn't going to rot their teeth. Similarly, if Max really didn't want to walk somewhere, we could take the car if practical. As Jill had said, Max wouldn't be with me for very long, so there was little point in 'making big changes'.

On Thursday my parents arrived in good time for me to collect Max from school for his medical and made a huge fuss of Paula as they always did. Dad gave me a bunch of flowers and then Mum produced a wonderful homemade fruit trifle and a pot of cream from a cooler bag for dessert. I thanked her, resisted the temptation to try it, and put the trifle and cream in the fridge, then made them a cup of tea, which they had in the garden. Before I left I reminded them to help themselves to whatever they wanted, and the time Adrian needed to be collected if I wasn't back. It was another warm, sunny day and I left the three of them in the garden, Paula in her element at having the complete attention of her beloved nana and grandpa.

I'd informed Max's school that morning that I'd need to collect him at 1.30 p.m. to take him to have a medical, and when I arrived he was already sitting in reception with his school bag. 'Good boy,' I said, and I signed us out.

'Is a medical like when I go to my doctor's?' he asked a little anxiously as we left the building.

CRUEL TO BE KIND

'Similar, but the clinic is in a different building to the doctor you go to. Don't worry, I've taken children to have medicals before and it is fine.'

'Will I have to have an injection?' he asked.

'No. The doctor just wants to check you over to make sure you are fit and well.'

I'd already explained to Max what a medical involved, but understandably he was anxious. He was quiet in the car and I reassured him again that there was nothing to worry about. Once we were in the health centre and he saw the other children, babies and toddlers waiting – a number of different clinics ran in the same building – he relaxed. Having given his name at reception, we were told to take a seat. Some of the children were playing with the toys provided at one end of the room, but Max just wanted to sit beside me. We chatted about school and the book he was reading. Shortly after our appointment time Max's name flashed on the digital display screen together with a recorded voice telling us to go to consulting room three. He slipped his hand into mine and we crossed the waiting area and then went down a short corridor until we came to a door marked Room 3. I knocked on the door and a female voice said, 'Come in.'

As we entered a young woman doctor rose from her chair behind her desk and greeted us with a warm smile. 'Hello, lovely to meet you. I'm Doctor Seema Jhaveri.'

'Cathy Glass,' I said, returning her smile. 'And this is Max.'

'Hello, take a seat.' I saw her look Max up and down and then frown.

We sat in the two chairs at right angles to her desk and she opened the file in front of her and read what looked like a letter of referral. 'You are his foster carer?'

'Yes.'

'And Max is six.'

'Yes.'

'He's badly overweight,' she said, looking up – first at Max and then at me.

'I know.' I suddenly saw an ally. 'He won't be with me for long, so I've been told not to do anything about it.'

'Why ever not?' she asked, shocked.

I glanced at Max. I didn't like talking about a child in front of them but there was no choice, so I phrased it as best I could. 'His mother doesn't see there is a problem and his social worker doesn't want her upset.'

'But that's ridiculous. The child is obese and probably has been all his life. He should be on a diet and exercise programme. It's cruel for him not to be.'

'Thank you,' I said, relieved. 'I feel like I've been fighting a lone battle. I wanted to make changes to his diet but I've been stopped.'

She frowned again. 'That's not good. Does he eat a lot of sweet and fatty foods?'

'Usually, yes.'

'I see from here', she said, referring to another page in the folder, 'that he has already had four teeth extracted due to decay. And there are two more that might need to come out. That's appalling for a young child.' I nodded in agreement. 'Does he have a lot of fizzy drinks, squashes and juices? You know the acidity in fruit juice is as bad for teeth as sugary drinks.'

'Yes, I know. He was used to having fizzy drinks, but I mainly give him water with the occasional glass of juice. We only have fizzy drinks as an occasional treat.'

'That's all right. But a lot of the damage will already have been done, as I'm sure the dentist would have told Max's mother. And he has asthma,' she said, reading on.

'It's been diagnosed, but he's only needed his inhaler once since he's been with me – when he first arrived.'

'He was probably stressed. Have you heard him wheezing?'

'No. He gets out of breath easily, but there's no wheezing.'

'He would get out of breath, carrying all that extra weight around. It puts a huge strain on the cardiovascular and respiratory system. To overfeed a child to this extent is a form of abuse.'

I glanced at Max again. I felt uncomfortable that he had to hear all of this, but it was the truth, after all. 'He's only been with me a short while,' I said, feeling culpable.

'Does he exercise?' Dr Jhaveri asked.

'Not a lot. He joins in PE at school, but he doesn't like walking.'

'That's because it's uncomfortable for him, but walking is a good form of exercise. Incorporate it into his daily routine.' I nodded. 'So what has his social worker told you to do?' She looked at me.

'To keep everything as it has been and leave it to his mother to deal with once he's home.'

'Clearly his mother hasn't been dealing with it so far,' Dr Jhaveri said firmly. 'What makes her think it will be different in the future?'

'I don't know.'

'Is his mother badly overweight too?'

'Yes.'

'Any siblings?'

'Three older sisters.'

'All obese?'

I nodded.

'I'm really shocked that no one has been advising the mother on her children's health, especially when the social services are involved. I see families here. We have a clinic that offers advice and support, and a weekly weigh-in. Obesity is a massive problem in the Western world and we are storing up huge health problems for the next generation. Is his mother in good health?'

I shook my head. 'She's in hospital now, that's why Max came to me.'

'What's the matter with her?'

'She had two toes amputated – I understand it's a result of type 2 diabetes.'

She let out a heartfelt sigh. 'Yet she's allowed her son to go the same way.' Dr Jhaveri was clearly a conscientious paediatrician whose outspokenness was a result of her concern for Max. 'I'll speak to his social worker. Perhaps she's not aware of the help available. I have her contact details on the letter of referral.' She then turned to Max. 'Hi, Max. How are you today?'

'OK,' he said quietly, obviously chastened by what he'd heard.

'Pleased to have the afternoon off school?' she asked, being friendly.

Max wasn't sure what to say.

'He likes school,' I said. 'He's doing very well and he loves reading.'

'That's good. My children like reading too. So do I. Now, I'm going to examine you. I expect you had an examination at your doctor's when he prescribed the inhaler.' Max nodded. 'We'll start by looking in your ears. Can you hear all right?'

'Yes,' Max said.

She took an otoscope from the top drawer of her desk and looked first in one of Max's ears and then the other. 'That's fine,' she said. Returning the otoscope to the drawer, she took a wooden tongue depressor from a sealed packet and then asked Max to open his mouth wide so she could look in. 'Thank you,' she said. Throwing the used spatula into the bin, she picked up the ophthalmoscope from where it lay on her desk and looked in his eyes. 'Do you have glasses for reading?' she asked. Max shook his head.

'And you can see the board the teacher writes on?'

'Yes.'

'Good. Can you read the letters on that chart?' she asked him, referring to the Snellen wall chart. Max read all the letters without any problem.

'Excellent.' She returned the ophthalmoscope to the desk and, looping her stethoscope around her neck, listened to his chest and then his back. 'His chest is clear,' she said and made a note on the form for the medical that Jo had sent. 'Now, let's measure you,' she said to Max. 'Can you take off your shoes and stand just here for me?' She took the few steps to the height recorder as Max leaned forward and began struggling to take off his shoes. It wasn't that he lacked the motor skills to undo the Velcro and pull off his shoes, but the fat around his middle stopped him from leaning far enough forward. I helped him and he padded across to the doctor. She gently placed him in front of the height bar and then lowered the ruler so it was just touching his head. 'Three feet, eleven inches,' she said. 'That's average for his age.' She went to her desk, made a note on the form and then returned to Max. 'Now, let's weigh you. Stand on here, please.' Max stood on the scales. I watched and waited. I knew he was overweight, but I had no idea by how much. It came as a huge shock. 'One hundred and nineteen pounds,' she read out. 'That's eight and a half stone – more than twice the weight he should be.' Then, as she walked to the desk to record the figure, she frowned. 'Do you realize that's the weight of the average fourteen-year-old? Perhaps the social worker will do something now.'

CHAPTER ELEVEN

STRESSED

D r Jhaveri didn't say anything further about Max's weight and continued the medical by asking him to lie on the couch so she could examine him. She placed a step-stool by the couch and helped Max clamber up and onto it, and then lie down. Movements that would have been completed easily by a child of normal weight were cumbersome for Max, who lacked agility. She felt the glands in his neck and then undid his shirt and the top of his trousers so she could feel his stomach. As she ran the palm of her hand over his stomach, gently pressing the flesh to feel his internal organs, the fat rippled.

'Do you do a poo each day?' she asked him. It was a stand-ard question asked by most doctors giving a child a medical.

He nodded seriously. 'It's OK, love,' I said. 'You're doing very well.'

Once Dr Jhaveri had finished the examination she helped Max into a sitting position and then off the couch. He waddled back to me, tucking his shirt in, and we sat side by side again as the doctor wrote on the forms. Coming to the end, she set down her pen and looked at me. 'Do you have any concerns about Max's health?'

'There are a couple of things I wanted to mention. His mother thinks he may have an allergy, as he comes out in a rash sometimes. I haven't seen the rash and as far as I know there has been no diagnosis.'

'It could be an allergy, although it could also be from sweating. Overweight people sweat more. Does he bath or shower regularly?'

'He does now,' I said.

'If the rash appears while he is living with you, take him to your doctor to get it checked. He'll need to see the rash to make a diagnosis.'

I nodded. 'The other thing is his snoring. It's very loud and continues intermittently for most of the night.'

'Does it wake him?'

'No. Just everyone else.'

She smiled. 'Some children do snore and they grow out of it. It can be a sign of enlarged tonsils or adenoids, but his tonsils looked fine when I examined him. Has he been referred to the hospital?'

'Not as far as I know. I'm sure I would have been told if he had.'

'The most likely cause of his snoring is that he's overweight and unfit. Fatty tissue around the neck and poor muscle tone contribute to snoring – in children and adults. Once he starts to lose weight and is healthier and taking more exercise, I'm sure the snoring will improve. But obviously, if you have any concerns, see his doctor.'

'I will. Thank you.'

'I'll give you some diet and exercise sheets for him to follow, although a lot of it is common sense.' She stood and crossed to a metal filing cabinet up against one wall and, opening the second drawer, took out some printed sheets. 'Plenty of vegetables, lean meat and fish,' she said, handing the sheets to me. 'Carbohydrates are a necessary part of a balanced diet, but go easy on the pasta, bread and potatoes. And generally limit the size of his portions. He might complain he's hungry to begin with until his stomach shrinks back to a normal size. Exercise should be light to start with – walking, swimming, a little skipping. Play hopscotch – make it fun. His stamina will gradually increase. Hopefully his mother will continue what you begin.'

'I hope so too,' I said, folding the sheets and tucking them into my bag.

She smiled at Max. 'Nice to meet you, young man,' she said, bringing the appointment to a close. 'Do as Cathy says and we'll have you fit and healthy very soon.' Max managed a small smile.

I thanked the doctor and we left. I felt she had spoken a lot of good sense, but I wondered what Jo and Caz would make of it. I also wondered what I was supposed to do: implement the suggestions she'd made, which is what I would have done had Max been my child, or follow Jo's instructions to keep everything as it was. I knew I needed to take advice, so I'd phone Jill first thing tomorrow.

'Am I still having cola tonight?' Max asked as we got into the car. I guessed he'd heard most of what the doctor had said and had understood the implications.

'Yes. The doctor said a fizzy drink occasionally is OK but not every day. It's about moderation; for example, just having one sweet, not the whole bag.' Although, of course, when Max was at the hospital I had no control over what he ate, and it would be asking an awful lot of a six-year-old who was used to eating as many sweets as he liked to self-moderate.

'Am I going to lose weight?' Max asked as I began the drive home.

'Would you like to?'

'Yes. I don't want to have toes like Mummy. They're horrible, red and smelly with yellow stuff coming out.'

I grimaced at the description. 'You won't,' I reassured him. 'We'll make sure you stay healthy.'

'Shall I tell my mummy she has to lose weight?'

'I think she already knows, love.'

But did she? I wondered as I drove. Do people with life-threatening conditions that are a result of poor lifestyle choices acknowledge the link, or are cause and effect too far apart? Like heavy drinkers with liver damage, for example, who literally drink themselves to death. Or smokers, who are aware of their increased chance of developing lung cancer, but never find the willpower to give up, believing it won't happen to them and citing the person who's smoked sixty cigarettes a day all their life and is in their nineties. Was Caz aware that being obese was killing her, and if she was, why didn't she do something about it? Easy for me to say, having never had a big weight problem. And judging from Max's comments about his dad liking big women, I didn't think he was going to give Caz much support if she did embark on a diet and fitness programme.

My parents had collected Adrian from school and were home just before us. I introduced them to Max and then made us all a cold drink, which we took into the garden. Mum and Dad made a point of including Max, talking to him about what he was interested in, as they did with all the children I fostered. I left them in the garden while I made dinner. My parents knew we were eating early, as Max would be going to visit his mother in hospital. Mum suggested Adrian and Paula could stay with them while I took Max, which met with much enthusiasm from my children. When I served dinner I gave Max a similar-sized portion to Adrian's and Paula's and one glass of cola, followed by one helping of Mum's delicious trifle with a little fresh cream. The trifle was so rich that none of my family wanted a second helping, and I didn't offer Max one.

Once Max was changed and ready to go he came with me to say goodbye, holding the bag of sweets and the box of fresh cherries I'd bought for him to take. Although I would be limiting Max's portions of food at home, I didn't think it wise to stop the sweets until I'd spoken to Jo, as Caz had specifically asked that Max take them to the hospital.

'Are those for your mother?' my father asked pleasantly.

'Yes,' Max said. 'She likes sweets.'

'Give her our best wishes,' Dad said. 'We hope she's better soon.'

Max smiled and we said goodbye. I felt considerably relieved that Adrian and Paula could stay with their grand-parents, rather than passing another evening whiling away their time in the hospital café. We left them in the living room, about to play a game of cards, with the patio doors open on a lovely evening and Toscha sitting on the step, watching the world go by.

* * *

At the hospital it was Summer who noticed that Adrian and Paula weren't with me and waiting in their usual place by the door of the ward. 'Where are your kids?' she asked me.

'At home with their nana and grandpa,' I said.

'That's nice,' she said. 'We don't have a nana or grandpa. They died.'

'I'm sorry,' I said. But I was pleased Summer was talking to me, despite her mother looking daggers at her.

Max put the sweets and cherries on the bed with the three other bags of sweets like a ritualistic offering. 'Cathy's parents said they hope you get better soon,' he remembered to say. I smiled.

'That's cute,' Summer said, while Caz just humphed.

'Watch out for the stones in the cherries,' I warned, mainly for Max's benefit. 'Have a nice evening.' And I left.

Upstairs in the café I bought a coffee and settled at a table, then realized I should have brought something with me to read. The time passed incredibly slowly without the children, although for a while I struck up conversation with an elderly lady who'd just visited her husband and was now waiting for her son to collect her and give her a lift home.

I returned to the ward at seven o'clock and as usual the bed was littered with sweet wrappers. Only Summer was there, sitting in the chair, her elder sisters having been allowed to go early. I thought Max was looking uncomfortable – sheepish – as if he had done something wrong.

'OK?' I asked him.

He nodded.

'I'll be speaking to his social worker first thing tomorrow,' Caz said, glowering at me. 'I'll get that paediatrician sacked. The rude cow!'

'Give it a rest, Mum,' Summer said, nibbling the tip of her little finger.

'And you can shut up,' Caz said, turning on her. 'It's not you she had a go at.'

I had wondered if Max would tell his mother some of what Dr Jhaveri had said, and apparently he had.

'Yes, discuss it with Jo,' I said amicably to Caz. 'That's for the best.' She was clearly annoyed and I wasn't going to enter into what was likely to be a heated discussion in front of Max.

He looked quite relieved that he was going and I thought Summer would have liked to leave too, but I didn't offer her a lift home, as I knew Caz liked her to stay until the end. I was sure Summer would have asked for a lift if she'd been allowed to leave early.

Max kissed his mother's cheek and then came to my side.

'Goodnight then,' I said.

'Night,' Summer replied. Caz elbowed her a warning.

As we left the ward Max slipped his hand into mine. 'I shouldn't have told Mum what the doctor said, should I?' he asked.

'It's not your fault. You can tell your mother what you like. Once she's had a chat with Jo I am sure she'll feel better about what the doctor said.' Or maybe she wouldn't, but I didn't want Max feeling guilty. So many children who come into care have secrets that they have been warned (sometimes threatened) by their parents not to divulge to the foster carer or social worker. It's confusing and worrying for the child, who constantly has to juggle what they can and can't say. I would therefore never tell a child not to tell their parents something, even if it might be the more diplomatic option. Caz was upset by what the paediatrician had said, but it was in her and her family's best interests to hear it and hopefully heed it. It was just a pity it had come from Max.

Once home, my parents stayed for a while and then said goodbye, as it was time for the children's bath and bedtime routine. I hadn't really seen much of them, but we'd get together again soon, and Adrian and Paula had clearly enjoyed spending time with their nana and grandpa. After they'd gone and before I took Max up to bed, he asked if there was any trifle left, meaning could he have some more. I said there was but we'd have it for pudding tomorrow, which he accepted.

The following morning, when I went to wake Max for school, he was already awake, not reading but sitting up in bed and looking worried.

'Are you OK, love?' I asked.

'I've got a tummy ache,' he said, giving his stomach a rub.

'Oh dear, I wonder what's caused that,' I sympathized. 'Get up slowly and see how you feel when you've had a drink and some breakfast.' I've found in the past, as I'm sure many parents have, that children can sometimes complain of minor pains and discomforts, which quickly pass off once they're up and about.

'Can't I stay here?' he asked, forcing a grimace as if in pain.

'Is it that bad?' He nodded. But he didn't look ill. He wasn't pale and when I felt his forehead it didn't feel as though he had a temperature. Then, from years of looking after children, I asked, 'Are you worrying about anything?'

A moment's hesitation and a small nod.

'Would it have anything to do with sports day this afternoon?'

Another small nod.

'What is it that's bothering you?' I asked, sitting on the bed. 'I thought you were OK about participating after Mrs Marshall spoke to you.'

'I don't want you to take a photograph,' he said. 'You said you'd bring your camera and take a photo for me to keep, but I don't want one.'

'All right,' I said. 'I won't take a photograph unless you want me to. I suggested it because I thought it would be a nice thing for you to keep. I usually take photographs of special events for Adrian and Paula and the other children I've fostered.'

'But they weren't fat like me.'

'Oh, love,' I said, taking his hand in mine. 'Is that why you don't want a photograph?'

'Yes.' His eyes filled and my heart clenched. 'I look funny in my shorts,' he said. 'I don't want to remember it. You can take a picture of me when I'm not fat.'

'I understand, but no one in your class has said anything to you, have they?'

'No, but they look. We have to have a class photo on sports day, but I stand at the back so just my head is showing. Don't tell Mrs Marshall, she doesn't know.'

I'm sure she does, I thought but didn't say. She was sensitive and perceptive. 'All right, love, I won't take my camera if you're sure. We'll just buy the class photograph.'

He perked up a little. 'You can take pictures of the other kids you foster that are cute and beautiful.'

'Max,' I said, giving him a hug. 'You are beautiful. It's the person inside that counts. That's where true beauty lies, and you are one of the most beautiful children I know. You are also very intelligent, so remember that.'

He gave a small, embarrassed laugh but looked pleased. I don't think anyone had said this to him before. 'I'll try to remember that,' he said. 'I guess it's the same for my mum and sisters too. We are all beautiful inside.'

'Yes. Absolutely,' I said, which I thought was very generous, considering Caz's hostility towards me.

Reassured that I wouldn't take a photograph of him in his PE kit at sports day, Max got dressed and came down to breakfast – I'd yet to address the issue of him having two breakfasts; I was thinking about what to do for the best. When I took him to school and we said goodbye I said I'd see him later at sports day and reminded him to look out for Paula and me sitting in the audience. I didn't know if any of Max's family would be going. Caz hadn't said anything, but they had the details.

As soon as I returned home from taking Paula to nursery I telephoned Jill and told her what the paediatrician had said at Max's medical, including how much he weighed, what a child of his age should weigh, that the most likely cause of his asthma and snoring was his obesity, and the diet and fitness programme she'd suggested.

'Do what she says,' Jill said without hesitation. 'Jo should be fine with it, as it's a doctor who's said he should be on a diet. But obviously don't overdo it. Hopefully, once Max is home, Caz and her family will join the programme at the clinic.'

'I was thinking of continuing more or less what I have been doing – giving Max normal-sized portions, but no second helpings and reducing the number of sweet and fatty foods he eats. The doctor said exercise should be light to begin with, like walking, swimming and playing outdoors.'

'Yes, that sounds reasonable. Keep a record of what you're doing. Weigh him, but only once a week. He's an intelligent child and you don't want him to become anxious about losing weight. Log it all in your diary.'

'Yes, I will. Thanks, Jill.'

'I'll speak to Jo. Any plans for the weekend?'

'Relaxing on Saturday – we'll go out if it's fine. On Sunday Adrian and Paula are out with their father, so I was planning on taking Max to buy some more casual clothes that I am allowed to turn up.'

'OK.' I heard Jill smile. 'Have a good one.'

'And you.' We said goodbye.

Jill is usually right about most things connected with good social work practice, but her assertion that Jo would be 'fine' was slightly off the mark. When Jo telephoned mid-morning she was even more stressed than usual. 'I've been on the phone all morning trying to sort this out – first Dr Jhaveri and then Max's mother. What on earth is going on? I didn't realize he was that overweight. Did you?' So I guessed Dr Jhaveri had given Jo some straight-talking.

'Well, yes, I knew,' I said. 'He's wearing clothes for twelve-year-olds and older.'

'Is he?' she asked, surprised, as if she'd only just been made aware of it.

'I mentioned it when Max first arrived.'

'Did you? I don't remember.' I thought Jo was always so stressed that it was a wonder she remembered anything.

'I've spoken to Jill and we think –' I began.

'Who's Jill?'

'My support social worker.'

'Oh yes. She phoned here while I was on the other line,' Jo said. 'I'll call her when I get a minute. What did she say?'

'That I should follow the doctor's advice but not do anything too drastic. We eat healthily here anyway, so Max will have the same food as us, but I'll limit his intake of sweet foods.'

'I'll have to try to explain this to Caz. Can you tell her?'

'She won't talk to me.'

'Why not?'

'I don't know. She probably resents the fact that I'm looking after her son.' I paused but Jo didn't comment. 'What shall I do about the bag of sweets he takes in each night, and all the sweets he eats during visiting time?'

'They don't eat that many, do they?'

'Four large bags, including the one Max takes in every evening.'

'But they're shared?'

'Yes.'

'You can't stop that.'

'So he still takes in the sweets? You know that apart from the issue of his weight his teeth are in a bad state. He's had four out and another two may have to come out because of his high-sugar diet.'

'The doctor said that?'

'Yes.'

'I'll tell Caz, but let him take the sweets in and she can have the responsibility of how many he eats.'

'All right. Also, Max always has second helpings of pudding at school, but to stop it the canteen staff need a letter from the parent. Can you send it to them, please?'

'Can't you?'

'I can, but I'm not sure it will be sufficient as I'm the foster carer.'

'Try. Tell them I said it was fine. I need to get back to Caz now.' She ended the call as stressed out as she'd begun it. Who'd be a social worker? I thought.

CHAPTER TWELVE

VULNERABLE

I wrote the letter to Max's school as Jo had asked, addressed 'To Whom It May Concern', and saying that a paediatrician had placed Max on a diet and it would be appreciated if he wasn't given second helpings of school dinners. I said his social worker was aware and could confirm this if necessary, and gave her contact details and also my own. I took the letter with me when Paula and I went to sports day and left it in the office. Then we joined other families who'd come to watch sports day on the playing fields at the rear of the school.

I looked around the small groups of spectators already sitting on the grass, but I couldn't see anyone I knew. The area where the events were to be held had been cordoned off with brightly coloured ribbon to form an arena. Some chairs had been set out at one end, but most of the spectators were sitting on the grass. I'd brought a ground sheet for this purpose and set it down in a spot where we could see the arena. Although there was some cloud cover, the ultraviolet rays in summer are very strong, so I'd already put sunscreen on us both before we left and Paula was wearing a sun hat. The letter from the school advising us of the arrangements for sports day had emphasized the importance of using sunscreen for both participants and spectators, and Max had taken a tube of children's sunscreen to school with him. I'd also come prepared with bottles of water, and the participants would be given water regularly as well. Two large water coolers stood on a table to the right of the seating area.

At 1.30 p.m. the children filed out of school and onto the playing field in their classes and then arranged themselves into their house teams. I spotted Max straight away, tucked into the line of children, and he was looking at the spectators, so I stood and gave a little wave. He waved back with a small smile. I could see him still looking around, possibly searching for members of his family, but as far as I knew they weren't there. The teams sat on the grass and the noise level gradually increased as the whole school assembled and the children chatted excitedly. Once all the children were on the field the Headmistress took a microphone into the middle of the arena and made a speech, welcoming the spectators and explaining the programme of events, which was also displayed on a large white board beside the table of drinks. As she finished speaking and opened the sports day a few latecomers arrived and among them I spotted Kelly, Max's seventeen-year-old sister. 'There's Max's sister,' I said to Paula, and I waved.

She appeared not to see us and began walking towards the chairs, but Mrs Marshall noticed and, going over to her, pointed to where we sat. I gave another wave and Kelly came towards us – a little reluctantly, I thought, but it would be nice for Max to see us all sitting together.

'Hi. Max will be pleased you've come,' I said as Kelly approached. I made room for her on the ground sheet.

'Yeah, well, someone had to come,' she said, removing her earbuds and switching off her music. 'I don't have classes on a

Friday afternoon.' She heaved herself onto the mat with a strenuous sigh, and then straightened out her legs in front of her. She was wearing leggings and a long top and looked rather hot. 'Where is he?' she asked.

'Over there.' I pointed to where Max sat in his house team. He'd seen Kelly as she'd arrived and waved. 'Didn't he mind coming?' she asked, waving back. 'He had the day off last year. I thought he hated PE and sports day. I did.'

'Max's teacher had a chat with him and he's fine about it now. I'm pleased he felt he could participate.'

The Headmistress's voice came over the public address system again as she announced the start of the first event and reminded everyone to cheer loudly. 'What are they doing?' Paula asked as all the children stood and began moving. The arena had filled with activity and the teams lined up in front of their first event. 'They are going to have their first race,' I said. 'It looks like Max's team is going to run the obstacle course.'

Once the teams were ready the Head said, 'On the count of three …' and then blew her whistle. A roar went up from the spectators as we cheered our teams. I could see what Mrs Marshall had meant about it not being individually competitive. Each child did their best, but it was a team event so that no child was singled out as a winner, runner-up or coming last, as in a traditional sports day. The staff were timing how long it took each team to complete an event and points were awarded for the fastest and also the skill shown by the team in completing the event. So, for example, the team who were playing dribble hockey accrued extra points for how many balls they got into the net. As each team finished they sat down, and once all the teams were seated the staff conferred and allotted points, which were displayed on the white board.

'What are you studying at college?' I asked Kelly, taking the opportunity of the pause between events to make conversation.

'A foundation course,' she said. 'I didn't get many exams at school, so I'm doing catch-up.'

'Sounds good. Are you enjoying it?'

'It's OK. I just wish I'd got my exams first time, but I was off sick too much.'

'Oh dear, I am sorry to hear that. Are you well now?'

She shrugged. 'I guess.'

The Headmistress announced that the next race would start shortly, and then the teams moved to their next event. Max's team was now lined up in front of beat the goalie, where each child had three shots to try to get the football past the goal-keeper, who was a member of staff. The Head blew her whistle and everyone cheered their team on again. Paula got so excited that she began jumping up and down and calling out.

'She's sweet,' Kelly said, and I smiled.

It seemed that Kelly, like Summer (when I'd given her a lift home), was far more personable and happy to chat with me when away from her mother. Although I fully appreciated why they felt the need to show solidarity and loyalty to their mother and join in her hostility towards me.

When the race had finished there was another pause as points were allotted and noted on the board. Kelly straightened her leggings and then turned to me. 'You know what Max told Mum about losing weight?' I nodded. 'Do you think I should go on a diet too?'

I was taken aback. It was a very personal question and Kelly hardly knew me. 'Have you discussed it with your mother?' I asked.

She shook her head. 'No, she won't talk about it.'

I paused and thought carefully what to say. 'Perhaps you could discuss it with your doctor?'

She gave a desultory nod. 'When I kept being ill he said I should try to eat more healthily and take more exercise. But it's difficult at home. We always have loads of ready meals, takeaways and sweets, cakes and biscuits. I can't not eat them when everyone else is.'

'No, that would be very difficult,' I agreed.

'But other people manage to lose weight,' Kelly lamented. 'My friend at college has lost three stone since we started. She looks fantastic. I wish I could do that, but her mum made her meals each day.'

'I think it helps to have support, and you'd need advice on what to eat and how best to exercise. When I was at the health centre with Max the paediatrician mentioned a programme they offered for those who want to lose weight. They give advice, support and weekly weigh-ins. Perhaps you could look into attending that?'

'Is Max going?' she asked.

'Not at present. The paediatrician gave me some information sheets on diet and exercise and I know what to do. But it's easier in my house as we don't have lots of ready meals, sweets and sugary drinks. We have them sometimes, but not every day.'

'Perhaps I should come and live with you,' Kelly said jokingly.

I smiled. 'I think your mother would have something to say about that. It would be good if your whole family could enrol on the programme. Why don't you talk to Jo about it?'

'Yes, I could. She gave me her phone number if I needed it. Dad isn't fat, but he smokes. Mum says that's why he's thin. Perhaps I should start smoking.'

'Absolutely not!' I said. 'You're sensible, Kelly, I'm sure you could follow a fitness plan with support, and your mother and sisters may want to join in when they see what you are doing.'

The next races began and we concentrated on the games again, cheering and clapping as appropriate. Kelly said she was thirsty, so I gave her one of our bottles of water, as she hadn't brought any with her and I had plenty. At half-time, while the children had a rest and a drink, Mrs Marshall came over to us to say hello and commented on how well Max was doing. She also made a point of asking Kelly how she and her family were, before moving on to say hello to another family with a child in her class.

'She's nice,' Kelly said after she'd gone.

'Yes, very.'

'She's been here for ages – she taught me and my sisters. Although I never liked school.'

The second half began fifteen minutes later and all the events were finished by 3.30. There was then a gap of about ten minutes as the staff added up the points before the presentation of the trophy. Max's team didn't win, but as the Head said in her closing speech it was participating that counted, and it was fantastic that everyone had a chance to compete and enjoy themselves. She thanked the spectators again for coming and asked that we remain on the field while the children went inside to collect their belongings and then they'd return to us.

Kelly, Paula and I stood, I put away the ground sheet and then we walked towards an area closer to the exit where others were waiting. As we did I heard a woman behind us say, 'Look at the size of her.' For a moment it didn't register who she was talking about until she added, 'Her sisters and brother are the same. They live near us. They're always in the chip shop. Don't know how they afford it on benefits.' I felt a surge of anger and protectiveness for Kelly and her family, which, through fostering Max, I had temporarily become part of. I turned and looked pointedly at the woman, who had the decency to look away. I glanced at Kelly. If she had heard she wasn't showing it, but I was hurt on her behalf. How dare that woman assume the right to comment out loud when she might hear? Kelly was obese, but she wasn't without feelings. It was probably a small indication of what she and her family had to contend with every day.

When Max appeared we congratulated him and told him how well he'd done. He glowed with the praise. 'Did you see me score the goals?' he asked excitedly.

'Yes, you did so well for your team,' I said.

'Well done, Max,' Kelly added.

Like most of the children, he was hot and sweating, but there wouldn't be time for him to shower before we had to leave to go to the hospital. Kelly walked with us and as we left the school grounds I asked her if she'd like a lift home – it wasn't out of my way – and she did. She said she was exhausted and that there was no way she was going to the hospital tonight, as she needed a rest.

'I'm sure your mother will understand,' I said.

To save time I didn't take Kelly right to her door but dropped her off at the end of her road, and then continued to Adrian's school, where I collected him from the production rehearsal. I asked him if it had gone well, and he said it had but then broke into fits of laughter as he told me that they'd been messing around and a boy had stepped off the stage and onto the piano keys, running to the end before jumping off. He could barely tell me for laughing, although they'd all had a telling-off, for as the teacher had pointed out it was dangerous and could also damage the piano. But I smiled too; I could picture the scene of overexcited children letting off steam. 'He has piano lessons, Mum!' Adrian cracked up. 'But you'd never have guessed from the noise he made.'

We were so short of time that I decided to stop off at a fast-food drive-through on the way home, where we bought burgers, chicken and chips to have at home. Greasy and high in calories, salt and hidden sugars, but absolutely delicious for a change. And there lay our excuse: it was 'a change', not our staple diet, so we could enjoy it without a guilty conscience.

That evening, when we arrived at the hospital, to my surprise Caz was sitting in the chair beside her bed. Paris and Summer were sitting on the bed. Kelly wasn't there and Caz clearly wasn't happy with the excuse she'd sent with her sisters. She was in the middle of a heated exchange with Paris.

'She doesn't need a rest! She's only been watching sports day,' Caz continued. 'She could still have come here tonight.'

'Will you stop going on?' Paris said, rolling her eyes. 'Or I'll go home. Be grateful we've come. It's Friday night. We should be out.'

'So you'd rather see your friends than your sick mother?'

'You're not sick any more,' Paris snapped. 'They're letting you out next week.'

'That's not the point,' Caz retaliated. 'Kelly should be here. It's hurtful that she's not.' She looked genuinely sad.

'Max did very well at sports day,' I said. He was standing in front of her, proffering the sweets and peaches and being ignored.

Caz and Paris glanced at him before continuing.

'If you want to nag someone about coming to visit you, why don't you nag Dad?' Paris said. 'He's only been here twice.'

'You know he hates hospitals,' Caz said, 'and he can't smoke in here.'

'I don't like hospitals either, but I'm here, aren't I?' Paris retorted with attitude.

'So am I,' Summer put in. 'Every night. At least you don't have to stay to the end.'

Max inched the sweets and fruit onto his mother's lap.

'I'll see you later,' I said. Then to Caz, 'Nice that you are up and about.'

She ignored me, concentrating instead on opening the bag of sweets Max had given her. I threw him a smile, said a general goodbye and crossed the ward to where Adrian and Paula were waiting by the door. If Caz was being discharged next week then there would be no more hospital visiting, I thought with some relief. It wasn't only Caz's daughters who were feeling the strain of being here every night; I was too. Indeed, the only person who didn't seem to mind was Caz, languishing in hospital, but that was probably unfair.

Upstairs in the café Adrian, Paula and I passed the time as we had been doing with a mixture of reading, games, chatting, and a drink and a biscuit. They were seeing their father on Sunday and he'd asked them to think about what they wanted to do for the day. Despite my personal feelings about John leaving – for another woman – I appreciated that he did try to give the children a fun day out. Adrian usually decided what to do and Paula went along with it. Adrian said that for this Sunday he was thinking of suggesting they went to an activity park in the area, or, if it was raining, the cinema. It wasn't always easy to find an activity that suited both a seven- and a three-year-old, but the activity park would work well. They'd been there with me and it catered for all age groups.

At seven o'clock we returned to the ward. Only Max was still there, bless him – a captive audience, I thought. Standing dutifully beside his mother's chair, he was watching the door, looking for us, and seemed relieved when we appeared. Without his sisters it must have been difficult. I doubt many six-year-old boys could generate meaningful conversation with their mother in hospital, especially every night for an hour and a half. I went over. Caz was still sitting in the chair beside the bed but was now moving her legs and shifting as if uncomfortable. Unprotected by her entourage of teenage daughters and with her heavily bandaged foot clearly giving her some discomfort, she appeared vulnerable – a side of her I hadn't seen before.

'They've all gone and left me,' she said. 'Now you're taking Max, I may as well get into bed. Can you tell a nurse on your way out that I want to get back into bed?'

'Yes, of course.'

'They don't always come when I buzz.'

'I'll tell them,' I said. 'I expect they're very busy.'

'It's not that,' she said, shifting again. 'They say I have to do more for myself. But they haven't had their toes off. It bloody hurts.'

'I'm sure it does,' I said sympathetically, although I wondered how she was going to cope at home if she couldn't make the couple of steps from the chair to her bed without help. 'Do you know which day you will be going home?' I asked.

'Some time next week.' She shifted again and grimaced. 'Can you get that nurse now?'

'Yes, of course.' Max and I said a quick goodbye and on the way out I stopped at the nurses' station where one nurse sat working at a computer; the rest were occupied on the ward. 'Sorry to trouble you, but Caz would like help getting back into bed,' I said, feeling I was intruding.

'I'll be with her in a moment, although she needs to be doing it herself,' she said, without looking up from the screen.

'Thank you,' I said, and continued with Max to where Adrian and Paula were waiting by the door. It wasn't for me to comment on what the nurse had said. I'd delivered the message, although I did wonder … Most people who go into hospital for an operation or because they are ill can't wait to return home. Yet I hadn't seen that in Caz and the nurse's words seemed to confirm it. She wasn't helping herself as much as she could. True, Caz's progress had been slowed by some initial complications, but I wondered why she wasn't pushing herself now to do all she could to return home. How could being in hospital possibly be preferable to being at home with your family?

CHAPTER THIRTEEN

DAN

The weekend flew by. On Saturday morning we made a quick visit to our local grocery store (we walked), and then on our return I helped the children erect the tent, and they played in the garden for the rest of the day. I made 'pot' lunches for a picnic, which we ate under the shade of the tree. In the air-tight containers I put chopped hard-boiled eggs, pasta, peas and halved cherry tomatoes with a light dressing of mayonnaise, to be eaten with a plastic spoon. I find that if foods a child wouldn't normally eat are presented attractively and made easy to eat then they are more likely to be eaten. Almost anything can be put into a pot for a picnic or a packed lunch, savoury or sweet, and there are plenty of recipe sugges-tions and tips for healthy eating in my book, *Happy Mealtimes for Kids*. Now I had the backing of the paediatrician, I was more confident in making changes to improve Max's diet, rather than keeping the status quo as Jo had initially instructed me to. Hungry, Max ate the lot without complaint, followed by a plain yoghurt with no added sugar.

During the afternoon, as well as playing in the tent – a largely sedentary activity – I took the bats and balls, skipping ropes (we had one each), the skateboard and hula hoop from the shed and encouraged Max to play with them. He said they had hula hoops at school but he'd never tried them, as he felt it would make him look silly. However, in the privacy of our garden he was less self-conscious and gave it a try. And yes, he did look funny as he gyrated his hips, trying to keep the hula hoop around his waist, but then so did we all as we took it in turns. Adrian had only recently mastered the technique earlier in the summer, while Paula's hoop clattered straight to the ground the moment she let go of it. Mine stayed up for a few twirls, but gradually migrated down my legs. It was good fun and exercise; we laughed and the mood was light.

I made sure the children had plenty of water to drink as they played, for as well as keeping them hydrated it also had the effect of taking the edge off Max's appetite. He said a couple of times that he was hungry (the paediatrician had warned me to expect this) and a cool drink helped. The children had fruit mid-afternoon and we ate dinner early as we were going to the hospital: chicken and noodle stir-fry.

When we arrived on the ward Caz was in the chair again and all three daughters were perched on or leaning against the bed. They'd apparently already exhausted conversation. Kelly and Paris had their earbuds in and Summer was examining her nails while absently dipping into one of the open bags of sweets. Caz said hi to Max. He presented her with his offering of sweets and fruit and Summer grabbed the bag of sweets.

'Greedy!' Caz said, snatching it back. 'They're for me. I'm the one in hospital, I have first pick.' She was like a child in her wish to have the sweets first and I saw Paris roll her eyes.

I asked Caz how she was today and she shrugged and said OK. I said goodbye and crossed to where Adrian and Paula were waiting by the door. Paula was yawning and rubbing her eyes; she was exhausted. Roll on discharge day, I thought again. Tired after a day of running and playing in the garden in warm weather, she could have done with a relaxing evening at home, an early bath and bed. But that wasn't going to happen. We made our way up to the café and once we had our drinks she snuggled up on my lap and then nodded off. I had to wake her when it was time to collect Max, as she was too heavy to carry all the way to the ward. 'We'll soon have you home in your own bed,' I soothed. Adrian looked tired too.

Kelly and Summer were both still with their mother, so I guessed Kelly was making up for not visiting her the evening before. They said goodbye to Max and we left.

On Sunday, after a good night's sleep, the children woke refreshed. Once Adrian and Paula had left with their father, I took Max into town to buy him some more casual clothes (that I could adjust without Caz complaining). We went to a large department store that had an extensive children's section. Max and I chose a selection of clothes for him to try on in the changing rooms; they were all for age twelve and above. Among them I'd included a pair of loose-fitting jogging bottoms, elasticated at the waist and ankles, as I thought they might be a better fit than tailored trousers. But when he tried them on they looked awful, far too long, and because they were held in at the ankles the legs ballooned out, making him look even bigger, like the Michelin Man. It was really difficult, finding clothes that looked good on him, although I made light of it. The trousers and shorts we eventually bought would need half the legs cut off to make them fit, but there was no alternative for a child Max's size.

* * *

On Monday, after a pleasant weekend, we began what would be the last full week of school before the long summer holidays. The children were excited and I was looking forward to getting out of the routine of the school run. That morning I mentioned to Max that in order to help him lose weight he wouldn't be having any more second helpings of pudding at school; I didn't want him going up to the counter and being refused. He understood and accepted it. I'd decided that as it was so close to the end of term I'd leave the breakfast arrangements as they were. If Max was still with me in September when the new term began we could start afresh with him only having one breakfast, either at home or school. I hadn't booked for us to go away during the summer holidays, but I planned to have plenty of full days out, although I was aware that with the present contact arrangements – arriving at the hospital at 5.30 p.m. – we couldn't go too far away.

On Monday afternoon Jill telephoned with some important news, having just taken a call from Jo. Usually, when a foster carer works for an Independent Fostering Agency (IFA), as I did, the child's social worker informed the carer's support social worker (in my case, Jill) of any important decisions, changes or meetings in connection with the child, who then advised the carer, so the agency was informed as well. It's slightly different for carers who work for their Local Authority (LA) – they are often updated directly by the social worker – but the end result is the same. And what Jill had to tell me was important news.

'Caz is being discharged tomorrow,' she said. 'Jo is calling a review on Thursday. Ten o'clock at the council offices.' Children in care have regular reviews and the first one should usually be within a month of the child being placed with the carer. The child's parent(s), social worker, teacher, foster carer, the foster carer's support social worker and any other adults closely connected with the child meet to ensure that everything is being done to help the child, and that the care plan (drawn up by the social services) is appropriate. Very young children don't usually attend their reviews, though older children are expected to. 'Jo says Max needn't go,' Jill added. 'His parents will be invited.'

'All right,' I said, making a note of the day and time on the pad I kept by the telephone.

'One of the issues that will be discussed is how long Max is likely to be living with you,' Jill said. 'Caz will have been home a couple of days by then so will have a better idea of what she can and can't do. It may be he'll go home straight away, but I doubt it. Jo said Caz's recovery has been slower than anticipated, and she needs a lot of help. The physiotherapist and dietician at the hospital will continue to support her for a while after her discharge, but clearly the social services will need to be satisfied that Max will be properly looked after. She is the main caregiver. Obviously, contact will be at the family home once she's discharged.'

'Yes, so I'll take Max to see her at the hospital as normal this evening?'

'Yes, then tomorrow there won't be any contact, as Jo can't be sure what time Caz will be going home. It will also give Caz a chance to settle back in at home. On Wednesday you are to take Max home for contact at the usual time – five-thirty to seven. We'll review the future contact arrangements when we meet on Thursday. Jo said that once school has broken up it would make sense for Max to see his family in the afternoon rather than the evening.'

'Yes, as long as it's not every day,' I said. 'I was planning on having some day trips out.'

'I think Caz will want to see him every day, but we'll discuss the timing on Thursday.' Which I accepted, although I would stand up for what I'd said. It wouldn't be fair to Adrian and Paula if they couldn't enjoy some days out because of Max's contact arrangements. Sometimes fostering is a juggling act between the needs of the child and those of the carer's own family, who can all too easily be overlooked.

Jill asked how our weekend had gone and then, winding up, said she'd see me on Thursday for the review. After we'd finished I made a note of the day and time of the review in my diary, that there was no contact on Tuesday and contact on Wednesday was from 5.30 till 7 p.m. at Max's house. I then began working out the logistics of taking Max to and from contact with Adrian's school production running from Tuesday to Thursday evening. It's in situations like this when single-parent foster carers can struggle. Had I a partner then the arrangements could have been simplified and shared between us.

When I collected Max from school that afternoon I told him that his mother would be leaving hospital the following day and when he would see her.

'So tonight is her last night in hospital?' he said happily.

'Yes, she'll be pleased.' Yet even as I said it I had my reservations. Would Caz be pleased she was finally going home?

Apparently not.

When we arrived on the ward that evening she was in bed, not in the chair, complaining to her daughters about the plans for her discharge. They were only half listening. 'The community nurse will only be coming in three times a week to change my dressings, but that's not enough. They do it every day here. And how am I supposed to manage without a home help? You only get one if you've had a major amputation, like your leg or arm off.' Caz was talking about the state-funded provision for post-operative support at home. 'No one seems to care a toss what happens to me,' she lamented.

'We do,' Paris said with an exasperated sigh. 'I've told you, Dad is pleased you're coming home.'

'It'll be another excuse for him to go to the pub,' Caz said, unimpressed. 'Well, he'll have to stay in tomorrow. I've no idea what time the ambulance will bring me home. It depends on their schedule.' From which I deduced she was using the hospital's patient transport service to go home.

'You'll be pleased it's your last night,' I said positively as she finally acknowledged Max standing there. He placed the sweets and box of grapes on the bed. 'See you later then,' I said. With considerable relief that this would be our last night in the hospital, I returned to Adrian and Paula waiting by the door and we trudged up to the café.

With drinks and an ice cream each for Adrian and Paula, we passed the time by playing the games I'd brought from home: cards, pocket-sized ludo, and paper and pens for hangman and similar guessing games. Even so, the children were tired and looked at the clock, willing the time to go by. I was even more determined to stand my ground at the review on Thursday, when future contact arrangements would be discussed, and negotiate arrangements less disruptive to Adrian and Paula.

When we returned to the ward only Max was there, sitting in the chair, his sisters having gone home early. Doubtless they, too, would be relieved to have their mother home again and be able to return to their normal routine.

'Good luck for tomorrow,' I said to Caz as Max stood. 'It's bound to be a bit of a struggle to begin with, so just give yourself time.'

'I still need looking after,' she said in a slight voice, her expression child-like and vulnerable. 'I wanted to go to a convalescent home, but they said my operation didn't merit it.' So Caz was in no rush to go home, I thought.

'I'm sure your daughters and husband will help,' I said.

'Dan? I doubt it,' she said, deriding the possibility. 'Him and the girls can't do anything.' Although, of course, they must have been looking after themselves to some degree all the weeks Caz had been in hospital.

'Have you been given advice on post-operative care – the dos and don'ts?' I asked.

'They gave me a sheet,' she said quietly.

'I think it's important to follow it.'

She nodded meekly. Without her entourage, her bravado had largely gone and I wondered how much of her hostility towards me was insecurity – a defence mechanism.

'Well, good luck for tomorrow,' I said again. 'See you on Wednesday.'

'Yes. Thanks.'

Max said goodbye and then suddenly hugged her. She looked taken aback and smiled, embarrassed. Now I came to think of it, I hadn't seen any spontaneous displays of affection between any of them, but then families are different – some are more tactile than others. It doesn't mean they love each other less.

'See you,' she said to Max but didn't return his hug. So we left her as we'd seen her on that first night, propped up in bed with a blanket cradle supporting the covers. I wondered again how she would manage at home.

On Wednesday morning, when I returned from taking Paula to nursery, there was a message on the answerphone from Jill confirming that Caz had been discharged from hospital the day before and contact this evening would be at the family home from 5.30 till 7 p.m. As it turned out, the evenings that week weren't the nightmare I'd anticipated of having to be in two places at the same time. Max didn't have contact on Tuesday, so the three of us had watched Adrian's school production, which was excellent. Then on Wednesday I dropped Adrian off at school for five o'clock – the time the cast had to be there for the second showing – and had plenty of time to continue to Max's home for contact.

I'd bought a bunch of flowers for Max to give to his mother as a welcome-home gift, and he plodded stoically up to the front door with them held aloft. Paula slipped her hand into mine, uncertain about being somewhere new. The small front garden was unkempt, mainly concrete, with weeds growing through the cracks. A wheelie bin for rubbish stood by the front door, and the door needed painting, although the original windows, like the others on the estate, had been replaced with modern uPVC ones. Net curtains hung at the ground-floor windows.

I rang the bell and as we waited for it to be answered I looked at Max. He hadn't said much on the way there, but he was clearly pleased to be going home again, although he understood that he would still live with me until his mother was well enough to look after him properly. No one answered the door, so I pressed the bell again. 'Perhaps they're out,' Max said, his brow furrowing with concern.

'They're expecting us,' I said. Unless, of course, there'd been an emergency – for example, Caz having to be readmitted to hospital – and no one had told us. I pressed the bell again and then a few moments later a man's voice sounded gruffly from the other side of the door.

'All right, hold your horses! I'm coming.'

'That's Dad,' Max said.

'Good.'

The door opened and Dan, whom I knew to be forty, stood framed in the doorway. Of average height and build, he looked as though he could have just got up: unshaven, barefoot, with a sleeveless vest hanging loosely over his jeans. His bulging biceps were heavily tattooed and his blunt expression suggested he wasn't pleased at being disturbed.

'Hello, I'm Cathy,' I said pleasantly. He frowned, puzzled. 'Max's foster carer,' I clarified.

'Oh yeah. Go on in, lad,' he told Max. 'Your mother's put herself to bed.' I caught the smell of beer and cigarette smoke on his breath.

As far as I knew Dan hadn't seen Max since he'd come into care, and I would have expected a warmer welcome, but Max seemed unfazed and, stepping past his father, disappeared down the hall. Paula's hand tightened in mine.

'Is Caz all right?' I asked, concerned.

'Yeah, she's fine. Why shouldn't she be?' he replied defensively.

'You said she's in bed.'

'She's always in bed,' he returned.

'She's not ill?'

'No, just lazy. I expect I'll have to get my own dinner again.' And maybe take some to Caz, I thought but didn't say. 'Are the girls in?'

'Summer is. Why?'

'I just wondered. Please say hi to her and Caz.'

He gave a curt nod. He clearly wasn't going to invite us in so I said, 'I'll come back and collect Max at seven then.'

'If that's what you've been told.'

'It is.' I raised a smile and said goodbye, but the door was already closing.

I try not to make a snap decision or value judgement when I meet someone for the first time, but I'd taken an instant dislike to Dan. He came across as brash, uncaring and brutish, although clearly he must have some hidden charms that appealed to Caz. Perhaps I'd caught him on a bad day, but Paula deftly summed it up with the honesty of a young child. 'Is that Max's dad?' she asked.

'Yes.'

'He's not like Max. I like Max, but I don't like him.'

There was enough time for Paula and me to go home briefly before we had to return to collect Max, after which we had to collect Adrian from school at the end of the second showing of the production. A similar arrangement would apply to the following evening – the final night of the production. Hoping I would have a chance to see Caz and wish her well, at seven o'clock Paula and I returned to Max's house to collect him. As I pressed the bell, Paula tugged at my arm. 'We won't go in, will we?'

'Yes, if we're asked. Don't worry, it will be fine,' I reassured her. Perhaps Dan would be more hospitable, or maybe Caz or one of her daughters would come to the door and invite us in. We didn't know how long Max would be staying with me and it would help if the contact arrangements were relaxed and cordial. I felt that towards the end of Caz's stay in hospital some of her hostility towards me had gone, and of course I'd got along with Kelly and Summer when they'd been by themselves, so I was hopeful. As we waited for the doorbell to be answered a tortoiseshell cat joined us, rubbing around our legs. 'I remember Max telling me they had two cats,' I said. Its presence seemed to make the house more welcoming and homely.

'He likes us,' Paula said, dipping down to stroke him, and also partially reassured.

The front door opened, the cat shot in, and Max stood before us. 'Bye!' he called over his shoulder.

'Bye!' one of his sisters – I think it was Summer – returned from inside.

I looked down the hall to see if anyone was going to come to the door to see him off, but no one appeared. He came out and closed the door behind him. He seemed very young to be seeing himself out, and I saw Paula looking at him, concerned.

'Did you have a nice time?' I asked him as we walked down the short path to the car.

'Yes.'

'What did you do?'

'I sat in my room and read a book, like when I live at home,' he said matter-of-factly.

'Did you see your mum?'

He nodded. 'I gave her the flowers and she said thank you, then she was tired so I went to my room.'

'Was your dad in?'

'For a bit, then he went out.'

'And your sisters? Were they there?' I asked as I opened the car door for Max and Paula to get in.

'Summer and Kelly were there watching television,' Max said, clambering into the back seat.

'While you read in your bedroom?'

'Yes.' Although this wasn't the welcome-home family reunion I'd envisaged for him, I accepted that it was his family's way of doing things and they felt comfortable with it. Providing there was a responsible adult looking after Max – he was, after all, only six – there shouldn't be a problem. Although I was mindful that the reason he'd come into care in the first place was that he'd been left at home alone.

'So your sisters and mum were in all the time, although they weren't in the same room?'

He nodded. 'But Kelly was disappointed because I didn't bring any grapes.'

'Really?' I asked, surprised, as Max fastened his seatbelt. 'So she liked the grapes?'

'Yes, and the other fruit. We all did. Can I take some with me tomorrow?'

'Yes, I'll buy some.' I smiled to myself. Of course, they could have bought their own fruit, but clearly Max taking in a nicely presented box of fruit to the hospital every evening had been appreciated after all.

I checked the children's seatbelts, closed the car door and went round to the driver's door and got in. Max's little voice came from the back. 'Oh yes,' he said as nonchalantly as he could. 'While I was in my room reading, I ate a whole packet of biscuits. That wasn't good, was it?'

I glanced at him in the rear-view mirror as I started the engine. 'I think one or two biscuits would have been better, don't you?'

'I know, but once I started I couldn't stop. I needed you there to just give me two.' Bless him.

I could see this being a problem in the future: that any improvement in Max's diet could be undone during contact if he lay on his bed every evening and ate his way through a packet of biscuits. It was asking a lot of a young child who had unlimited access to snack food and was used to snacking to limit his intake and self-regulate. Caz, and ideally the whole family, needed to be involved and committed to a healthier eating plan if Max was to have any long-term success. Hopefully, there would be a chance to talk about this at Max's review the following morning, assuming Caz was there.

CHAPTER FOURTEEN

FIRST REVIEW

The timing of Max's LAC (looked-after child) review at ten o'clock on Thursday was perfect for me, as Paula was at nursery. Reviews usually last about an hour, which meant I would be back in time to collect her when nursery finished, although I had my friend with a child at the nursery on standby just in case. She'd take Paula home with her if necessary and look after her until I arrived. If I have to attend a meeting at the social services, I always have a back-up plan, as I know the meetings can start late or overrun.

I was dressed smart-casual, in light grey cotton trousers, a blouse and black kitten heels. I parked the car in the council offices car park and arrived in reception with ten minutes to spare, where I waited for Jill. I had a manila folder with me containing some notes and the eating and fitness plan the paediatrician at the clinic had given to me. I knew from experience I'd probably be asked to speak near the start of the review and say how Max was doing so that everyone present was brought up to date. I had a fair idea of what I wanted to say.

A couple of minutes later Jill arrived. 'Hi, Cathy, how are you?' she said with her usual cheerfulness.

'Good, thanks, and you?'

'Pleased it's nearly the summer holidays.' She, too, had children and was looking forward to the break.

We signed the visitors' book in reception and then made our way up the stairs to the second floor, where the meeting was to be held. 'Hopefully, we'll find out how long Max is likely to be with you,' Jill said as we went. 'I've had a referral for another child who needs an experienced carer. I'd like her to go to you, if possible.' Jill wasn't being dismissive or marginalizing Max, but there is always a shortage of foster carers, so often as one child leaves another arrives. She was caring and professional, although she didn't have the emotional attachment that a foster carer develops towards the child. At present I could only think of Max, so I nodded absently as she told me the few details she had about the new child and we continued to the top of the stairs. We turned left, went down a short corridor and to the meeting room. Jill gave a perfunctory knock on the door before opening it and we went in. A woman sat alone at one end of the table with a pen and folder in front of her. 'Are you here for Max's review?' she asked hopefully.

'Yes,' Jill said.

'Good. I was starting to think I was in the wrong room. I'm Cindy Ashmore, the IRO.' LAC reviews are chaired by an independent reviewing officer (IRO), who also minutes the meeting.

'I'm Cathy, Max's foster carer,' I said, smiling as I sat down.

'Jill, Cathy's supervising social worker from Homefinders Fostering Agency,' Jill said, sitting next to me.

'Pleased to meet you both.' The IRO had social work experience with additional training. She glanced at the clock on

147

the wall. 'I hope we're not too late starting. I have another review at twelve.'

It was exactly ten o'clock and Jo should have been here by now. Leaving the IRO sitting alone in a meeting room wasn't really acceptable.

'I'll make a note of your names while we're waiting,' she said, picking up her pen and opening the folder she had in front of her. She would minute the names of all those who attended.

We gave her our full names and roles and then she thanked me for returning the review forms. These are short question-naires – one for the carer to complete and one for the child – sent out just before the review to give feedback on how the child is settling in. The door opened and Jo came in.

'Sorry I'm late,' she flustered. 'Max's mother is on her way. I've had to organize a taxi for her – we've agreed to fund it.' So I assumed that's what had occupied her. Social services help with funding in some circumstances, and it was impor-tant Caz attended her child's review so she could have a say in planning Max's future.

'His mother is out of hospital then?' the IRO asked. She would have been briefed on the case some days before.

'Yes, just,' said Jo. Sitting down with a sigh, she deposited the folders she was carrying onto the table in front of her with a thud. 'Tuesday, late afternoon.'

The IRO nodded and made a note of Jo's name. She would know her from other child-care cases they'd worked on together. 'Do we know who else is coming?' she asked Jo.

'Max's teacher was invited but she can't attend, as it's the last day of term,' Jo explained. 'She's given me an update. I think one of Caz's daughter's might be coming too.'

'And Max's father, Dan?'

'Not as far as I know,' Jo said. There was a short silence and then Jo asked me, 'How did contact go last night?'

'All right, I think. I didn't go into the house. Max's father came to the door when we arrived, and I didn't see anyone when I collected him. Two of his sisters were in and Caz was in bed.'

'But Max spent time with her?' Jo asked.

'Yes, briefly, then he went to his bedroom and read for most of the evening. He also ate an entire packet of biscuits,' I added indulgently. Jill gave a light-hearted tut, but Jo didn't comment. She seemed preoccupied.

'Max was all right after contact?' Jill asked. Sometimes children become upset after seeing their family. They hold it all together and appear to cope with being in care and then this brief, bittersweet reminder of home unsettles them.

'He seemed to take it in his stride, as he does most things,' I said.

Suddenly a phone began to ring loudly from somewhere in the room, making us start and look around. Jill spotted it first – on the floor in one corner. I wasn't even aware that these meeting rooms had phones; I'd never heard one go off before.

'Shall I answer it?' Jill asked, looking at Jo as the ringing continued. I suppose Jill felt it was Jo's prerogative, as she worked in the building.

Jo shrugged.

'I think you'd better,' the IRO said. It was making quite a noise.

Jill stood, crossed to the phone and, lifting the handset, said, 'Hello?' She listened and then said, 'Yes, it is.' Then listened again before turning to Jo. 'It's reception. Caz has arrived. She's asking if there's a wheelchair available?'

'I've no idea,' Jo said, immediately stressed. 'How did she get from the cab into reception?'

Jill asked the receptionist on the phone, 'What is Caz using now?' And after a moment she said, 'Crutches.'

'So she can use those to get to the lift, can't she?' Jo asked. 'I don't know if there's a wheelchair here or not.' I could see her stress level rising.

'Can she use the crutches to get to the lift?' Jill said more diplomatically into the phone. There was a pause as the message was relayed to Caz. I saw the IRO glance at the clock again; it was now 10.15.

'OK. Thanks,' Jill said, and replaced the handset. 'She said it's painful using crutches, but her daughters are going to help her to the lift.'

I thought I heard Jo sigh.

'Perhaps the council needs to look into making a wheel-chair available in reception?' the IRO suggested to Jo. 'I know some authorities have one.'

Jo nodded, although I thought this would probably be the last thing on her mind with her busy work schedule, as most wheelchair users would arrive with their own. We waited in silence and Jo checked something in one of the folders she had in front of her, then presently we heard voices in the corridor outside, followed by a loud knock on the door.

'Come in!' the IRO called.

The door opened. Paris entered first and then held it wide open so Caz could come in, followed by Kelly. Caz was clearly struggling to use the crutches; it was taking a lot of effort, not helped by her size. It was the first time I'd seen her standing; at the hospital she'd either been in bed or sitting in the chair beside the bed. She wasn't tall and the strain on her arms as she transferred her weight from one crutch to the other was enormous. Her face was bright red. Jill, who was sitting closest to the door, stood. 'Here, Caz,' she said, pulling out a chair to make it easier for her to sit down.

Caz heaved herself to the chair and sat down. Jill and I then moved round so she and her daughters could sit together. I was touched by the way Kelly and Paris were helping their mother and looking out for her. Childlike in her endeavours to make herself comfortable, they helped manoeuvre her chair closer to the table and straighten her bandaged foot, which now had a protective post-operative boot covering it. They then positioned her crutches either side of her.

'Are you comfortable?' the IRO asked politely, once they'd settled. 'I'm sorry there wasn't a wheelchair available.'

'It's OK,' Caz said.

'Let me know if there is anything you need during the meeting or if you want to take a break.' Caz nodded. 'I know it must have been an effort for you to come here, so thank you for making it.' Caz nodded again. 'Can I take your full name and that of your daughters, please, for the minutes?' Caz told her and she made a note. 'Your husband's not coming?' she asked.

'No. He doesn't have to, does he?' Caz said a little defensively.

'No, but I'd have waited for him before starting the meeting if he was.'

'He's busy,' Paris put in.

'Thank you,' the IRO said, smiling at her. 'I've noted his apology for absence.' Which is the standard way of minuting those who have been invited to a meeting but can't attend.

'Is Summer coming?' Jo asked Caz.

'No. Her school hasn't broken up yet.'

'That's your other daughter?' the IRO clarified.

'Yes,' Caz said.

'So let's start with introductions,' the IRO said. 'I'm Cindy Ashmore, the reviewing officer for Max. I think you'll have been given some information on my role and the nature of the review.' Caz nodded. The IRO now looked at Jo to introduce herself. Jo gave her name and said, 'Local authority social worker for Max.' Jill was next, then me, then it was Paris's turn. A little embarrassed, she said, 'I'm Paris, Max's sister.'

'Thank you,' the IRO said with another smile and then she looked at Caz.

'I'm Max's mother,' she said.

'Thank you,' she said, making a note.

'Kelly, Max's sister,' Kelly said, stifling a self-conscious grin.

'Thank you,' the IRO said again, and finished noting their names. She then addressed us all. 'This review is about Max, who at present is living with Cathy, a foster carer. He's accommodated under a Section 20. That hasn't changed, has it?' she asked Jo.

'No,' Jo confirmed.

'I'd like to start by hearing how Max has been settling into his foster home. Then we'll hear from everyone else in turn who wishes to speak.'

Although there were only a few of us, reviews tend to be formal and I straightened in my chair and glanced at my notes. I always start with the positives. Even if a child is behaving badly and has been excluded from school, I find something positive to say. In Max's case it was easy, as there were plenty of positives. 'Max is a lovely boy, intelligent, caring and thoughtful,' I began. 'He's settled well into my household and plays nicely with my children, Adrian and Paula, although he obviously misses his own family. He understands why he is in care and seems to be taking all the changes in his stride.'

'He never says much,' Caz put in, and the IRO nodded.

'He's eating and sleeping well, and is happy to join in my family's outings and activities,' I continued. 'I've met his teacher, Mrs Marshall, and he's doing well at school.' (I didn't elaborate on his progress at school, as Jo had a report from Mrs Marshall.) 'His teacher has been lending Max books, as he loves to read. We have plenty of books at home and we'll visit the library during the summer holidays.' I paused to allow the IRO, who was minuting, time to catch up.

'Health-wise,' I continued, 'Max has been diagnosed with asthma and has an inhaler, although he only used it on the first day he came to me. As far as I know he's only used it once at school too. He gets out of breath after exercise, but his chest isn't tight and he doesn't struggle to breathe, so he carries the inhaler with him just in case.' I paused again to allow the IRO time to write.

'Max snores very loudly when he's in a deep sleep,' I said, 'which I understand can be due to enlarged tonsils or adenoids. But the paediatrician found no evidence of this and said his snoring, breathlessness and the rash he sometimes gets are most likely caused by him being overweight. He hasn't had the rash since he's been with me, but I will take him to the doctor's if it appears to try to get a diagnosis.'

'The cause of the rash hasn't been identified then?' the IRO asked, glancing up from writing.

'No. Not as far as I know,' I said. 'Caz thought it might be an allergy.'

'It's always gone by the time I get a doctor's appointment,' Caz said, and the IRO nodded.

'The paediatrician said it might be due to sweating,' I said.

'Has the paediatrician's report arrived yet?' the IRO asked Jo.

'No, not yet,' Jo said.

The IRO looked to me to continue. 'During the medical, the paediatrician weighed and measured Max and said he was considerably overweight. She has put him on a diet and fitness plan.'

'How much does he weigh?' the IRO asked.

'Eight and a half stone,' I said.

She frowned. 'What does the average child of his age weigh?'

'Approximately three and a half stone,' I said, avoiding Caz's gaze. This was a sensitive subject, but it had to be said, as a review is concerned with all aspects of the child's wellbeing.

'What does the diet and fitness plan involve?' the IRO asked me.

'Nothing too drastic. I have a copy of the plan here,' I said, taking the printed sheet from my folder.

'I haven't got one,' Caz said.

I slid it across the table towards her so she could read it.

'Perhaps you could photocopy it when we've finished,' the IRO said to Jo, 'so Caz has a copy and we have one on file.'

'Yes,' Jo said.

'Thank you, Cathy. Is there anything else this review should know about Max's health?'

'The paediatrician tested his eyesight and that was fine,' I said. 'He doesn't need glasses, but he may need to have some

154

more teeth extracted. He had some teeth out before he came into care and the doctor said he might need to have more. I understand he's under his own dental surgeon.'

'Yes, he is,' Caz said. She'd taken a brief look at the diet and fitness plan and had passed it to Kelly to read.

'When is his next appointment at the dentist?' the IRO asked Caz.

'In a month or so,' Caz said. 'I can't remember the exact date.'

'We don't know if Max will still be with Cathy then,' the IRO said to Caz, 'but if he is, she can take him if you wish. Let Jo know.'

Caz nodded. She seemed more placid and less confrontational than she had been in hospital. Perhaps it was the formality of the review, although in my experience it rarely stopped parents speaking their minds.

'Thank you, Cathy,' the IRO said. 'Is there anything else you want to say? I see from the questionnaire you returned that generally you feel Max is happy.'

'Yes. He has settled in well.' I would raise the matter of contact arrangements later, once everyone had given their reports.

'And Max can stay with you for however long the placement is needed?' This was a routine question.

'Yes,' I confirmed.

The IRO now asked Jo to give her report and Jo began by stating that Max was in care under a Section 20, and briefly summarized the safeguarding issues that had brought him into care: that while Caz was in hospital he had been left unattended at home. I saw Caz glare at her daughters as if they were responsible, but to my mind surely Max's father was more culpable? Jo confirmed that the care plan was for Max to return home once Caz, the main caregiver, was well enough to meet his needs and offer appropriate supervision. Jo would be visiting the family the following week to make an assessment. She said that in respect of Max's education, Mrs Marshall had described him as 'studious' and a pleasure to teach. The end-of-year test results, which would be included in the school report and sent home on the last day of term, showed that Max was well above average, especially in literacy. His reading age was ten.

'That's very good,' the IRO said, glancing up at Caz.

'Don't know where he gets that from,' she said, almost embarrassed. 'His father and I don't read books.'

Jo continued by saying that Mrs Marshall was encouraging Max to join in more with class discussion and interact with children outside the classroom. She was pleased he was now following a diet and fitness plan, as the school encouraged all children to have a healthy lifestyle. She would be his teacher again in September, as the teachers were moving up with their classes. Jo confirmed as a matter of formality that there had been no exclusions from school. Then she moved on to contact, saying it had taken place at the hospital from 5.30 until 7 p.m., but now that Caz had been discharged it would be at the family home.

'And these arrangements are working well and will continue?' the IRO asked.

'Yes,' Jo said. 'Although during the school holidays contact will take place in the afternoon. Caz goes to bed very early.'

I glanced at Jill, who said, 'Cathy would like to take the children on some day trips during the summer holidays, which would be difficult if contact was every afternoon.'

The IRO nodded thoughtfully and then said, 'Perhaps we could alternate afternoon and evening, or is that going to be confusing?'

There was a few moments' pause and then Jill said, 'So if it was alternated, contact could be in the evening on Monday, Wednesday, Friday and Sunday – five-thirty to seven. Then in the afternoon on Tuesday, Thursday and Saturday, say two to three-thirty. How would that work?'

'I can mange that,' I said. It would still be a lot of toing and froing, but at least it would give us the freedom to go on day trips. Max had a high level of contact because he was going home, so the bond between him and his family was maintained. Children who can't or are unlikely to be able to return home – often as a result of abuse or neglect – have a lower level of contact and it's usually supervised at a contact centre.

The IRO was now looking at Caz for her response, and I was half expecting her to object and say that she wanted to see Max every afternoon, but to my surprise she said, 'Yeah, but write it down for me or I'll never remember.'

'Jo will send you a letter with the revised contact times,' the IRO said. 'They will start once school has broken up.'

As Caz seemed to be in a good mood, amicable and open to suggestions, I grabbed the chance and said, 'It would be really helpful if Max's diet could be continued while he is at home during contact.'

'Yes, that would make sense,' the IRO said, and she looked at Caz.

Her cheeks flushed. 'You really think I can stop him eating? Look at the size of me!'

CHAPTER FIFTEEN

MEETINGS

There was an embarrassed silence when no one seemed to know what to say or where to look, then Kelly said, 'I want to do what Max is doing.' Which allowed us to look at her. 'I was going to phone you,' she said to Jo. 'I want to go on a diet and fitness plan. Cathy told me I could get help at the health centre.'

The IRO smiled encouragingly and said to Jo, 'Do you have details of the help available?'

'No, I'd have to find out,' she replied.

'The paediatrician mentioned that support was available when I took Max for his medical,' I confirmed.

The IRO nodded and then said to Jo, 'Can you look into it and let Kelly and her mother know the details?'

Jo nodded and made a note.

There was another short pause. The atmosphere was still a bit awkward. My question hadn't been addressed and I didn't feel happy pursuing it, although of course it was in Max's interest to keep to his diet during contact. Caz was gazing at the table. Then Paris said, 'I'll go with you, Kelly.' Which was commendable but didn't really help Max with his diet. Then Kelly added, 'And I'll try and stop Max stuffing himself in his bedroom.'

'Thank you.' I smiled at her.

'See if you can stop me too,' Caz said dryly under her breath.

'I'm sure support would be available,' the IRO said. 'We're all becoming more health-conscious as a nation.' Which was tactful and diplomatic.

'Easier said than done,' Caz said in the same deadpan voice.

'I can appreciate that,' the IRO said gently. However, the review was about Max – now wasn't the time to explore Caz's eating issues – so moving the review on, the IRO said, 'I'll minute that Max will be encouraged to maintain the diet and fitness plan recommended by the paediatrician while he is at home during contact.' We waited as she wrote and then she asked Jo if she wanted to say anything else. Jo didn't. 'And you're satisfied that Max is receiving a good level of care with his foster carer?' she asked Jo.

'Yes,' Jo said. The question is always uncomfortable for the carer(s) but is considered necessary, although in practice if there was any doubt that the carer(s) was falling short in their care of the child, it would be addressed immediately and wouldn't wait for the next review.

It was now Caz's turn to speak and she didn't know what to say. Embarrassed, she pulled her cardigan protectively across her chest and looked down.

'Is there anything you want to add?' the IRO asked. Caz shook her head. 'Are you happy with the standard of care Max is receiving? Obviously, as his mother, you would do some things differently, but generally are you satisfied he is being well looked after?'

'Yes,' Caz said.

'Anything you would like to say in particular, possibly about Max's routine?' she asked.

I wondered if Caz would hark back to her initial complaints, but she shook her head. The IRO made a note and then said, 'Kelly, Paris, would you like to add anything to this review?'

'Is Max getting his pocket money?' Paris asked a little defiantly. 'My dad says that the foster carer gets money and some of it has to go to the kid.'

Jill replied. 'That's right. The carer has a clothing allowance for the child, who at Max's age will have his clothes bought for him. There is also an element in the carer's allowance for pocket money, which Cathy has been saving for him.'

'Why doesn't he get it?' Paris asked.

'Because I have been buying Max everything he needs,' I said. 'He puts the money I give him each week into a money box in his bedroom, which he knows he will take with him when he leaves.'

'Thank you, Cathy,' the IRO said. Then to Kelly and Paris: 'Do you have any more questions or comments?'

They shook their heads.

'Jill?' the IRO asked. 'Would you like to add anything?' The supervising social worker usually attended the review, but their report was often short.

'My role is to supervise and monitor Cathy in all aspects of her fostering,' she said, looking at Caz, Kelly and Paris as she spoke. 'I visit her regularly and we discuss Max's needs and how Cathy is meeting them. I check her record-keeping is up to date and advise her on further training. She is a conscientious and experienced carer who provides a high level of care. We are also in regular contact by phone and I know she will ask for advice and help if necessary. I have no concerns and am happy with the level of care Max is receiving.'

'Thank you,' the IRO said, making a note. She looked at her checklist and then at us. 'Has Max had any accidents or illnesses since he came into care?'

'No,' I said.

'And he hasn't run away?' A standard question.

'No,' I said again.

'Are there any complaints from anyone?' She glanced at each of us in turn. This was another standard question, and while Caz had had plenty of complaints to begin with, they seemed to have fizzled out. There was silence. 'I'll write none then,' she said. Then looking at Jo: 'When are you next visiting Max?'

'Next week,' she replied.

'So am I,' Jill said.

'Well, if no one has anything further to say, all that remains is to set the date for the next review in three months' time. If Max is home by then, it's likely the review won't be needed, but we can confirm or cancel nearer the time.' She opened her diary and chose a date at the beginning of October, which Jo, Jill and I noted. Then she thanked everyone for coming and closed the meeting. 'Have arrangements been made for your transport home?' she asked Caz.

Caz looked at Jo, who said, 'I'll call a cab now.' She stood and so did I.

'I'm dashing off,' I said. 'I have to collect my daughter from nursery.'

'Thank you for coming,' the IRO said.

'I'll phone you,' Jill said.

'See you later,' I said to Caz.

'If I'm not in bed,' she returned. 'I'll be exhausted after this lot.'

I smiled sympathetically and, calling goodbye to everyone, left the room. Although the meeting had started late, I still had time to collect Paula from nursery. Overall, I felt the review had gone well. The minutes would be typed up and a copy sent to all of us who had attended. That Kelly and Paris had volunteered to help Max stick to his diet during contact and were going to attend the health centre themselves I thought was very positive. Perhaps they'd persuade Caz to go too. She hadn't said much at the review, but at least she seemed reasonably amicable. There had definitely been a change in her over the last few days, so I assumed that her bad humour while in hospital was probably a result of frustration and anxiety about her operation.

That evening, when I took Max to contact, Kelly let him in. She said her mother was resting on her bed but would get up when Max arrived. Their father was out. Adrian, Paula and I had time to go home briefly and when we collected Max I left them sitting in the car directly in front of the house, with the pavement-side door open to let the air in and so I could see them clearly. Kelly saw Max out and Caz, who was sitting out of sight in the living room watching television, shouted goodbye.

'How are you?' I called.

'Uncomfortable!' she returned. 'Kelly! Can you fetch me another cushion on your way back?'

Kelly sighed in mild exasperation and rolled her eyes. 'She was less of a problem in hospital,' she said affectionately.

I smiled, called goodbye to Caz down the hall and we left.

* * *

The next day was Friday and that evening, before Max had his bath, I took the scales from where I stored them in my bedroom into the bathroom and weighed him. I was weighing him once a week as I'd been advised to and was keeping it all very low-key. I didn't want him to become fixated or anxious and to start counting pounds or become disappointed if he didn't lose weight one week. The diet wasn't drastic, just healthier eating with fewer sweet and fatty foods and more exercise, so change was likely to be slow. He'd actually lost four pounds, but I simply said, 'Well done.' I left the bathroom for him to finish getting undressed and returned the scales to my bedroom, then I waited on the landing until he'd finished his bath. Max had a bath every evening now as part of his bedtime routine, just as Adrian and Paula did. Later, I recorded his weight in my fostering log.

For the next few evenings, when I took Max to contact, one of his sisters answered the door when we arrived and saw him out when he left. After Kelly's comments about fruit, I was now buying extra again so that Max could take some with him, as he had done at the hospital, but not the bag of sweets. When I asked him if he'd had a nice time he always said he had and that he'd shared the fruit with his sisters before going to his room to read. From what he told me, he spent most evenings in his bedroom because he didn't like watching the television as his mother and sisters did. While this seemed isolating to me, it was what he was used to and happy with, although I suspected that had they all played a game of cards, for example, or watched a good children's film or wild-life documentary, which Max loved, he would have joined in. He had started leaving some books in his bedroom at his home so he didn't have to keep taking the one he was reading at my house. He brought them back when he'd finished them and exchanged them for different ones.

On Sunday we visited my parents and, as usual for a Sunday, Mum cooked a full roast dinner, followed by delicious homemade apple pie with melt-in-your-mouth pastry, served with a choice of warm custard or vanilla ice cream or both. I'd already had a quiet word with Mum and asked her not to offer us second helpings, as Max was on a diet. Mum loves to feed her family. She didn't offer second helpings, but the portion sizes of the first servings were so generous that we couldn't have eaten any more anyway. We had to leave at 4.30 p.m. so we were back in time for Max's evening contact.

School broke up the following week and Max and Adrian came out of school very excited and with bagfuls of schoolwork and their end-of-year reports. At home I read the reports while they played in the garden and then later congratulated them individually. Adrian's was very good; Max's was outstanding. He was way above average in all core subjects and his test results showed he was working at the age of a nine- or ten-year-old. Mrs Marshall mentioned in her summing-up how pleased she was that he had maintained his progress throughout the year, despite some unsettling changes at home. Her only criticism – if it could be called that – was that she would like to see Max interacting more with other children his age, which she'd mentioned to me when I'd met her. I'd asked Max if he had some friends he'd like to invite home to play during the summer holidays (Adrian and Paula would be seeing their friends sometimes), but he said he didn't. If Max was still with me in September when the new school term began, I'd up my efforts to encourage him to bring home some friends. I appreciated how important it was for children to interact and socialize with their peer group, not just to make friends; it helps them to be able to get along with people in adulthood too – at work and in their personal relationships. Children and adults who aren't at ease in company often struggle.

I received a copy of the new contact arrangements in the post and transferred them to my diary. The first day of the summer holidays fell on a Thursday, so according to the new arrangements Max was seeing his family in the afternoon between 2 and 3.30 p.m. He took all his schoolwork with him and his school report for his family to see, and when I collected him he said his mother had read his report and was very pleased. Fantastic, but she'd rewarded him with a box of chocolates! Of which he'd eaten the entire top layer before Kelly had stopped him. Pity his poor teeth and glucose levels, I thought, but I didn't say anything: old eating habits die hard.

On Friday Jill and Jo visited us. It was unusual to have the social worker and the supervising social worker visit on the same day, but they were both about to go on their summer holidays so wanted to squeeze in their statutory visits before they went. Jill's visit was at 10.30 a.m. and Jo's at 1.30 p.m. I knew Jill wouldn't be late and would want to see the children, so I kept them in the living room playing until she arrived. She said a bright and relaxed 'Hi' to them and then sat chatting informally to us all, during which time she would be observing Max, my children and me to see how well we were all interacting and getting along. Although it could be said we were on our best behaviour, Jill was experienced enough to see through any pretence, and she knew me well enough to know that I'd raise any problems I might be having in fostering, not hide them. Supervising social workers also make at least one unannounced visit each year so that the carer isn't expecting them and doesn't have time to prepare for their visit.

She talked with Max for a while as he played. Although he was quieter than many children I'd fostered, she did manage to engage him in a conversation about books and what he liked to read, and some card and board games I was teaching him. She also talked to Adrian and Paula, who knew her from her previous visits with other children we'd fostered, so they were less shy. I knew she'd want to talk to me alone at some point, so when she'd finished talking to the children and was taking out her notepad and pen I suggested they went into the garden to play.

'Can I go too?' Max asked quietly.

'Yes, of course,' she said. I guessed he realized that Jill's visit was specifically about him.

Adrian automatically offered Max his hand to help him stand, which he found difficult to do from the floor or a low seat. While it was a kind gesture and done naturally, it seemed to highlight Max's lack of agility due to his weight. I saw Jill watching him as with Adrian's help he hauled himself to his feet and then, the last to leave, took hold of the edge of the patio doors to heave himself over the small step.

'How's the diet and fitness plan going?' she asked when he'd gone.

'Well,' I said. I opened my fostering folder and read out his weight loss, which she wrote down.

'He looks healthier,' Jill said.

'Can you see a difference already?'

'Yes. He's brighter-eyed and his skin has lost that pastiness. Cutting out much of the junk food and encouraging him to play actively outside is bound to have a positive effect.'

I was pleased Jill had already noticed a difference, for it wasn't just about Max losing weight, but generally being healthier. We spent a little while discussing the type of meals I was giving him and his routine, then I told Jill about his very good school report and she asked how Adrian had done. I updated her on contact. Although I'd mentioned this at the LAC review, I now gave Jill more detail, including that Max was coping with contact well and wasn't upset afterwards, but that he was spending a lot of time during contact alone in his bedroom. Jill said she'd mention it to Jo. The agency had some printed sheets that they gave to parents containing guidance on making the best of contact, for obviously it was a different situation to when a child was living at home. Jill then asked if there had been any changes to my household, which was a standard question at each supervisory visit, and I said there hadn't. We discussed the training I'd attended and was due to go on. I usually attended training one or two days a month, but it had stopped for the summer holidays. She asked if I needed any additional support to look after Max, which I didn't.

She then checked and signed my log notes and handed me a printed copy of the minutes from her last supervisory visit, which I had to check and sign to say they were correct. We got out our diaries to arrange a date for her next visit in four weeks' time, although Jill said she'd telephone me when she returned from her holidays in two weeks. If I needed any help or advice in the meantime, I could telephone the agency and speak to one of her colleagues or the local authority duty social worker. Before she left she called goodbye to the children, and then I saw her to the front door, where I wished her a relaxing and well-deserved holiday. Some of those working in social care think that support social workers (compared to those working in child protection) have an easy time of it, but in my experience they work just as hard. Jill had twelve foster carers to supervise and support, which included visiting them regularly at home, attending meetings with them, writing reports on them, assessing them for their annual review, participating in training, liaising with the child's social worker, as well as taking turns on the rota to cover out-of-hours calls, as the agency offered twenty-four-hour support every day of the year. It's surprising how often they're needed in the middle of the night and even on Christmas Day.

We had lunch indoors – cold chicken salad – and then sat in the living room, as Jo was expected at 1.30 p.m. But when it got to two o'clock and she still hadn't arrived and the children were asking to go outside I let them, with the proviso that they came in when called. Jo finally arrived nearly an hour late, full of apologies, stressed and with indigestion. She'd had to attend an emergency strategy meeting at twelve and had then grabbed a sandwich, which she'd gobbled down while driving to me. I fetched her the glass of water she asked for as she settled in the living room.

'Our flight is in twenty-four hours and I haven't started packing yet,' she said. 'More stress!'

'Where are you going?' I asked, sitting opposite her.

'Greece. If we ever get there. They'll all just have to help.' I assumed she meant her family. She took a pen and large notepad from her bag and I asked her if she wanted me to call Max in from the garden, but she said she'd talk to me first.

Like Jill, she would have a checklist to work through, although the child's social worker's agenda was slightly different to the carer's supervising social worker, as their responsibility was primarily with the child and establishing a relationship with them, whereas Jill was responsible for the welfare of my family and me as well as the child. Jo began by asking about Max's routine, including his bath and bedtime, then his self-care skills (which were good). She asked if we all ate together as a family (which is considered very important), what he liked to do in his spare time and how the new contact arrangements were working. I said they'd only begun the day before when the children broke up for the summer, which she seemed to have forgotten. I told her what I'd told Jill about contact and that Jill had said her agency had notes for parents about making the most of their time together.

'She's sending them to me, right?' Jo asked, glancing up from writing.

'I think so. She was certainly going to speak to you.'

'OK. And you're not going away during the summer?' she asked, moving on.

'No. We're having some days out.' Which had been my main reason for asking that contact wasn't every afternoon.

'And you'll be taking Max?'

'Yes, of course.'

'Who lives here again?'

'My children, Adrian and Paula, Max and myself. And our cat, Toscha.'

'No issues with his health?' she asked, racing through her checklist.

'Yes.' I reminded her that Max had been diagnosed with asthma, although he rarely used his inhaler, and that this and his snoring and rash could be due to his obesity. I also reminded her that he may have to have further teeth out, and that he was now following the diet and fitness plan recommended by the paediatrician (although all of this had been covered before at the review).

'What paediatrician?' she asked.

'The one you arranged to give Max his medical when he first came into care. I gave you the details of what she'd said at the time.'

'Oh yes. It must be on file. That's what Kelly and Paris were talking about yesterday, which reminds me, I have to phone them.' She hastily scribbled another note at the top of the page and drew a large circle around it to remind her. 'Go on.'

I told her of Max's weight loss, which she noted, and that Max's school report was with his mother. 'Hopefully, his teacher will remember to send a copy to the department,' she said, starring what she'd just written. It's usual for a copy of the child's school report to be on their file at the social services.

'No other issues?'

'I don't think so.'

'I'll see Max now then,' she said.

'Shall I leave you two alone?' I asked. The child's social worker usually wanted to see the child alone in case there were any issues the child wanted to raise that they didn't feel comfortable mentioning in front of their carer.

'Yes, please.'

I called Max in and once he was settled on the sofa beside Jo, I said I'd be outside if I was needed. Going out through the patio doors, I joined Adrian and Paula in the garden, who were doing some puzzles on the ground mat in the shade of the tree.

The amount of time the child's social worker spends alone with the child varies. They need to satisfy themselves that the child is happy and is being well looked after, and the child or young person may have a lot they want to say or nothing much at all. Max reappeared through the patio doors after about fifteen minutes. I stood and left the mat. 'She wants to see you,' he said as he drew near.

'OK, love. Thanks.'

As Max joined Adrian and Paula on the mat I heard him ask Adrian, 'Will you have to see her?'

'I don't think so,' Adrian replied. 'She is your social worker, like Jill is ours.' Which summed it up pretty well.

In the living room Jo was putting away her folder and pen. 'He showed me his bedroom,' she said. The child's social worker usually sees the child's bedroom at each visit. 'He seems comfortable enough, and he's coping all right?'

'Yes, I think he's coping very well.'

I sat down, for although Jo had packed away she'd made no move to go. 'There's something I want to ask you about,' she said. And from the seriousness of her tone and her expression I assumed it was something negative, possibly something I'd done wrong or that Max was struggling with. But, tucking her bag on the floor by her feet, she said, 'I'm thinking of leaving my post and becoming a foster carer. What do you think?'

CHAPTER SIXTEEN

STRANGE, THE WAY THINGS TURN OUT

Taken off guard by Jo's question, I opened and closed my mouth in a good impersonation of a fish before I found the words I needed. 'The two roles are very different,' I said. 'Why are you thinking of changing?'

'Less stress.'

'Fostering can be very stressful, although it's probably a different stress to yours.'

'In what way? You always seem pretty chilled.'

'That's for your benefit,' I said with a smile, but it wasn't returned. 'We have to appear calm and in control for the sake of the child or children in our care, but some of the issues we deal with are very stressful. And remember, we're on call every hour of every day. You can go home in the evening and recharge your battery, ready for the following day.'

'But that's the same with your own children, it's twenty-four/seven.'

'Yes, but fostering a child is more intense and stressful than looking after your own child. The foster child comes with history and baggage that you are never fully aware of, so you have to be hyper-vigilant to meet their needs, especially in the early weeks. With your own children you know their history and there is little they can do to shock you. But many of the children who come into care have unsafe and dangerous behaviour because of their early years' experiences. And to hear what they have been through first-hand – the abuse they've suffered – is heartbreaking. I've had many sleepless nights.'

'So have I,' Jo put in.

'I'm sure. Dealing with the child's parents is also stressful for foster carers. No one wants their child to go into care. At best they resent it and often they are very angry.'

'But they don't hate you like they do social workers,' Jo said.

'Many do,' I said. 'They see us as part of the system that's working against them to take their children from them. And remember, foster carers don't have the support of colleagues like social workers do. You can see a client in your office if necessary, or if you make a home visit, you can take a colleague with you. Carers don't have that. We meet the parents regularly at contact and sometimes they wait outside their child's school. If they are angry, the foster carer is an easy target. We have no protection. I've been on the receiving end of plenty of anger and abuse, some of it threatening, which has left me very shaken and stressed.'

'So why don't you report it?' Jo asked

'We do if it's very bad, but nothing happens. There aren't the resources to provide foster carers with back-up each time they take a child to contact or school. So we defuse the situation as best we can and try to build up a relationship with the parents, just as you do. Sometimes it works, but other times the parents remain angry, especially if the child isn't able to go home. They blame the carer as much as they blame the court and social services.' I wasn't trying to put her off, but she needed to know the reality.

'Hmmm,' she said reflectively. 'But carers only have one child or a sibling group to look after. Our case loads are ridiculously high.'

'I know, I sympathize, I really do, but remember, the children we foster are often very distressed, even disturbed, with challenging behaviour. We are here day and night for them, sometimes with very little progress at the start. Don't get me wrong, I love what I do – you couldn't do it if you didn't – but there are a lot of issues to consider. Fostering isn't really a job, more a vocation. Have you thought about the financial implications?'

'Foster carers get an allowance, don't they?' she said, clearly having already considered this.

'Yes, but all the expenses for the child, including their food, clothes, leisure activities, holidays, transport and so on, has to come out of it. We only receive the allowance when a child is living with us, so you can't view it as a regular income.'

'How do you manage then?' she asked.

'I have to be very careful with money. I also have a small part-time admin job, which I can do from home. I fit it in around the children – when they are at school or in bed.'

'My husband works so we have a good standard of living,' Jo admitted. I nodded. She looked thoughtful. 'I came into social work with such high hopes. I didn't have the best childhood myself and I wanted to help others. But the reality is I'm spread so thinly I can't help anyone. I dash from one meeting to another and then beat myself up over the decisions I have or haven't made. I'm so stressed when I get home I don't have time for my own family.' She shrugged. 'Perhaps I just need a holiday.'

I nodded and glanced down the garden to where the children were now playing on the bikes. 'Have you discussed fostering with your family?' I asked.

'Not properly. I mentioned I was thinking about it. They weren't that keen to have someone else living with us the whole time, but the foster child would be my responsibility.'

I looked at her carefully. Jo seemed rather naive when it came to fostering. 'It doesn't work like that. Fostering includes the whole family, so everyone has to be fully committed. It's not like having a lodger. The child is a member of your family for however long they are with you. You know when you visit a child in a foster home one of the things you look for is that they are fully integrated into the family and included in all family activities. It can't work if any of the family is half-hearted about fostering or doesn't want to.'

'You're right. I'll have to talk to them about it again.'

'I would. Everyone needs to be committed. It's such a juggling act to make sure your own children have their fair share of attention. It's so easy for them to resent the intrusion when their lives have been disrupted and turned upside down.'

'How are they disrupted? Other than having someone living with them,' Jo asked.

It wasn't difficult to find an example. 'Take Max. He's a lovely boy and has fitted in well and we all think the world of him. But since he arrived my children haven't had an evening to themselves when they could relax at home and play because of the contact arrangements. I've been collecting Adrian from school, driving to Max's school to collect him and returning home with just enough time to eat dinner (which I've been having to prepare earlier to save time). Then we've all been getting back in the car to take Max to the hospital, where Adrian, Paula and I have had to while away an hour and a half in the hospital café every evening. Adrian has been trying to do his homework there, but it hasn't been easy, and I've had to keep Paula amused and awake. She's usually in bed at seven o'clock. After collecting Max from the ward and coming home, there's been just enough time for a snack before their bath and bedtime routine.'

'And your kids didn't mind?' she asked, amazed. 'Mine would kick up a right stink.'

'Adrian and Paula are used to it, although I'm sure they'd rather have been at home playing, given the choice. But as you know, contact takes priority and overrides any plans the foster family may have. It might be easier for you, as you have your husband who can help,' I added.

'I doubt it; he works long hours too,' Jo said.

I had clearly given Jo plenty to think about, and although what I'd said was true I thought I needed to balance it a bit. 'On the positive side,' I said, 'the joy of seeing a child improve and knowing that in some small way you have helped them towards a better future is immeasurable.'

'That's what I used to think about social work,' she said, her voice flat.

'Why don't you have a chat with some other foster carers and ask them for their views?' I suggested.

'Yes, I might do that when I get back from my holidays. Anyway, thanks. I'd better go now and start packing. I hope you have a good summer.'

'And you.'

Standing, she crossed to the patio doors where she called goodbye to the children, then I saw her out. It was now 3.45 p.m. and although I didn't have the school run during the holidays, I still had to make dinner early so there was time to eat before we left to take Max to contact. As I made my way through the living room to check on the children and see if they wanted another drink Adrian came dashing in. 'Mum, come quickly! Max has fallen off the bike and he's crying!'

I rushed outside and down the garden to where Max was sitting on the grass beside the overturned bike, head in his hands and crying quietly.

'Where are you hurt?' I asked, kneeling beside him. He was wearing shorts and his legs, apart from being a bit grubby, didn't appear cut or grazed. I couldn't see his face properly, but that didn't appear cut either.

'Max, love,' I said, touching his arm. 'Where are you hurt? Show me.' Although he'd fallen onto the soft grass, I knew that if you fell heavily or at a funny angle it was possible to hurt yourself badly or even break a bone. He was now rubbing his eyes, so both his arms were obviously working and not causing him pain.

'Show me where it hurts, love,' I said again. Adrian and Paula were standing watching and looking very worried.

'I'm all right,' Max said with small sob, but he made no attempt to get up. Usually when a child takes a tumble while playing they soon jump up, brush themselves down and carry on with the game. But Max didn't.

'You're not all right,' I said, holding his arm. 'You're upset. Can you tell me what's wrong?' There was no reply. I then wondered if his distress was more to do with hurt pride rather than any physical damage, and perhaps he'd feel better without an audience. 'Adrian, Paula,' I said, glancing up at them. 'Could you go and sit on the patio for a few minutes while I help Max?'

Without further ado Adrian took Paula's hand and they walked up the garden to the patio.

'What's the matter, love?' I quietly asked Max, shifting my legs to sit more comfortably. 'Can you tell me?'

He let out another small sob. 'I want to ride a bike like Adrian, but I can't. I'm too fat.'

I could have easily cried too – for Max. The poor child. What he'd said was true. I'd realized soon after he'd arrived that he would struggle to ride a child's bike of any size due to his weight, and he wouldn't be able to reach the pedals on an adult bike. He couldn't easily ride a scooter or skateboard either – I'd seen him try. The fat on his thighs stopped him from working his legs to gain the necessary momentum for these types of activities. He also had very poor balance. It requires agility and core stability to master the skills required, as well as muscle tone, especially in the lower limbs, which Max simply didn't have. But what could I say to him to make him feel better?

'I know some of these activities are difficult for you at present, but it will get easier. Jill said to me this morning how much fitter and healthier you looked, and that's just after a few weeks.'

'But I want all this to go now,' he said, prodding the fat on his thighs and stomach. 'I want to be like Adrian and the other kids at school, so I can run and play football and hockey and cricket and score goals and win points in high jump.'

'We're not all good at sports, Max. Some children excel at sports, but I never did.' I was concerned that Max could be laying too much at the door of losing weight.

'And you weren't fat?' he asked.

'No, I just wasn't good at sports. Many children aren't.'

'Did they like you at school?' he asked, his face sad and serious.

'Yes, I think so. Why? Has someone said something to you at school?'

'Not really.' He sniffled. 'But I'm not popular like the kids who are good at sports. Everyone wants to talk to them and be in their game.' I remembered from my own school days how those who excelled at sports were very popular and always seemed to be on the stage collecting trophies and medals.

'We can't all be good at everything,' I said. 'You are very good academically, which will take you a long way, Max. Your school report was excellent. Do you know what I mean by academic?'

He nodded. 'It's when you're good at most subjects and know things, then go to university to study.'

'Yes. I can see you going to university.'

'I'd like that,' he said, finally looking at me. 'I like books.'

'I know you do and I'm pleased, but I'm also pleased you are out here in the garden playing. That's important too. I'm sure there will come a time when you can ride a bike very well, but in the meantime, don't let it upset you. Life's too short.'

'That's what Mrs Marshall says sometimes.'

'Sensible lady.'

I helped Max to his feet and waved to Adrian and Paula to come down from the patio to join him. Satisfied he was all right, I went indoors to begin making dinner. I had a good view of the garden from the rear window of the kitchen and as I peeled potatoes and other vegetables I repeatedly glanced out to make sure they were all OK. They'd left the bikes and were now playing with the bats and a ball. There were no rules as such; it was just a matter of hitting the ball to someone when it was hit to you. I could see both my children surreptitiously helping Max. Adrian wasn't hitting the ball with the force he would usually use, but more pushing it towards Max to give him the best chance of returning it. If Max missed the shot, which he did quite often (even a game of bat and ball requires agility), Paula would quickly pick it up and bat it to Max so he could have his turn. I'd noticed before, when they'd been playing in the garden and park, that Adrian and Paula often tailored their playing to assist Max. Most children would; they do it instinctively. In some respects, and I hesitate to say this, it was as if they were helping a child with a disability. Whether Max realized they were making allowances for him I didn't know. If he did then hopefully he appreciated it was because they cared about him, very much.

After we'd eaten I gave Max the box of peaches I'd washed for him to give to his family and we left for contact. As before, I parked directly in front of his house and left Adrian and Paula sitting in the car with the door open onto the pavement so I could see them. The front door to the house was opened by Max's father, Dan, who was on his way out. No more charming than the first time I'd met him, he gave a curt nod in my direction, tapped Max on the head in a vague gesture of acknowledgement and disappeared off. Max waddled down the dark hall. 'Hello, anyone in?' I called.

Summer appeared in the hall. 'Me and Paris are here. Mum's having a rest.'

'OK. See you at seven.'

When we returned it was Summer who saw Max out.

So our holiday routine continued. We still had a lot of toing and froing in the car, with Adrian's and Paula's afternoons or evenings being disrupted by contact, but at least there wasn't the frantic rush there had been during the school term. We didn't always go home when Max was at contact but instead went to a local park. As promised, on the days when we had evening contact I arranged day trips out: to the zoo, castle ruins, the adventure park and even a day trip to the coast, when we had to get up at the crack of dawn to make it worthwhile. Max had only been to the seaside once before when his family (minus his father) had rented a caravan with an aunt. We took buckets and spades, built sandcastles, paddled in the sea and had fresh fish and chips while sitting on the beach. It was fun, we all enjoyed it, and the complete change made it feel as though we had been away for much longer than a day.

On the days when contact was in the afternoon time was limited, so I organized games at home, both indoors – like painting and clay modelling – and outdoors. Sometimes I just let the children amuse themselves, as I knew it was important that they weren't organized every minute of every day but had the space and time to use their imaginations and create and develop their own play. They also spent some time each day with a book: Max and Adrian reading, while I read Paula a story. Max also read while Adrian and Paula were watching children's television in the early evening. He didn't have any interest in television, which I think was due to it being on constantly at his house. It had gone from being a source of entertainment to an irritation, and as a result he'd completely rejected it.

Max liked non-fiction books as well as fiction and we were going to the library regularly to change our books. He loved the library – the smell of books, the muted sounds – and basked in its atmosphere of quiet learning. I think he would have happily spent the entire day there if lunch had been provided. His family weren't bookish, so they never went to the library. His only experience of libraries was the small school library and the visit his class had made to this library when they'd been shown around and read a story. As I'd got to know Max I'd realized he had a thirst for knowledge and seemed to retain facts and figures much more easily than the average six-year-old. He could also use reason and logic better than any young child I'd known. I didn't think he was a child prodigy, but he was bright and had taken refuge in books and learning. He'd been given the opportunity to learn a musical instrument at school the following term and he'd chosen the violin – not the obvious choice for a six-year-old. But he liked classical music and if I had it on in the background at home or in the car, he'd ask me about the piece of music and the composer.

At the start of the third week of the summer holidays my parents asked if Adrian and Paula would like to stay with them for a few nights. They'd done this before in the school holidays and naturally they were delighted. It was a real treat for them, and my parents always spoilt them with their time and affection. I'd miss them, of course, but it would only be for a few days and I could give Max some one-to-one attention. So on Wednesday Mum and Dad arrived, stayed for lunch and then took my two very excited children with a case each back with them. The plan was that on Sunday Max and I would go there for dinner and then bring them home. It's strange, the way things work out, for had they not gone they would have been in the car when I took Max to contact, which means I wouldn't have accepted the invitation into his house and learnt what was really going on in there.

CHAPTER SEVENTEEN

ABUSED CHILD

Their front door was opened unusually by Caz. Leaning heavily on her crutches, her mobility apparently no better than the last time I'd seen her, she was clearly in a lot of discomfort. 'Hi, Mum,' Max said, offering up the box of fruit.

'Put them in the kitchen, will you?' she said. 'I haven't got any hands free.'

'How are you?' I asked. Max disappeared into the darkness of the hall.

'Not good,' Caz said, grimacing.

'Oh dear. What's the matter?'

'Everything,' she sighed. 'But I won't keep you. You've got your kids waiting.'

'Actually, I haven't,' I said. 'They're spending a few days with their grandparents.'

'Do you want to come in then?' she asked in the same despondent tone.

'Yes.' I smiled, pleased that I was being asked in and Caz appeared to be making an effort to get along with me. I waited on the doorstep as she awkwardly turned, easing her crutches around in little jolts until she was facing down the hall.

'Shut the door behind you, will you?' she said. I did as she asked and with no natural light the hall became darker still. 'Light bulb's gone,' she said. 'I can't get up there to change it.'

'Is no one else in?' I asked.

'They're all out. Could have done with resting myself. My feet are killing me.'

'Oh dear,' I sympathized. 'You should have phoned me – we could have cancelled contact tonight.'

'Not likely! And let that social worker think I'm not coping? Quickest way to lose your kids, I'd say.'

We were now in their open-plan living room, which smelt of cigarette smoke despite the window being wide open. A large plasma-screen television stood against one wall with a sofa and two armchairs grouped in front of it. A kitchen area at the other end of the room was separated by a Formica-topped breakfast bar. I could now understand why Max went to his room to read; it was impossible to have privacy or escape from the television in this room. The television was on now, its bright lights and constantly moving images and loud dialogue dominating the room. Max had made a space for the box of fruit on the work surface and was waiting, uncertain of what to do next, presumably because his usual routine had been disrupted by me coming in. Caz noticed and said, 'You can go to your room. Cathy can make me a drink if I want one.'

With a brief smile he turned and plodded off upstairs and a few moments later I heard his bedroom door close. Caz eased herself down into one of the armchairs, then lifted her feet onto the footstool. 'They told me at the hospital I should keep my feet elevated when sitting,' she said. Both her feet were bandaged now and her slippers had been cut to fit.

'Is there anything I can do?' I asked. 'I could change the light bulb in the hall.'

'No. One of them can do it when they get back. It's always going. It gets left on all night. Sit yourself down.'

The other armchair was occupied by one of their cats, so I sat on the sofa where I was at right angles to Caz. She picked up the remote and lowered the volume on the television until it was just a hum in the background. In front of me was a glass-topped coffee table littered with teenage magazines. A bright-red glass fruit bowl stood in the centre, but instead of containing fruit it held an attractive display of sweets – small packets of Smarties and Jelly Tots, lollipops and sherbet dips and so on. Very tempting indeed. I could picture Caz and her daughters in the evening watching television or flicking through the magazines while popping sweets, as they had done at the hospital. Jo had said it was what they did – a little family ritual. The rest of the room contained the detritus of six people living in a relatively small house where the main caregiver was incapacitated. Pans were in the sink, the draining board was stacked with cutlery and crockery, while the work surface was littered with takeaway pizza boxes and half-empty bottles of fizzy drinks. A number of beer cans had been stacked beside the overflowing bin. 'Sorry about the state of the place,' Caz said, nodding towards the kitchen 'They just eat and leave me with their mess.'

'Where have they gone?' I asked, making conversation.

'Dan's out with his mates, drinking, and the girls have gone to the community hall. They put extra entertainment on in the summer. I used to go. It's nice. You can meet people and have a cup of tea and a chat. But I haven't been able to get there since I've been ill.'

'You'll be able to go again soon, once your foot is properly healed,' I said encouragingly.

She looked downcast and shrugged. 'Not so sure. They've put me on antibiotics again. My other foot is playing up. Two toes on that foot might have to come off.'

'I am sorry,' I said, shocked. 'What a worry. Hopefully the antibiotics will start to work soon and it won't be necessary.'

'The nurse who changes my dressing didn't seem too hopeful.' Caz's face clouded and she suddenly burst into tears.

'Oh, Caz,' I said, standing and going to her. 'You poor dear.' I went to take her hand but she pulled away. 'Is there any other treatment you can have? Have you talked to your doctor?'

She shook her head despondently and, taking a tissue from her cardigan pocket, quickly wiped her eyes as if she didn't have the right to cry or be upset.

'I am sorry,' I said again, at a loss to know what comfort I could offer.

'It's not just that,' she said. 'I feel so worthless. Sometimes I think everyone would be better off without me.'

'Caz, don't say that. Your family loves you lots. I saw that at the hospital. Not many teenagers would give up every evening to go to the hospital, even if it was their mother. I think you should speak to your doctor about how you are feeling. I am sure he'll be able to help.'

'It's not the girls, it's him,' she said in the same flat voice, and for a moment I thought she meant Max.

'Max?' I asked, wondering what he could possibly have done to upset her.

She shook her head. 'No. His father. Anyway, it's not your problem.' She blew her nose and tucked the tissue into the sleeve of her cardigan.

'Do you have someone you can talk to?' I asked, returning to my chair.

'Yes, but talking doesn't do any good.' There was a few moments' silence, which I broke by telling her Max was coping well and enjoying the summer holidays – something most parents of children in care want to hear. But Caz's face clouded again and her bottom lip trembled. I made a move to go to her, but she waved me away.

'It's OK. You're doing a good job with Max. Better than me.'

'I'm doing my best to look after him until you are better,' I said. 'But I won't ever replace you. You're his mother.' For I wondered if this might be contributing to her upset – that I was fulfilling her role. It worries many parents with children in care. 'Max misses you very much, although he puts on a brave face. He seems to take everything in his stride, but I know he'll be pleased when he can come home.'

She managed the faintest of smiles. 'He's certainly a deep one, that kid. I don't know where he gets it from, but I think he'll do well, don't you?'

'Yes, I do.'

She looked thoughtful for a moment and I saw pain in her eyes. 'Does Max ever talk to you about his father?'

'Not really,' I said honestly.

'He doesn't tell you about how he treats me?'

'No.' I looked at her carefully and waited.

'It's not right, him seeing his father treat me like he does. It sets him a bad example.' I nodded and waited again. 'I'm unhappy, Cathy, dreadfully unhappy, so I comfort eat. I have done most of my life.'

'Because of Dan?' I asked gently.

'He's one of the reasons. He treats me like crap.' Her brow creased.

'Does he hit you?' I asked.

'Sometimes, but it's what he says that hurts more. That does the real damage. He calls me names, horrible dirty names, and in front of the kids, like slut, bitch and whore. He says I'm worthless and I should be grateful he stays because no one else would.'

'Those are dreadful things to say,' I said. 'Especially in front of the children. It's abusing you and them. You don't have to put up with it.' Yet even as I said it I knew it wasn't that simple.

'But he's right. I am a slut. Not just because of how I am now, but because of who I was.' Her voice shook and she took a deep breath. I waited until she could continue, wondering what on earth she could mean. 'You see, I've got a past, a nasty one. Dan and me were seventeen when we started going out. He was my first boyfriend, although I wasn't a virgin. I told him everything, confided in him, and I was so grateful he still wanted me. Part of me still is. I was damaged goods, soiled. My stepfather had been having sex with me since I was nine.'

'Oh Caz,' I said, and instinctively reached out to touch her arm, but she withdrew it.

'When I met Dan my stepfather was still abusing me. I didn't know how to stop it. Dan did. He gave him a right thrashing and said if he came near me again, he'd finish the job. I don't like being touched,' she added. 'Not even by my children.' Which explained why I'd never seen her hug them. Adults who have been sexually abused can shy away from physical contact and showing affection until they work through it in therapy.

I was reeling from what I'd heard and trying to think of what to say that might help. 'Did you tell anyone apart from Dan that your stepfather was abusing you?' I asked. 'You know it's never too late to go to the police.'

She shook her head. 'It is. He's dead. I told my mother at the time, but she didn't believe me, although I'm sure she must have had her suspicions. Then, when I told Dan and he beat up my stepfather, she threw me out of the house. I lived with Dan's family until we got our own council house. My mum is dead now, but look at what she's left me with – a life sentence. And my kids too.' Her face clouded and she began to cry again. I felt helpless just sitting there watching her and unable to offer her any physical comfort. 'Pass me the box of tissues, will you?' she said, nodding to the shelf beneath the coffee table.

I handed her the tissues and, taking a handful, she wiped her eyes.

'Does Jo know any of this?' I asked quietly. 'She may be able to offer you some counselling.'

'Some of it. But not about Dan and Paris.'

An icy chill ran down my spine. 'What about Paris?'

'Oh, he won't touch her again,' she said. 'He knows what will happen if he does. But she's his favourite. He's all over her, spoils her – it's not fair on the others.'

'Touch her again?' I asked. 'What did he do to her?'

'He tried to touch her breast. He was always making comments about her breasts. Paris said he kept going into her bedroom without knocking. Then one night before I went into hospital he came home drunk and staggered into her room. He claimed he thought he was in our bedroom. Anyway, she woke to find the duvet pulled back and him with his hand on her breast. Her boyfriend fitted a lock on the bedroom door, so it won't happen again.' Caz seemed pretty unfazed by this, but I heard alarm bells ringing. This was sexual abuse and a father who abuses his child once is likely to do it again. He would have had plenty of opportunity while Caz was in hospital.

'You need to tell Jo,' I said.

'Do I?' Caz asked naively. The poor woman had so many issues to deal with she was struggling, but protecting her children was paramount.

'Yes, Caz, you must,' I said. 'You wouldn't want the same thing happening to Paris that happened to you.'

She looked horrified. 'Good grief, no. He wouldn't do that. But if I tell Jo, he'll be furious and may leave us. I couldn't cope alone.' Unacceptable though this reason was, fear of being left alone and unable to cope is a reason why many women fail to report an abusive partner.

'Your children must come first,' I said.

'I know. I'll tell her,' Caz said too easily. She rested her head back with a heavy sigh, overwhelmed by all she was having to face. She was very different now from the controlling woman who'd sat propped up on her pillows in a hospital bed with her daughters in attendance and issuing her complaints and orders. Cocooned, looked after, and away from the problems at home, I could see why she'd been in no hurry to return.

'Is there anything I can get you?' I asked.

'You could make me a nice cup of tea,' she said.

'Sure. How do you like it?' I stood and crossed to the kitchen.

'Milk and two sugars. There should be some clean mugs in the cupboard above the sink.'

I opened the cupboard door, took out the mug – there was only one that was clean – and then filled the kettle and switched it on. As I moved around the kitchen making tea, Caz struck up a conversation from her chair at the other end of the room. 'Did you see that programme the other night about eating disorders?' she asked.

'No, I don't think I did.'

'It said that many people who have an eating disorder have experienced some form of abuse. It doesn't have to be physical abuse, it can be emotional – where a person puts you down the whole time. I wasn't always fat, you know. I started comfort eating because I was so unhappy at home and it's continued. My friend, Bet, says if I don't do something soon I'll eat myself to death. I think she could be right. How is Max doing with his diet?'

'Good,' I said, glancing in her direction. I couldn't see her face as the chair was facing away – towards the television. 'He's been losing about three pounds a week. He's eating well,' I reassured her, 'but taking more exercise.'

'Which I can't do,' she said flatly. 'Even if I went on a diet, I wouldn't lose weight. I can't even walk, let alone exercise.' She had a point.

'I know it must be difficult for you at present,' I said, placing a tea bag into the mug. 'But I'm sure the health centre would be able to suggest a diet and fitness plan to suit you. Did Kelly and Paris go?'

'Yes, but the classes aren't running now. They start again in September when the staff are back from their holidays.'

I concentrated on pouring the boiling water into the mug, then found some milk in the fridge. There was an opened packet of sugar on the work surface and I added two teaspoonfuls as Caz had wanted. It was on the tip of my tongue to ask her why she didn't use a sweetener instead, but that may have sounded rude. I carried the mug of tea to her. 'Don't you want one?' she asked.

'No, I'm fine, thank you.'

'You couldn't fetch me a biscuit as well, could you?' she said with a guilty smile. 'I find tea a bit wet without one,' she joked. 'There should be a packet of chocolate digestives on the work surface somewhere.'

I returned to the kitchen, found the open packet of biscuits and took it to her.

With her tea in one hand and the biscuits on her lap, she deftly took the top biscuit out of the packet and dunked it into her tea before taking a bite. 'Hmm,' she sighed, savouring the melting chocolate on moist biscuit. 'I know I shouldn't, but you need a few treats in life, don't you? Would you like one?'

'No, thank you.'

Taking a sip of tea, she peeled off the next biscuit and, dunking it, ate it with the same pleasure, then the next. As I watched her pop one in after another, absorbed in the pleasure, I saw the comfort eating of the abused child. With her shoulders always slightly rounded and her head hung forward, her posture was that of the victim, which she had been for most of her life. It was pitiful and demeaning, and as one biscuit quickly followed another I saw that Caz could no more stop eating them than she had been able to stop her stepfather's abuse.

'Here, take them away,' she said eventually when there was one left, and threw the packet to me.

I returned it to the kitchen. 'Shall I get Max a drink?' I asked. He hadn't appeared since we'd arrived.

'He'll come out and get one when he's ready,' she said.

I sat with her again, wondering if I should go now. There was still forty minutes of contact left, not enough time for me to return home, but I didn't want to outstay my welcome.

'Do you need anything?' I asked.

'New feet.' Her smile was bittersweet. Then suddenly she froze as the front door could be heard opening and then banging shut. 'Dan?' she said under her breath.

'I've forgotten me fucking wallet,' he cursed from the hall. 'None of them wankers at the bar would stand me a round. Supposed to be me fucking mates!'

'He's been drinking,' Caz whispered. 'You'd better go.'

Dan came into the living room with a lit cigarette between his fingers. 'Not more bleedin' social workers,' he cursed, referring to me. 'Haven't you got better things to do?'

'This is Max's foster carer,' Caz reminded him timidly and clearly unsettled.

He grunted an acknowledgement and, placing the cigarette between his lips, began searching the living room, presumably for his wallet.

'I don't think it's in here. I would have seen it,' Caz said. 'Try the bedroom.'

With another grunt he went out, leaving a trail of smoke behind him.

'You'd better go,' Caz said again. 'Take Max with you. There's not long left.'

'I could come back later for him?' I offered.

'No. I'll see him tomorrow and I need to lie down. Max!' she then called. 'Time to go.' And to me: 'If he doesn't appear, shout upstairs for him, will you?'

'I'll see you tomorrow then,' I said. 'You're sure you'll be OK?'

194

'Yes. You go,' she said, clearly wanting me out.

I went into the hall and to the foot of the stairs. Dan could be heard cursing as he searched the main bedroom. 'Max, we're going!' I called.

A moment later a door opened and then Max came down the stairs, carrying a bag of sweets. 'I only ate half of them,' he said proudly, holding the bag up for me to see.

'Good boy.'

'I like to treat him,' Caz called from the living room. 'Bye.'

'Bye,' we returned. 'Bye, Dan,' I added. There was no reply.

We went down the dark hall and I let us out. The fresh air greeted us and I drew a deep breath – to rid myself not only of the cloying smell of cigarette smoke, but also the oppressive atmosphere of unhappiness that pervaded the house, which could only be alleviated, it seemed, by comfort eating. It was depressingly sad.

CHAPTER EIGHTEEN

REPORTING CONCERNS

I drove home with a very heavy heart and my thoughts coursing with all that I'd seen and heard at Max's house. The living and kitchen area could have done with a good clean and tidy, but it wasn't the worst I'd seen – far from it. I was irritated that Caz had been leaving Max bags of sweets as treats in his bedroom when she had agreed to him being on a diet. I assumed this was because she was still refusing to truly acknowledge and address the connection between over-eating and obesity, so giving Max sweets wouldn't be seen as counterproductive to his diet. Of course she would want to treat him, but to be honest, from what I knew, I thought the best treat she could give him was her company: to find time to sit and talk with him about what he'd been doing and was interested in, or play a card or board game, instead of letting him go to his bedroom every visit.

But the thoughts that dominated most and were of greatest concern were those of abuse: all those years when Caz had been raped by her stepfather, and now Dan's abuse of Paris. Caz was afraid of Dan; it had shown in her eyes and demeanour when he'd come home unexpectedly. A woman who is afraid of her partner is not going to be able to stand up to him and protect her children. What was she going to do? Not throw him out. She'd said herself she couldn't manage without him. The dismissive language she'd used when describing his abuse of Paris had a normalizing element: 'He was always making comments about her breasts ... he kept going into her bedroom without knocking ... Anyway, she woke to find ... his hand on her breast.' It had fallen to Paris's boyfriend to fit a lock on her bedroom door. Also, when Caz had told me of the terrible abuse she'd suffered at the hands of her stepfather I noticed she hadn't used the term rape, but had said her stepfather had been having sex with her. This has a different connotation and implies that it was in some way consensual, which rape *never* is.

Last but not least in my doom-laden thoughts was that as Caz was the victim of domestic violence so, too, were her children. What parents often don't realize is that domestic violence has as much – if not a greater – impact on their children as it does on the adult victim. Children, scared witless, have to stand by and watch their parent being abused and are powerless to intervene and protect them. It often leaves a lasting legacy and the social services view domestic violence as a form of child abuse in itself, with grounds for removing the child from the home.

Deep in thought, I suddenly found myself outside my house and I pulled onto the driveway. Max hadn't said anything during the journey home either.

'Are you OK?' I asked, glancing at him in the mirror.

He nodded, but as we got out he said, 'It's strange without Adrian and Paula.'

'Yes, it is,' I agreed.

I unlocked the front door and as we went in Max passed me his bag of sweets for safekeeping. 'I think I've had enough today,' he said.

'Good boy. You can have some more tomorrow.'

It was even stranger in the house without Adrian and Paula than it had been in the car, and to be honest I didn't like it. Max didn't either. 'Four sleeps until they're home again,' he said gloomily. Adrian and Paula were either side of his age, so he always had someone to play with.

'Roll on Sunday when we collect them,' I said, then caught myself. 'But we are going to have a nice time before then. Think about what you would like to do. Tomorrow we just have the morning, as you have contact in the afternoon, so we can go somewhere close.'

'Library?' he suggested, without giving it much thought.

'Or would you like to go to a museum? There is a small one not far from here.'

His eyes lit up. 'Yes. I like museums. I went to one with the school on a coach.'

'That'll be the City museum. This is a smaller one, not far away and worth a visit.'

'Can I take my sweets with me?' he asked.

I smiled. 'Yes, a few. And we could have lunch out. There's a café next to the museum.' I had brightened, too, at the prospect of an enjoyable day out rather than sitting at home, missing Adrian and Paula. Although I would have liked them to come too, I knew they were having a fantastic time with their grandparents. I'd phone them in the morning to say hi.

Max had a bath and then read in bed while I went downstairs and wrote up my log notes. I included the details of contact and what Caz had told me, using her words as far as possible when she'd described Dan's sexual abuse of Paris. Once I'd finished I returned the folder to the lockable drawer in the front room. Max sometimes fell asleep with the light on and his book open on his bed, so I always checked on him after an hour. Sometimes he was still awake and I had to tell him it was time to go to sleep or he would be tired in the morning, but tonight he was fast asleep. Flat on his back, snoring lightly, his cherub-like features relaxed in sleep. My heart went out to him, as it often did; he was such a lovable, unassuming and good-natured child who asked for very little. Odd that in so many ways he was very different from the rest of his family, although I could see a likeness, especially between Max and his mother. His sisters clearly cared for him, but I didn't see a lot of warmth from Caz, but then, of course, she was having to deal with a lot of problems of her own, including being abused and her present poor health and limited mobility.

I placed the book Max had been reading quietly on his bedside cabinet, repositioned Buzz Lightyear so that his arm wasn't digging into Max and then came out of his room, drawing the door to behind me. Perhaps it was my imagination, but I thought Max's snoring was becoming less pronounced. I doubted he'd lost enough weight to make a significant difference, but the time he was spending playing outside in the fresh air would certainly be helping, as would living in a smoke-free household.

Despite ending the day on a positive note, I didn't sleep well that night. As soon as I lay down Caz's words about abuse came back to haunt me. All those years of suffering – from the age of nine. How had she survived? It was horrendous.

Little wonder she'd taken to comfort eating – it had probably been her only solace. I assumed from what she'd said that her stepfather had died before he had been brought to justice. Had his death allowed her some closure or had it left a gaping wound? Some survivors of abuse find that seeing their abuser prosecuted helps set them on the road to recovery, but Caz had been denied that. My thoughts then went again to Paris and what Caz had said about Dan's abuse of her. Summer had told me in the car when I'd given her a lift home from the hospital that Paris was their father's favourite. Apart from thinking that a parent shouldn't show favouritism, I hadn't given it any more thought. It certainly hadn't crossed my mind that there was a darker, more sinister implication. Were Kelly and Summer aware of their father's abuse of their sister? If so, had they been told not to say anything? When I'd told Caz that Jo needed to know she'd agreed – too readily, I thought – but what if she didn't tell her? Jo had to know. I'd never forgive myself if Dan's abuse wasn't reported and he went on to do it again or was even still abusing her now. I shivered at the possibility. As well as feeling responsible on a personal level to report the abuse, I had a duty as a foster carer to report any safeguarding issues. It was a part of fostering I didn't like, but it had to be done. The social services would then decide what action, if any, needed to be taken.

After a restless night I rose early, fed Toscha, got the laundry on, had breakfast with Max and then at nine o'clock settled him with some puzzles at the table in the kitchen-cum-diner, while I went into the living room to use the phone. Jill and Jo had both returned from their holidays now, although I hadn't heard from either of them. I knew there would be staff at the fostering agency, so I phoned there. A colleague of Jill's answered and passed the phone to her.

'Sorry, Cathy,' Jill said straight away. 'I was going to call you later. It's been manic here since I got back.'

'Don't worry. Did you have a good holiday?'

'Yes, but the day we returned my son managed to fall out of a tree and break his arm. Today is my first day back at work.'

'Oh dear, I am sorry to hear that. How is he?'

'Fine now. He thinks it's great fun having a plaster cast on his arm, although he was in a lot of pain at the time. Just as well it wasn't a foster child or I'd have had a lot of explaining to do!'

Jill was right. If your own child accidentally hurts themselves you're obviously concerned, you seek medical help and possibly blame yourself for not being more vigilant, but that's usually where it ends. When a foster child has an accident there are wider ramifications. As well as informing the fostering agency of the incident as soon as possible, it has to be entered in detail in the carer's log, then an accident report form has to be completed, a copy of which is sent to the agency and the child's social worker. The child is spoken to by their social worker to check that your account tallies with theirs, and if there are any inconsistencies or a suggestion that the carer(s) may have been negligent then more questions will be asked and their safer-caring policy reviewed. If doubts remain, the carers could be suspended from fostering or even barred completely, although this is unusual. In addition, the child's parents, already angry and upset at having their child in care, are often quick to blame the carer for negligence or even of intentionally harming the child. It's extremely stressful and worrying for the carer(s), who are probably already blaming themselves. Consequently some activities – for example, contact sports – are not usually offered to foster children to minimize the risk of an accident. The children are kept ultra-safe – safer than the carer's own children.

'So are you having a nice summer?' Jill asked.

'Yes. We've having some days out and activities at home on the other days. Adrian and Paula are staying with their grandparents for a few days just now. I collect them on Sunday.' I wasn't just making conversation; Jill, as my supervising social worker, should know what we were doing and of any changes in my household, even temporary ones.

'They'll enjoy that,' she said.

'Yes. Jill, there is something I need to make you aware of in respect of Max.'

'Yes. Go ahead. What is it?'

'Yesterday evening, when I took him for contact, only his mother was at home and she invited me in.'

'That's progress.'

'Yes. In a way. Unfortunately her other foot is causing problems now and she may need another operation; her mobility is very limited. I made her a cup of tea and sat with her. She wanted to talk and at one point she was quite upset. She told me she'd been badly abused as a child by her step-father, who has since died. She also said that her husband, Dan, the children's father, has been making comments about Paris's breasts and one night he'd gone into her bedroom and touched her breasts.' I heard Jill take a sharp breath.

I continued by telling Jill all that Caz had told me and Summer's comment about Paris being their father's favourite.

I then said that Caz had admitted Dan hit her sometimes, and I'd seen how scared she was of him when he'd suddenly arrived home unexpectedly.

'Thanks, Cathy,' Jill said as I finished. 'I know there are some ongoing safeguarding concerns around the amount of supervision the children have at home, but I'm sure Jo isn't aware of Paris's allegation against her father. Nor of the domestic violence. Indeed, the last I heard the care plan was to return Max home before the start of the new school term.' She was silent for a moment, then, 'Max hasn't said anything to you about his father's behaviour?'

'No. He hardly talks about his family.'

'All right. I'll phone Jo now. She'll probably want to speak to you later.'

We said goodbye and I replaced the receiver with some relief that I'd made the call. It was out of my hands now. Jo and the social services would investigate further and take any necessary action.

I went to check on Max doing his puzzle at the table and told him I was going to quickly phone Adrian and Paula, then we'd go to the museum.

'Can I talk to them?' he asked.

'Yes, of course, love.'

Leaving the puzzle on the table, he came with me into the living room and sat beside me on the sofa. I keyed in my parents' telephone number and Dad answered. Even before I asked he said that Adrian and Paula were fine and keeping them busy. Mum was making them all a cooked breakfast before they went out for the day. He called Adrian to the phone first. 'Hi, Mum,' he said.

'Hi, love. How are you?'

'Great. Nana and Grandpa are taking us to a model village today. It has a real working train set.' I could hear the excitement in his voice. I knew the place he meant; we'd been there some years before when he'd been much younger. The model village was the life's work of a railway enthusiast. It was situated in his back garden and he had opened it to the public to raise money for charity. Adrian then asked how Max was, so I put him on and Max said a shy and polite, 'Hello, Adrian. How are you?'

They only spoke for a few moments. Max seemed a bit awkward and self-conscious using the phone, so I guessed he hadn't had much opportunity to use it at home. But he was satisfied and smiled as he passed the handset back to me. My father then put Paula on to speak and she said, almost in a whisper, 'I miss you lots, Mummy,' which choked me up.

'I miss you too, love,' I said. 'But you're having a nice time at Nana and Grandpa's, aren't you?'

'Yes, but I still miss you. I told Nana I missed you last night when it was bedtime so she read me lots of stories and cuddled me until I went to sleep.'

'Good. So that was fine then, wasn't it?'

'Yes. Nana is cooking eggs and sausage. Can you smell it?'

I smiled. 'No, love, not down the phone. But I'm sure it smells and tastes delicious.'

'Can I speak to Max like Adrian did?' she asked, not wanting to be left out.

'Yes, of course. He'd like that.'

I passed the phone to Max again and in his best telephone voice he said, 'Hello, Paula, how are you?'

She must have said well for then he said, 'I am well too.'

And handed the phone back to me. 'She's gone to have break-fast,' he said.

Dad came to the phone and I thanked him for all he and my mother were doing, said I hoped the children weren't wearing them out and wished them a pleasant day.

Before Max and I left for the museum I locked the back door, put Toscha out for a run and remembered the bag of fruit for Max to take to contact, as there wouldn't be time to return home after we'd been to the museum.

The museum is on the other side of town. It's only small and is staffed mainly by part-time elderly volunteers who are happy to explain all about the artefacts on display, many of which were discovered locally. Max loved it, as I thought he would. He liked facts and history and this was history coming alive. Children can complete a questionnaire if they wish, the answers to which are somewhere in the museum; for example, *What was a corn flail used for?* The answer was on a card beside the exhibit: *The corn flail was used to separate the grain from the husk, circa 1850.* The children were awarded a sticker at the end for completing the questionnaire.

At one o'clock we left the museum and went next door to the café for lunch, and from there I drove straight to Max's home for contact. It was with some nervousness and trepida-tion that I approached their house and then rang the doorbell. Had Jo had time to speak to Caz about the concerns I'd reported, and if so, how had she taken it? I was expecting the worst and when Kelly answered the door and said, 'Mum wants to talk to you,' I assumed my fears were about to be realized.

With mounting anxiety, I followed Kelly down the dark hall (the light bulb hadn't been replaced) and into the living room. To my surprise, Caz was sitting in her armchair with her feet up, watching the television. 'Hello, Caz,' I said tentatively.

'Hi,' she called. 'I love this programme.' Without taking her eyes from the screen, she waved for me to go over. I crossed to her chair. Meanwhile, Max had put the fruit on the work surface in the kitchen and Kelly was eating it.

'Can you do me a favour?' Caz asked, her gaze momentarily shifting from the screen as she passed me a slip of paper. 'That's the name and address of Max's dentist. He has an appointment next week. Can you take him? I won't be able to.'

'Yes, of course,' I said, relieved. 'Anything else?'

'He could do with a haircut.'

'Yes, I agree. I was going to ask you about that. I'll take him to our barbers.' Carers should generally ask the parent first if they can take the child to have their hair cut, as it can be a contentious issue. A child suddenly arriving at contact with a haircut, new hairstyle, or wearing new clothes or shoes are stark reminders to the parent that they are no longer looking after their child.

'Is there anything else?' I asked.

'No.' Her gaze had returned to the television and she laughed heartily. 'I love this programme,' she said again. I felt dreadful, for clearly she hadn't been told of the concerns, and I knew her happiness would be very short-lived.

CHAPTER NINETEEN

WHEN WILL I SEE MUMMY AGAIN?

I decided to return home while Max was seeing his family, as there didn't seem much point in going to a local park without Adrian and Paula. A tight knot had formed in my stomach as I thought of Caz laughing at one of her favourite television programmes, blissfully unaware of the ball I had started rolling, which would reach her very soon. While she didn't know yet, it wouldn't be long. If Jill hadn't managed to speak to Jo about the concerns I'd raised then she would have spoken to her line manager. Child protection issues – which Dan's abuse of Paris was – can't be left until the next day. Paris and Summer hadn't been at home, but I thought nothing of this. It was their school holiday, so they would be out making the most of it.

I let myself into my house, which was resoundingly silent without any children. Straight away I saw the light on the answerphone on the hall table flashing, signalling a message. Pushing the door to, I pressed play. The message was from Jill: 'Cathy, can you give me a ring, please, as soon as you get in? I'm at the office.' Timed fifteen minutes before.

It was urgent. Although Jill hadn't said much, I knew from the terseness of the message and the tightness in her voice that something had happened. Remaining by the hall table, I picked up the handset and pressed the agency's office number. Jill answered with, 'Homefinders fostering services.'

'Jill, it's Cathy. I've just got in.'

'Is Max at contact?' she asked.

'Yes. I've just dropped him off.'

'What time do you collect him?'

'Three-thirty.'

'Can you collect him earlier this afternoon? I've just finished speaking to Jo. She is on her way there now and she thinks it's better if he is with you.'

'Yes, of course. What time?'

'As soon as we've finished. There has been a development. Paris has put herself into foster care.'

'Really? When?'

'Late this morning. She and Summer went to the social services' offices and asked to speak to Jo. Paris told Jo that her father has been sexually abusing her and she didn't feel safe at home any more. She asked if she could live with you, but I had to tell Jo you didn't have the room, so we've found another carer. She's going with Jo now to collect some clothes from home.'

'So just Paris is going into care, not Summer as well?' I clarified.

'That's right. Summer is returning home, for now at least, but obviously there will be concerns about how safe the other children are. Summer and Paris share a bedroom and Summer substantiated what Paris said.'

'So it's a coincidence that this has happened today? It's not a result of what I reported?'

'Correct. About an hour after I'd spoken to Jo in respect of the concerns you'd raised, Paris and Summer arrived at the office. Caz hadn't been told then. Apparently Kelly knew they were going and tried to stop them, but Paris said she'd had enough. It seems the incident Caz told you about wasn't the only time Dan abused Paris. He's been going into their bedroom a lot and trying to get into bed with Paris, usually when he's been drunk. Paris said that although her boyfriend put a lock on the bedroom door, she didn't feel safe at home any longer.'

'No, indeed. Thank goodness she had the courage to report it.'

'Yes, although she might have opened up when Jo interviewed her after what Caz told you. Paris and Summer are saying their mother didn't know what was going on, and they didn't tell her because they didn't want to upset her when she was ill. But the girls are covering up for her, because we know from what Caz told you she was aware of at least one incident of abuse and that Dan had been talking to Paris inappropriately – referring to her breasts – for some time.'

'So despite all Caz went through as a child, when her mother failed to protect her, she's done the same,' I said sadly.

'Worrying, isn't it? Max will obviously remain with you for now. If his parents do try to remove him – he's in voluntary care – the social services will apply to the court for a care order. The police will take a statement from Paris, very likely tomorrow, and then, if there are grounds, Dan will be arrested.'

'All right,' I said with a heavy sigh. 'I'll collect Max now and try to explain to him what is happening.'

'Yes, please. You know where we are if you need us.'

We said a quick goodbye and, replacing the handset, I opened the front door and returned to my car. It's not unheard of for a young person of Paris's age to ask to go into care. Their request is usually taken seriously, unless it's the result of a minor fallout with their parents, which can be resolved, and the young person feels able to return home. It must have been bad for Paris to have gone to the social services and ask to go into care – clearly a last resort. So often in fostering, situations change and aren't as they first appear. Max had originally come to stay with me while his mother was in hospital after his sisters had left him home alone. There'd been no mention of him being unhealthily over-weight, which had been a shock, and the first issue I'd had to address. Now plans to return him home were on hold. Summer and Kelly might be brought into care too, for if one child in a family is known to have been abused then the other children are considered to be at risk. In covering up for Dan, Caz stood to lose all her family, which was heartbreaking, but protecting one's children has to be paramount for any mother. Sadly, I could see only too clearly how this had happened. If Caz had not been burdened by ill health and her mother had set a good example in protecting her, she would have been in a much stronger position to protect her own children when it had become necessary. Yet, while Caz was a victim as much as Paris, it didn't excuse her. Indeed, having suffered herself, surely she should have been more alert and protective of her family?

* * *

It was just before 3 p.m. as I drew up outside Max's home. My pulse had stepped up a beat and my mouth was dry. Jo's car was already there, parked directly in front of mine. I hate confrontation, but I couldn't see how it could be avoided given what must be going on inside the house. Opening my car door, I got out and began walking along the pavement and then up the short path. The front door was closed, but a downstairs window was open and through it came raised voices, one of which I knew was Kelly's, shouting hysterically. I pressed the bell and waited. The voices stopped for a moment and then the front door opened. A cat shot out and a woman of middle age with a careworn expression looked at me questioningly.

'I'm Cathy Glass, Max's foster carer,' I said.

'Oh yes. Come in,' she said, her voice flat. 'I'm a colleague of Jo's. We're in the living room.' Social workers sometimes work in pairs.

The shouting had begun again. I closed the front door and followed Jo's colleague down the still-dark hall. Mayhem greeted us in the living room. Kelly, Paris and Summer were standing at various points around the room, shouting accusingly and jabbing their fingers at each other. Caz was sitting on the sofa, red in the face and her eyes bloodshot from crying. Jo sat next to her, trying to console her but looking stressed and out of her depth. There was no sign of Dan or Max.

'What about Mum?' Kelly was now shouting at Paris and Summer, her bottom lip trembling. 'You didn't think about her when you went off and reported Dad, did you?'

'Of course I did, but what else could I do?' Paris cried, throwing up her arms in despair. 'I can't force her to chuck him out, so I've got to look out for myself.' I assumed 'him' was Dan.

'Me, me, me!' Kelly retaliated. 'Never mind the rest of us. He's going to be furious when he finds out. But you won't be here, so you needn't worry.'

Jo went to say something, but Paris was already answering. 'You can come too, if you want. You don't have to put up with his shit. Jo told you she could find you somewhere to go.'

'And who's going to look after Mum?' Kelly yelled back, her eyes glistening with tears.

'Why don't you come?' Paris now asked Summer.

Clearly Summer, thirteen, and the youngest of the girls, didn't know what to say or do for the best. She looked lost and was visibly shaking. 'I want us to stay together,' she said and began sobbing.

'Now look what you've done!' Kelly accused Paris.

'Girls, this is not helping,' Jo's colleague, who was still standing beside me, said.

'It's not me!' Paris shouted at Kelly. 'It's him you have to blame.'

'But we've managed this far,' Kelly said, her voice dropping slightly.

'I know, but I can't take any more,' Paris replied, tears springing to her eyes. 'I've had enough!'

'Where is Max?' I asked Jo's colleague.

'He went to his room.'

'Shall I go and collect him now?' Clearly I couldn't do much to help here.

'Jo,' she called. Jo looked over. 'Probably best if Max goes now?'

Jo nodded.

'I want to say goodbye to Max,' Paris said, tears spilling onto her cheeks. 'I don't know when I'll see him again.'

'We'll arrange something,' Jo's colleague said.

I turned and left the room, greatly saddened by witnessing a family being torn apart. Paris came with me. 'Are you all right?' I asked her, touching her arm. She gave a small nod. 'Jo will arrange contact so you can all get together.'

'I hope so,' she said, her voice breaking. She began walking up the stairs and I followed. 'I hope I've done the right thing,' she said anxiously, turning to me as we arrived on the landing. She looked so worried and upset, but of course putting herself into care and reporting her father was a momentous and very painful decision.

'You have done the right thing,' I said. 'I know it's difficult. You're being very brave. Once you've met your carers and settled in, you'll start to feel a bit better.'

'Jo said they were nice, but I've always lived here. This is my home. Perhaps I shouldn't have said anything.' Her face crumpled and she laid her head on my shoulder, sobbing. I took her in my arms and held her as she cried.

'You are doing the right thing,' I said gently as I comforted her. 'Abuse of any sort can never be tolerated. You've told the truth, that's all. It's never the fault of the victim. The abuser is always to blame, no matter what they might say.' Many children who come into care blame themselves for the abuse and the break-up of their family.

'It's not like I didn't warn him,' Paris said as she cried on my shoulder. 'I kept telling him if he didn't leave me alone I'd report him. He didn't think I would.' She suddenly drew back and, wiping away the tears with her hand, asked, 'Do you think Mum will get rid of him so I can come home? She won't, will she?'

'I don't know, love.' I thought it unlikely, though, as surely Caz would have done so when she first knew of the abuse.

'Will I be able to see Max at your house?' Paris now asked. She must have had so many questions and worries going through her mind.

'I don't see why not. Jo will arrange contact.'

'I've got to pack some of my things,' she said, her brow creasing. 'What shall I take?'

'Your favourite clothes, nightwear, toiletries and your music. Don't worry, I'm sure Jo will arrange to collect anything else you need, and your carer will have some emergency spares.'

She nodded and, putting on a brave face, said, 'I'll say goodbye to Max now.' She went to a door on the right and opened it. I followed her into Max's bedroom. He was lying on his bed face down, propped on his elbows and poring over a book, with his hands covering his ears. I wondered how often he'd had to lie there on his bed, blocking out arguments and other things he didn't want to hear.

He sat up immediately when he saw us and looked slightly surprised and relieved. 'Is it time to go?' he asked.

'Yes, love. Paris has come to say goodbye.'

'Why?'

She went over and sat next to him on the edge of his bed. 'I'm going to live with a foster carer, like you, but I'll see you again soon.'

'When?' he asked.

'As soon as I can. But I won't be living here any more.'

He nodded. I guessed he must have been aware of at least some of what was going on downstairs, for he didn't seem unduly surprised by this.

'Give me a hug,' Paris said. Slipping her arms around him, she drew him to her. They weren't a tactile family and seeing the two of them sitting on the bed, clasped in a farewell embrace, brought a lump to my throat.

'Will someone look after you like Cathy looks after me?' Max asked her.

'Yes, I hope so.' Her voice broke and I could see she was fighting back more tears, trying to stay brave for Max's sake.

'I'll miss you,' he said.

'I'll miss you too,' Paris said. She quickly kissed his cheek and stood. 'I've got to go and pack now.' She headed for the bedroom door. As she passed me I saw tears streaming down her cheeks.

'Take care, love,' I said, but there was no reply.

I went over to Max and took a deep breath to steady my own voice. 'Come on, young man, time for us to go. Do you want to bring that book with you to finish?'

'No. I'll leave it here for next time.'

I didn't say anything, but it was quite possible there wouldn't be a next time and that future contact would be supervised at a family centre. Dan had abused Paris and assaulted Caz, so all the children would be considered at risk.

I offered Max my hand and he took it. Together we left his room and went downstairs to the living room. The shouting had stopped as anger had given way to tears. Kelly, Summer and their mother had tissues pressed to their faces, their expressions those of abject misery and disbelief. If ever there was a snapshot of what abuse can do to a family, it was this scene, agonizing and raw. Abuse enters a home like a rat in the night and gnaws its way through everything held dear by the family until there is nothing left but pain, recrimination, guilt and a lifetime of trying to come to terms with what happened.

'Bye, Mum,' Max said quietly from across the room.

'Oh, are you going now?' she asked, pressing the tissue to her eyes.

'It's for the best,' Jo said. 'You'll see him again soon.'

'Will you give me a kiss?' Caz asked him pitifully.

Max plodded over to her side, planted a kiss on her cheek and then threw his arms around her in a heartfelt embrace, as he had done that once at the hospital. I saw her flinch and momentarily draw away – the legacy of the abuse she had suffered as a child – but then force herself to stay, stiff and awkward as he hugged her.

'Be a good boy,' she told him as he lowered his arms.

'I'm sure he will be,' Jo said.

Max returned to my side.

'One of us will be in touch,' Jo's colleague said to me.

I nodded and, taking Max's hand, we left the room and went into the dingy hall, even darker now with the anguish and despair unfolding behind us.

Outside we walked in silence to my car and I opened the rear door. I waited while Max climbed in and fastened his seatbelt, then I checked it was secure. As I got into the driver's seat a cat strolled across the road in front of us, going towards Max's house.

'There's Smokey. Will someone let him in and feed him?' Max asked, focusing on the tangible and familiar.

'Yes, love.'

I fastened my seatbelt, started the engine and pulled slowly away. As we passed Max's house Smokey could be seen sitting on the doorstep, waiting patiently to be let in – the epitome of the cosy family home if you didn't know the heartache going on inside.

As I drove Max sat in silence, gazing out of his side window, while my thoughts returned to his family. I wondered if Summer would be taken into care – at her age it was highly likely. Kelly, seventeen, while technically a minor, would probably make her own decision on where she lived because it's impractical (and virtually impossible) to force an older teenager into care if they really don't want to go, unless they are considered a danger to themselves or others, when they can be sent to a secure unit or hospital.

The girls' loyalty and solidarity towards their mother had now been fractured by what Kelly saw as Paris's betrayal of their family, although of course Paris had done the right thing. However, I didn't blame Kelly; she just wanted the security of what she knew and was familiar with, even though it was at times abusive. Right now they were all in shock, struggling to come to terms with social services' intervention and the break-up of their family, but I hoped that in time Kelly would see who was really to blame. Her comment, 'He's going to be furious when he finds out,' was very worrying and suggested she, too, was afraid of her father. How did he show his anger? Who did he take it out on? But that was for Caz, with the support of the social services, to address. I had no control over that and needed to concentrate on Max.

'Are you OK, love?' I asked him, glancing in the interior mirror.

He nodded.

'When we get home I'll explain what has happened, all right?'

He nodded again, and then continued silently looking out of his side window for the rest of the journey home.

Once indoors I made us both a cold drink and then took Max into the living room, where we sat side by side on the sofa. In a calm and gentle voice I said that his sisters and mother had been upset, but he wasn't to worry, as Jo would look after them. Children in care often fret dreadfully for their families and assume responsibility far beyond their age permits. I then explained that Paris was going to live with a foster carer because their father had been saying and doing things that he shouldn't have. I wouldn't demonize him. He was still Max's father and it was quite possible they'd continue to see each other at supervised contact. I thought this was sufficient detail for a six-year-old and I'd answer any questions he had as they arose.

'When will I see Mummy again?' he immediately asked.

'I'm not sure yet. I expect Jo will phone us tomorrow.'

He nodded, accepting this in this usual stoical manner. But I now wondered how much of his stoicism was a result of the things he'd heard and witnessed at home: an inbuilt survival mechanism for dealing with trauma and upset. I didn't question him about what he may have seen and heard. He'd had enough to deal with for one day, and Jo would doubtless want to speak to him in due course. As he didn't have any further questions, I suggested he choose a game from the cupboard while I made a quick phone call. I needed to update Jill and also ask her about contact arrangements.

She was expecting my call and when I'd finished updating her she asked how Max was. She then said she'd speak to Jo in the morning when she was back in the office and then phone me.

That evening I kept Max occupied by playing board games with him before and after dinner so he didn't have time to worry. I was slightly relieved, though, when I could start his bath and bedtime routine. I felt emotionally exhausted, and although Max didn't say, I thought he must be too. As I saw him into bed he asked again when he would see his mother.

'I don't know yet, love,' I said. 'I'll speak to Jo tomorrow.'

'Mum said social workers don't always do what they say, so if Jo doesn't phone you, will you phone her?'

'Yes, love. Please try not to worry. I'll take care of it.' Which was the only reassurance I could give him.

CHAPTER TWENTY

COMFORT EATING

Needless to say, I had another sleepless night thinking about Max's family, and the following morning, when I went into his room, it seemed he had too. I hadn't heard him snoring much during the night and had taken this as a positive sign of his improving health, but of course to snore you have to be asleep. Max was sitting up in bed reading and said he'd been awake since half past three. There was a clock on his bedroom wall and he knew how to tell the time. 'When am I seeing Mummy?' he asked, closing the book.

'I don't know yet. I'll speak to Jo later.'

'Can you phone her now?'

'No, love, it's only seven-thirty. She won't be in her office yet.'

'Can you phone her at her home?'

'No. Try not to worry. If she doesn't phone me, I'll phone her.'

But he did worry. Max was an intelligent and sensitive child and was aware that his family was in turmoil and his mother probably wasn't coping.

'Will Summer go with Paris?' he asked as he got up.

'I don't know, love. Possibly.'

'Will Kelly stay at home and look after Mummy?'

'Yes, I'm sure she will.'

'Mummy has a friend, Aunt Bet. Will she help Mummy?' he asked as we ate breakfast.

'Yes, I expect so.' Caz had mentioned Bet to me. 'But try not to worry. The adults will sort it out.' Which sometimes needed to be stated. This was the adults' responsibility, not Max's.

He'd paused from eating and looked at me thoughtfully. 'I wish I was an adult, then I could help sort it out.'

Bless him. I smiled and, changing the subject, asked him about the book he'd been reading in bed. Max was always happy to discuss a good book.

Interestingly, but not surprisingly, with his ready playmates Adrian and Paula away and Max anxious about his mother, he began craving food as a comfort, which had been the norm in his house. We'd only just finished breakfast when Max came to me rubbing his stomach theatrically and saying he was hungry and could he have a snack. I gave him a piece of fruit, but ten minutes later he said he was hungry again and asked if he could have some biscuits like he did at home. He'd brushed his teeth, so I wasn't really happy about giving him sweet foods and I suggested we waited until nearer mid-morning – around eleven o'clock – when we usually had a snack. I arranged some puzzles on the table to keep him occupied, while I had a quick tidy-up. But every so often he came to me, hand on his stomach, claiming he was hungry. I gave him a glass of water to help alleviate the feeling of hunger and said I'd make a snack soon. Then a few minutes later, when I returned from hanging out the washing in the garden, I found him in the kitchen, gazing longingly up at the cupboard containing the biscuit tin. It was nearly mid-morning so I told him to sit at the table, and I made him a snack of grated cheese on crackers with sliced cucumber, then offered him the biscuit tin to choose one.

As soon as he'd finished the snack he asked (as he had been doing on and off all morning) if Jo had telephoned yet and if he was seeing his mother that evening. I said again that I didn't know and reassured him that Jo would sort something out and if I didn't hear from her, I'd phone her. I knew she'd have a lot to do and either she or Jill would telephone me. For the next hour Max was either asking for food or asking when he would see his mother, despite my best efforts to keep him occupied. At twelve o'clock I made an early nutritious and filling lunch – rotelle pasta with diced hardboiled egg and halved cherry tomatoes with a dash of salad oil (pages 62–3 of *Happy Mealtimes for Kids*) – for us both. And Max was happily occupied for a good ten minutes. I felt that after lunch a small outing with a change of scenery would be a good idea, although I didn't want to go too far away in case Jo or Jill telephoned with last-minute contact arrangements, which I knew from experience could happen. Once I'd cleared away the lunch dishes I suggested to Max that we walk to the High Street to the barbers to get his hair cut, as his mother had asked me to. This would serve two purposes: his overdue haircut and some exercise.

Max's face lit up. 'Yes. I like going to the barbers,' he declared.

'Do you?' I asked, surprised. Most young boys I knew, Adrian included, didn't like going to the barbers, not one little bit. Having to sit still under a cloak in the chair for fifteen minutes or longer while the barber cut and clipped their hair, and then coming out scratching from hair clippings down their backs – for Adrian it ranked on a par with a visit to the dentist. But Max was visibly elated, as if I'd promised him a treat. Then I found out why.

'The barber has a big jar of lollipops,' he said, his eyes widening in anticipation. 'If you're good and sit still you can choose one at the end.'

Although the barber Max would have gone to was in a different part of town and not the one we used, ours also had a large jar of sweets, as I think many do. Pity they didn't use well-done stickers like the dentist for rewarding children, I thought.

I'd never seen Max move so quickly. With the promise of a sweet at the barbers, he had his outdoor shoes on and was waiting by the front door before I'd finished closing and locking the patio doors. Outside he set up a steady pace along the road towards the High Street. He was holding my hand as he usually did, but now, instead of feeling like I had a lead weight at the end of my arm as I encouraged him along he was now in step beside me – a little red in the face and perspiring, but nevertheless walking rather than slogging.

'Well done,' I said. 'You're getting much fitter. You'll be running along here soon.'

He smiled at the praise. 'I like sweets,' he said, referring to the sweet that awaited him at the barbers.

'Yes, I know, and you like vegetables and fruit now too.'

'Have you read Roald Dahl's *Revolting Recipes*?' he asked with a cheeky grin.

I laughed, pleased that his sense of humour was still shining through.

The bell on the door of the barber's shop clanged as we entered and the owner glanced in our direction. 'Hello, take a seat,' he said. 'Shouldn't be too long.' He and his assistant were both busy cutting hair and two men were sitting on the chairs waiting, although I assumed one to be the father of the boy who was having his hair cut.

'We'll have a little wait,' I said quietly to Max as we sat down. But he didn't mind. His gaze had settled on the large jar of sweets on the shelf by the cash desk, full of an enticing assortment of brightly coloured wrapped sweets.

The barber finished cutting the lad's hair and his father stood. Max watched intently as father and son went to the till and the father paid. I saw the boy had his gaze on the sweet jar too. Once his father had been given his change and had tipped the barber, the barber said to the lad, 'I expect you'd like a sweet?'

'Yes, please,' he replied.

With a little flourish the barber took the jar from the shelf, unscrewed the lid and offered it to the boy. Max watched intently as the boy dipped his hand into the jar and took one out.

'What do you say?' his father reminded him.

'Thank you,' the boy said politely.

Max's expression was of uncontained delight at the prospect of having a sweet and I felt like the wicked witch for only allowing him a few each day. He was such a lovely child that I could have easily showered him with treats, given him every sweet he ever wanted, as his mother had, but that wouldn't have been kind. Although Max didn't know it (or maybe he did), in limiting his sweets I was acting in his best interest.

The other man waiting now sat in the vacated barber's chair, so when it was Max's turn it was the assistant who was free. I gave Max a helping hand up into the chair, as it was quite high off the ground.

'My, you're a big lad!' the assistant quipped. 'No more ice creams for you.'

He was just trying to be friendly – the banter of a barber to his client – but I inwardly cringed. I glanced at Max's reflection in the mirror and he was wearing a polite smile. I guessed he was used to comments and jokes about his weight and this was how he dealt with it, but the remark stung me. No one should have to go through life wearing a polite smile to accommodate others' thoughtless humour. But there was worse to come.

Having told the barber Max just wanted a trim, nothing drastic, I returned to my seat and he began snipping. Presently Max became uncomfortable from sitting in one position for so long and shifted in the chair. It creaked, as I'm sure it did with many customers. Most men were a lot heavier than Max. But the assistant exclaimed jocularly, 'Whoa, mate! Steady on. Don't go breaking the chair.' And threw me a knowing look in the mirror. I looked away.

Then later, once the haircut was over with and Max was offered the jar of sweets, the assistant remarked pointedly, 'I think one is enough for you, mate.' And quickly snapped the lid back on the jar. The lad before had only been offered one sweet, but no comment had been made then because, of course, he wasn't overweight. Max showed no sign that the comment had hurt and we left the shop with him chewing happily on his sweet, although I didn't give the assistant much of a tip.

Outwardly, therefore, the comments appeared to have done little damage to Max. He wasn't looking hurt. But inside it was probably a very different matter. Those words would be another nail in the coffin for Max's self-esteem and respect, to go with all the others that had been hammered in – intentionally and unintentionally – since he'd been old enough to understand he was fat. Yet other than wearing a polite smile or ignoring such comments, what else could he have done as the butt of a joke about his size? If he'd said, 'That's rude,' or similar, it would have drawn attention to the comment, probably provoking a retort or a lecture on manners. As an adult I would have said a sarcastic, 'Thank you,' or a similar put-down. But this remedy wasn't available to a child, so I guessed Max's way of dealing with what was an insidious form of bullying (although I'm sure the barber's assistant hadn't seen it that way) was probably for the best – a polite smile. And, of course, Max had other worries occupying him at present. 'Am I seeing my mummy tonight?' he asked as soon as he'd stopped chewing.

'I'll find out when we get home,' I said.

Once home I telephoned my fostering agency. Jill was speaking to someone on another line, so her colleague said she'd ask her to phone back as soon as she'd finished. 'I think she's talking to Jo now,' she added. It was only a small office with six staff and they kept abreast of each other's cases so that they were up to date when they covered the emergency out-of-hours service. It was now two o'clock and ten minutes later Jill returned my call.

'Sorry, Cathy, I've only just managed to speak to Jo,' Jill said. 'At present Jo's not sure what's happening about contact. She's trying to arrange it for later this afternoon at the Family

Centre, but there's an issue finding transport for Caz. She says she can't use a taxi; her foot is too painful. If contact doesn't go ahead today, it will have to be next week. The Family Centre isn't open at the weekend. Can you prepare Max for that eventuality just in case, as he's used to seeing his family every day?'

'Yes, I will. Will his father and sisters be going to contact?'

'I don't know. If contact doesn't go ahead today, I suggested to Jo that Max phones his mother instead.'

'Yes. All right.' This was a reasonable second best. 'How is Paris?' I asked.

'Jo took her to her foster carer's yesterday, but she hasn't had a chance to speak to her today. At some point she'll try to arrange sibling contact, but that won't be this afternoon. I'll phone you as soon as I know the contact arrangements for Max to see his mother.'

'OK. Thank you.'

Having said goodbye, I went to Max, who was in the living room, and told him what Jill had said. 'What's a Family Centre?' he reasonably asked.

'It's a building with rooms like living rooms where parents and children can meet. There's a sofa, a table and chairs and lots of games to play with and books. A lady called a contact supervisor stays in the room while you see your mother in case you need anything.' She would also be monitoring them and making notes on the session, which she'd pass to Jo, but I didn't go into that now.

'Will Dad and my sisters be there?' he asked.

'I don't know yet.'

I'd no sooner finished telling Max about the Family Centre when the telephone rang again and it was Jill. She said that

contact wouldn't be going ahead today, as no suitable transport was available to take Caz to and from the centre. Jill said
I should phone Caz at six o'clock so Max could speak to her
and I wrote down the telephone number, as I wasn't sure if it
had been included in the essential information pack. Jill said I
needn't put the phone on speaker and monitor the call (as I'd
had to do with some children in the past), as there were no
safeguarding concerns about Caz speaking to Max, but that I
should stay in the room while he spoke to her in case he
became upset, which I would have done anyway with a child
of his age. She said I should also call Caz at the same time on
Saturday and Sunday so Max could speak to her, and
concluded by wishing us a nice weekend and reminding me
to phone their out-of-hours service if I had any urgent problems with Max. I wished her a happy weekend and we said
goodbye. As gently as I could I told Max that he wouldn't be
seeing his mother that night, but we could phone her at six
o'clock. He took this with his usual stoicism and then asked
for something to eat.

'Max, you know it's OK to be disappointed and upset?' I
said.

He looked at me questioningly.

'You've had a lot to cope with and you were hoping to see
your mother this afternoon, but unfortunately that isn't going
to happen. I'm guessing you could be feeling a bit hurt and
maybe angry. I think I would be.' I wasn't trying to upset him,
but I thought it was emotionally healthier for him to admit he
was upset, rather than asking for food to comfort eat.

'What's the point in being hurt and angry?' he asked. 'It
won't change anything. Adults do things and make decisions
that children can't do anything about.' Which was profound

for a child of six, true, and probably came from all the books he'd read.

'I understand it can be frustrating being a child,' I said. 'But it still helps to let out your disappointment, whether you're a child or an adult, rather than feeling unhappy and then trying to cheer yourself up with food.'

I saw a flash of recognition cross his eyes. 'That's what we do at home, isn't it?'

'I think it could be,' I agreed.

He looked thoughtful for a moment. 'When Dad gets in a bad temper I hide in my bedroom and eat lots of sweets. Then when he's gone I come out and Mum tells one of my sisters to go down to the shop and buy us something nice to cheer us up. She means sweets and cream cakes.'

I nodded, but I'd latched onto the words bad temper. 'Does your dad often get in a bad temper?' I asked.

Max nodded.

'While you've been going there for contact?'

'Yes, and before when I lived there. More then. What do you do if you're upset or angry?' he asked.

'Go for a walk,' I said. 'It helps clear my head.'

'I think I've done enough walking for one day,' he said quaintly, and I smiled.

'Max, you know when your dad gets in a temper, how does he show it?'

'He shouts very loudly at Mum and sometimes hits her.'

'That's very wrong of him. Does he hit you or your sisters?'

'Sometimes he hits my sisters, but I stay in my bedroom and he forgets I'm there.'

Little wonder they all comfort ate, I thought, living constantly under the threat of violence. I would be noting what Max had told me in my log notes and also notifying Jo. As far as I knew she wasn't aware of the extent of the father's violence and that it had been directed towards his children, as I hadn't been until now.

'Max, will you try to say more about how you are feeling, rather than keeping it inside?' I suggested.

'Yes. I'll try. I miss my mummy, but I'm still hungry,' he said pragmatically.

'All right, I'll get you a small snack to see you through to dinner.'

'A healthy one so I can lose weight?'

'Yes, of course.'

Max clock-watched for the rest of the afternoon and gave me regular updates on the progression of time towards six o'clock when he could phone his mother: 'Two hours to go'; 'An hour and a half'; 'One hour, Cathy'; 'Half an hour'; 'Fifteen minutes'; 'Five minutes.' So at one minute to six we were sitting side by side on the sofa in the living room and I keyed in Caz's number. I told Max I'd say a quick hello to his mother and then he'd speak to her.

One of his sisters answered with a tight, 'Hello.' I wasn't sure which one it was.

'It's Cathy, Max's carer. Is that Kelly?' I asked.

'Yes. I'll put Mum on,' she said curtly. So it seemed I was out of favour again.

A moment later Caz's voice came on and she said a very quiet, 'Hello.'

'Hello, Caz, how are you?' I asked sympathetically. 'Max is sitting beside me. I'll put him on.'

Immediately she began crying. I couldn't pass the phone to

him, as it would upset him to hear his mother weeping. He was watching me intently, already aware something was wrong. I waited, and after a few moments Caz recovered a little and said, 'I'll talk to him now.'

'Are you sure you feel up to it?' I asked. 'We could call back in a while.'

'It won't make any difference,' she said, her voice breaking again. I waited some more and once she felt better I passed the phone to Max.

'Hello, Mummy,' he said faintly.

She must have asked him how he was, for he said, 'I'm all right. How are you?'

Then he went quiet and looked very sad and eventually passed the phone back to me. 'She can't talk, she's crying.'

'Caz?' I said, taking the phone.

'I can't stop crying,' she said. 'I'll speak to him tomorrow. Kelly wants to talk to him.'

Kelly came on the line and I passed the handset to Max again.

She must have asked him what he'd been doing, as he told her of our day, including the visit to the barbers. But his tone was very flat and subdued; it wasn't a natural conversation, I think partly because he wasn't used to using a phone, but also because it wasn't a normal situation – he and Paris were in care and his mother was beside herself with grief. He said goodbye to Kelly, and Summer came on the line. He had a similar short and flat conversation with her and then said goodbye. He returned the handset to me, but the line was already dead. Caz had my telephone number, so she could phone if she felt up to speaking to Max later.

'We'll phone her again tomorrow,' I said encouragingly. He looked so sad.

Far from reassuring him, the telephone contact had unsettled him, and although we'd only just had dinner he complained he was hungry and began agitating for food.

'You're not hungry,' I said. 'You're worried about your mother.'

'Yes, you're right, Cathy,' he said in his quaint, old-fashioned way. I suppose when emotion and food have been interlinked all your life it's difficult to separate them.

I then telephoned my parents, as I hadn't spoken to Adrian and Paula the evening before. Dad answered, as Mum was playing with Paula. They'd all been to the cinema that afternoon and when Dad put Adrian on he excitedly told me all about the animated Disney cartoon they'd seen. He then chatted to Max and told him about the film, which helped cheer him up. After we'd all spoken and said goodbye, Max said he'd like to go to the cinema; he'd been once when Paris had taken him, but that was some time ago. I said we'd go tomorrow afternoon – Saturday – which gave him something else to think about until bedtime, when his thoughts returned anxiously to his mother.

'Who's looking after Mummy?' he asked, one hand on Buzz Lightyear.

'Kelly, Summer and probably her friend, Bet,' I said.

'Bet doesn't like my dad,' he said. 'Do you like him?'

'I don't know him,' I said carefully. 'I've only met him a couple of times. But I don't like the way he has been treating you and your family. A man is supposed to look after his wife and children, not hurt them.' For, like any child growing up with domestic violence, Max had been shown a very poor example of fatherhood and not one he should follow when he grew up.

'Why doesn't Adrian and Paula's dad live here?' he asked. 'Was he horrible too?'

'No, not like that.' It wasn't the first time a child I was fostering had commented on John's absence. A direct question deserves an honest, age-appropriate reply.

'He lives with another lady,' I said. 'Although he still loves Adrian and Paula.'

'I wish my daddy lived with another lady,' Max said, and I could see he meant it, which shook me. It was sad and shocking for a young boy to feel that way about his father; that Max wished him gone gave a good indication of just how damaging Dan's presence was in their family.

CHAPTER TWENTY-ONE

UNEXPECTED TURN
OF EVENTS

Max enjoyed the film and enjoyed the popcorn even more. He'd looked slightly surprised in the foyer when I'd said he could have a box of popcorn and a fizzy (zero-calorie) drink. But it was part of the treat of going to the cinema, and like all treat foods, having it occasionally wasn't going to harm him as long as he ate healthily the rest of the time, which he was now doing generally.

That evening telephone contact with his mother was a little easier. Caz, expecting the call, answered and managed to hold it all together. I asked her how she was and she said a flat 'Getting by'. I passed the handset to Max and although his mother didn't have much to say, Max told her about our trip to the cinema, including the large box of popcorn, which he said was bigger than the microwave popcorn they made at home. Summer and Kelly also spoke to him. Kelly asked him if he'd heard from Paris and he said no. Then she asked him if I had Paris's foster carer's telephone number and Max asked me. I said I didn't and his mother should ask Jo on Monday about arrangements for talking to and seeing Paris. Max repeated this to Kelly. When they'd finished he said goodbye and hung up, then asked if he could phone Paris.

'I'll ask Jo when I speak to her next week,' I said. 'She will tell us about the contact arrangements.' I couldn't promise that he'd be able to phone Paris, but I thought it was very likely. I'd had experience in the past of sibling phone contact with children I'd fostered, as generally it's considered important for siblings to maintain their bonds. It could be that he would have face-to-face contact with Paris, but at this point I simply didn't know what arrangements Jo would make.

On Sunday morning we left straight after breakfast to go to my parents' house to collect Adrian and Paula. I was so pleased to see them again, as was Max. It was lovely that they'd had this special time with their nana and grandpa, but I'd missed them more than I cared to admit. They'd only been away a few days and I'd had Max to look after, but I'd felt as though part of me was missing. It was a stark reminder of the unbelievably huge adjustments parents of children taken into care have to make.

Mum and Dad made a fuss of Max, and Adrian and Paula were pleased to see him again. Mum made a roast dinner and then we went for a short walk to their local park, then left at four o'clock to return home. Mum and Dad had to be up early in the morning as they were going on a coach outing for the day to the coast. 'Remember to take your buckets and spades,' Adrian joked as we left.

'We will!' my father returned.

Paula was quiet in the car and I asked her if she was OK. 'I'll miss Nana,' she said, pulling an unhappy face.

'I'm sure you will. You've had a lovely time, but we'll see her and Grandpa again soon.' She would have been spoilt with all the one-to-one attention, whereas at home my time was split between the three of them. Another side effect of fostering as a single parent.

But once home Adrian and Paula were pleased to be reunited with Toscha, all their toys and to be in their own bedrooms again. They were still up there playing when it was time for Max to telephone his mother. I called him down and we went into the living room, where we sat side by side on the sofa and I keyed in the telephone number for his home. Kelly answered and said with some attitude that Max couldn't talk to his mother, as she was in bed ill, as if it was my fault.

'Oh dear, what's the matter with her?' I asked, ignoring the slight.

'Don't know.'

'Have you spoken to a doctor?'

'No. Bet came round and said she was run down and needed a rest, and to tell the nurse tomorrow when she comes to change her dressing.'

'OK.' So I assumed that Bet would seek medical help if necessary, and I passed the phone to Max, explaining that his mother was having a lie down.

He spoke to Kelly first and then Summer, telling them both that we'd been to see my parents and had a big roast dinner, and Adrian and Paula were home now and he was playing with them. Just having them here had brightened his mood. However, unfortunately, Summer told him that he and Paris would be able to go home soon. I didn't know why she said that, probably she was just trying to think of something positive to tell him, but it was unrealistic and unsettling.

Once they'd finished and had said goodbye Max repeated what she'd said: 'Paris and me can go home soon.' He was smiling. I had to explain that Jo would decide when they

236

could go home and as far as I knew it wasn't yet, as she'd need to be sure that his mother was well enough to look after him. Although Max was in care under a Section 20 (as Paris would be) and technically Caz could remove them from care when she wanted to, Jo had said that with the revelations about their father's abuse she would apply for a court order to keep them in care, if necessary. No social worker would return a child to a parent who was known to be violent and had sexually assaulted his daughter.

'Why did Summer say that?' Max asked.

'I think she's missing you and hoping to see you soon.' Which he accepted. Later I overheard him telling Adrian that Paris was also with a foster carer and he hoped to see her or speak to her on the phone soon, so I thought he'd accepted what I'd said.

On Monday morning, when Max woke, he asked me if he would be seeing his mother that day. I said I hoped so and I'd tell him as soon as I'd heard from Jo. Once up, and with Adrian and Paula home, he was gainfully occupied so didn't keep asking me when he could see his mother or if he could have food. All three children played nicely together in the garden and at eleven o'clock Jill telephoned. I took the call in the living room from where I could see the children through the patio doors. Jill asked me if we'd had a good weekend, how Max was and if I'd heard from Jo. I said I was waiting to hear from her about the contact arrangements. She said she'd phone her now and get back to me. She also made an appointment to visit us the following week for one of her supervisory visits.

Jill phoned again after lunch and said she'd spoken briefly to Jo – she was very busy – and there was still an issue with transport – getting Caz to and from the Family Centre – much as there had been on Friday. The social services could provide a cab to take and collect her, but Caz was insisting she needed an ambulance with a wheelchair, as it was too far for her to walk from a cab into the centre. She'd told Jo that ambulance transportation was provided for her hospital appointments, so she needed it if she was going to get to the Family Centre. I suppose her request was reasonable, although she had been getting around on crutches at home. Jill said they were still trying to find transport, but she doubted contact would take place this afternoon. I didn't say anything to Max until we knew for certain. Jill called back an hour later to say that no suitable transport was available until the following day, so contact had been set up from two o'clock to three-thirty the next day – Tuesday.

'I'll tell Max,' I said. 'Should he phone his mother this evening?'

'Yes, I would think so,' Jill replied. 'I'll let Jo know.'

'Do we know what's happening about contact for the rest of the week?' I asked. I hoped it wasn't going to be two to three-thirty every day, as it would stop us having further days out. There were only two weeks left until the new school term started and I wanted to make the most of it.

'No, not yet,' Jill said.

Having said goodbye, I went into the garden and, taking Max to one side, I said that he'd be able to speak to his mother on the telephone that evening, and then tomorrow he'd see her at the Family Centre. He took the news with his usual fortitude and returned to play with Adrian and Paula.

* * *

I know from experience that arrangements and situations can and do change quickly in fostering. One of the requirements of being a good foster carer is adaptability. However, even as an experienced foster carer I was taken aback by the swiftness of the change of events that now followed. At six o'clock Max and I took up our usual positions on the sofa, ready to telephone his mother, while Adrian and Paula stayed in the garden, playing. I keyed in Max's home phone number and one of the girls answered with a quick, 'Hi.' As usual I wasn't sure if it was Kelly or Summer.

'It's Cathy,' I said.

'Hi, Cathy,' she said brightly. 'How are you?'

'Fine, thanks,' I said, slightly thrown by her upbeat tone.

'It's Paris.'

'Paris! What are you doing there?'

'I've come back home.' My heart sank.

'But why? You should have given it longer. It takes time to settle into a foster family. What about your father and all the reasons you put yourself into care?'

'He's not here,' she explained.

I glanced at Max, who was watching me closely. 'Just a minute,' I said to Paris. Then to Max: 'Can you go and play in the garden with Adrian and Paula for a few moments, please? I'll call you when it's time for you to speak.' Aware there was a drama unfolding at home, he was reluctant to leave. 'Now, please,' I said more firmly. I didn't want him hearing this until I knew what was going on. With a small sigh, he heaved himself off the sofa and went out through the patio doors.

'Sorry, Paris,' I said. 'I'll put Max on in a moment to talk to you. You said your father isn't there now, but I'm assuming he'll be back later this evening. Then what?' I was obviously concerned for her safety.

'No, you don't understand,' she said, her voice rising. 'Mum has thrown him out. She's not going to let him come back. Ever.'

'When did this happen?'

'This afternoon. She's done well, hasn't she?' In a way, yes, I thought. It must have taken a lot of courage for Caz to stand up to the man who'd been bullying and assaulting her for years. But I knew it wouldn't be that simple.

'Does Jo know?' I asked.

'Not yet. Mum's going to phone her tomorrow. The office is closed now. I've only been back an hour.'

'Does your foster carer know?' It occurred to me that if Paris had just disappeared, her carer would be worried sick.

'Yes, she tried to stop me. She wanted me to wait until tomorrow when we could discuss it with Jo. But the only reason I left home was because of him and he's gone now.'

'Paris, can I talk to your mother, please? Is she able to come to the phone?'

'Yeah, sure. She's here. I'll speak to Max when you've finished talking to her, yeah?'

'Yes. But could I ask you not to tell him he'll be going home?'

'OK. Why not?'

'We don't know for certain when that will be. You're older, it's slightly different for you. But the reason Max came into care was because he wasn't being looked after while your mother was in hospital and was left at home by himself.'

'Oh yeah. But we won't do that again, and Mum's not in hospital any more.'

'I know.'

'Here she is. I'll put her on. I'm going to unpack.' I could hear the jubilation in Paris's voice. Of course she was happy to be home.

'Hi, Cathy,' Caz said, coming to the phone. 'I've done well, throwing that bastard out, haven't I? The girls are proud of me. Ouch, my foot's killing me. But I can cope with anything now. Can't wait to have Max back.' I'd never heard her sound so positive and upbeat.

'Caz, I've asked Paris not to tell Max he's going home yet.'

'Why?'

'I think you need to discuss the time frame with Jo first,' I said diplomatically.

There was silence.

'And perhaps you could ask Kelly and Summer not to mention it to Max either. He'll be so disappointed if he thinks he can return home now like Paris, and he can't.'

'Why shouldn't he? I'll phone Jo first thing in the morning and tell her I want him home tomorrow. I assume you can bring him in your car with all his belongings?'

'Yes, if that's what Jo wants me to do.'

'No problem then. I agreed to Max going into care voluntarily after he got left home alone. There's no court order, so I can have him back when I want.'

'Yes, but talk to Jo first.'

'OK. You know, sometimes it takes a shock to make you realize what you stand to lose. I've spent all my adult life believing I couldn't manage without that bastard after he rescued me from my stepfather. I chose to ignore what was going on under my own eyes until Paris put herself into care. That was the shock I needed to stand up to him and put my kids first. He's gone and he's not coming back.'

'What if he returns?' I asked. 'Presumably he has a key.'

'Bet's going to have the locks changed, but he won't be back. He knows when he's well off.'

'Well off?' I asked, puzzled. I couldn't see how being thrown out of your home made you well off.

'Paris told him that she wouldn't make a statement to the police as long as he stayed away.'

'I see.' So he'd been let off, I thought but didn't say.

'So he's gone for good, with his tail between his legs,' Caz said. 'He can cry on *her* shoulder now. Well, good luck to her, I say. She's welcome to him.'

'He has someone else?' I asked.

'Yes, didn't you know?'

'No.' There was no reason why I should.

'She's got two kids by him, plus three of her own. I bet she doesn't let on to the benefits office that he's moved in. I put up with him being with her when he fancied because I felt I wasn't worth any better. So he won't be coming back here. Not if he knows what's good for him.'

'Does Max know of this other family?' I asked, surprised by this revelation.

'Not sure. He might have heard the girls and me talking about it. I never told him.'

Max was smart, so I thought he probably knew.

'What about Jo? Does she know?' I asked, for there could be safeguarding concerns there too.

'She does now. Put Max on, will you, so I can talk to him? He can speak to the girls after.'

I stood, went to the patio doors and called Max to the phone. I hoped Caz wouldn't tell him he was going home tomorrow. But she did. Almost immediately. He put the phone to his ear and within a few seconds he was grinning. 'Really? Tomorrow?' he said, looking at me for my reaction. But I didn't say anything until the very end, after he'd finished speaking to his sisters.

He told each of them in turn that he was going home tomorrow, so by the time he spoke to Paris, who went last, it was general knowledge and her promise not to tell him was redundant. Once he'd said goodbye he was eager to go into the garden to tell Adrian and Paula.

'Max, just a minute,' I said. 'Before you go I need to say something.' He looked at me questioningly. 'I've been a foster carer for a long while and some of the children who returned home didn't go as quickly as their parents would have liked. It might be that Jo says you can go home tomorrow, in which case I'll take you. Or it might be she wants you to stay here for a bit longer.'

'To make sure I don't get left home alone again?' he asked.

'Yes, and other things.'

'It was frightening being left all by myself without any dinner.'

'I know. So Jo needs to make sure that won't happen again.'

He nodded. 'Can I go and play now?'

'Of course, love.'

He went outside to join Adrian and Paula. Max was sensible and seemed to have accepted my cautionary message. I saw no need to tell him about the concerns there would be around his father – it was enough that he understood he might not be going home tomorrow. As it turned out, I'd been right to issue the warning, for Max didn't go home the next day – far from it.

CHAPTER TWENTY-TWO

SEA OTTERS HOLD HANDS

'Am I going home today?' Max asked the following morning when he woke.

'I'm not sure yet,' I said. 'We'll have to see what Jo says.'

'If I don't go home, will I see my mummy?'

'I hope so.'

I knew my replies sounded vague, but I'd learnt in fostering never to make a promise to a child about contact or going home unless it was 100 per cent certain, and then some.

At nine o'clock, around the time Caz had said she'd be telephoning Jo, we were all seated at the table having breakfast. I intended to telephone Jill once we'd finished to give her an update – that Paris had taken herself home and Caz wanted Max home today. However, at 9.30 a.m., just as I was clearing up the breakfast dishes, the phone rang and I answered it in the kitchen. The children were on their way upstairs to brush their teeth. It was Caz and she was so upset and angry that she could barely get her words out.

'Jo is off sick! I had to wait ages to speak to her manager. She says there's no way Max can come home today or this week. She says – and I can't believe this – that someone from the department will have to make a home visit, maybe more than one, so our case can be reviewed! Case! We're a case now!' Her voice caught and she had to take a deep breath. 'Jo's manager said they're short-staffed anyway and with Jo off sick and other social workers on annual leave, she couldn't say how long it would take. I hit the roof. I mean to say – I told her I'd send a cab for Max if necessary and do you know what she said?' I could guess, but I kept quiet. 'She had the cheek to say that if I tried to take him from you, she'd apply for a court order straight away. That's blackmail, isn't it?' Her voice faltered with a cry.

I waited until she'd recovered before I spoke. 'Caz, I know how upsetting this is, but if the social services have concerns, they would have to apply for a court order if you tried to take him. They wouldn't have any choice. I think Jo told you something similar a while ago.'

'Yes, but that was when his father was living here. I told her manager he'd gone and he wouldn't be coming back. But she said there were still certain safeguarding issues – like would he be looked after properly. Kelly says we should get ourselves a good lawyer and fight them.' Her voice broke again.

'Caz, I know you're upset. I would be. But the social services have to be certain Max will be looked after and that Dan won't be coming home.' Max wasn't within earshot so I felt I could speak freely to her.

'I wished I'd never agreed to Max going into care in the first place!' Caz blurted. I didn't comment, but had she not agreed the social services would have applied for a court order at the start to remove him from home. You can't leave a six-year-old unattended, as had happened to Max.

'Did Jo's manager give you some idea of the timescale?' I asked when Caz had stopped crying.

'No. She says she'll need to speak to Jo, as she's our case-worker, then set up the home visits and the review. I think she was talking weeks, possibly months, not days.'

'What about contact arrangements?' I asked. 'You're seeing Max this afternoon at the Family Centre and then when?'

'I don't know,' she cried, distraught. 'Could you find out for me?'

'Yes.'

'Thank you, Cathy. I can't cope with all this and my foot is killing me. I'm going to take some painkillers.'

It was the least I could do for her. Although dispassionately I knew the reasons Max couldn't go home at present, as a mother I sympathized with Caz – separated from her child and up against the social services, who had no immediate plans to return him. Adrian and Paula had been away for a few days and I was so pleased to have them back again. Not only was Caz separated from her son, but she had no control over when or even if he would be returned. Whether I could find out any more I didn't know, but first I needed to check on the children's teeth-cleaning.

I went upstairs, where they were all gathered in the bath-room, but I got as far as the landing when the phone began to ring again. I answered it in my bedroom. 'Is that Cathy Glass?' a woman asked.

'Yes.'

'It's Lorraine, Jo's manager. You're the foster carer looking after Max, aren't you?'

'Yes, that's correct.'

'Jo's off sick and I'm handling her caseload for the time being. I've just spoken to his mother, Caz. She wants to take Max home, but I've had to explain that's not possible now. I wanted to check the contact arrangements with you. I believe Max is seeing his mother this afternoon from two o'clock to three-thirty at the Family Centre. Are you able to take and collect him?' She sounded very efficient.

'Yes.'

'Good. I'm going to book the Family Centre and transport for Thursday this week too, at the same time.' I reached for a pen and paper and made a note. 'Then next week, and until Max returns to school, contact will be Monday, Wednesday and Friday, two o'clock to three-thirty at the Family Centre.'

'Do you want him to phone his mother on the evenings he doesn't see her?' I asked as I wrote. 'He has been doing.'

'Yes. If phone contact is going well, it can continue. I'll speak to Caz shortly with the arrangements. How is Max coping? He's bright, isn't he?'

'Yes, he's coping well. He misses his family, obviously, but he has a good understanding of why he is in care.'

'And he can stay with you for as long as necessary?'

'Yes.'

'Excellent. Thank you.'

'Lorraine, will Paris be staying at home?' I asked.

'I'm going to see her as soon as I can this week,' she said, and then ended the call with a pleasant and efficient goodbye.

It crossed my mind that Jo's absence could be stress-related. I wouldn't have been at all surprised. I wondered what Caz would make of the new contact arrangements. Until the last few days she had been used to seeing Max every day, but now – and for the foreseeable future – it would be three times a week. I knew there wouldn't be the funding for more supervised contact, as resources were stretched to the limit.

Usually only babies and toddlers who are being adopted or rehabilitated home have daily contact. But how would Caz take these new arrangements? It wasn't long before I found out.

The children had brushed their teeth and we were now downstairs. We'd had some rain, so they were rummaging in the toy cupboard for games to play indoors. When the phone rang, I answered it in the living room.

'Cathy!' I recognized Caz's voice. 'They're only going to let me see Max three times a week! It's shocking. They should be reported. I'm going to speak to …' I couldn't hear for the noise in the background. 'Paris! Turn the television down!' Caz shouted. The volume was reduced, but a banging sound continued. 'The lock's being changed on the front door,' she added. 'It's doing my head in. I can't think straight.'

'Hopefully it won't take long,' I offered.

'And we're being supervised the whole time!' Caz said, returning to the issue of contact. 'A stranger will be in the room with us constantly. It's not right.'

'It's standard procedure,' I said.

'But I have been seeing him at home.' Which was obviously true.

'Did Lorraine explain why the contact has been moved?' I asked.

'Sort of. It's because of *him* [Dan], and Max not being properly looked after before. But I told her Dan had gone, and although I can't get around properly, Max's sisters will be here to look after him.'

'I know, but the social services have to satisfy themselves that Max is safe and being properly looked after.'

'Of course he will be,' she snapped.

'You know that, but they need to be certain too.' I heard her tut and sigh. 'Caz, my advice would be to concentrate on enjoying your time with Max this afternoon. That's the most important thing, isn't it?'

'Yes, but ...' she began and stopped as one of the girls shouted.

'Mum! The nurse is here.'

'Oh drat, I forgot about her. I'll have to go.'

'I'll see you this afternoon then,' I said.

'Why? Will you be there?'

'Yes, I'll bring Max into the Family Centre, say hello to you and then leave. At three-thirty I'll come into the centre to collect him.'

'Oh good,' she said, brightening. 'I didn't realize you'd be there. See you later then.'

I was left thinking how much our relationship had improved since those first days at the hospital, that she now viewed me as an ally and welcomed my presence. I could appreciate it was daunting for a parent to have to see their child at a Family Centre with a supervisor watching, but I knew from experience that after a few visits they fell into the routine and were more relaxed and able to make the most of their time together. Indeed, some parents living in poverty actually prefer being at the centre rather than home. It's clean, comfortable, well equipped, the staff are friendly and in winter it's warm – which, sadly, some family homes aren't.

The rain stopped and the children went outside to play until lunch, then at half past one we set off in the car for the Family Centre. I stopped at a small grocery store on the way to buy some fruit for Max to take with him, as it had become a little ritual, and he chose a box of ripe peaches. 'Don't forget to wash them before you eat them,' I said as I paid. 'There's a kitchen at the centre. The supervisor will show you and your mum where it is.' The supervisor's role wasn't only to monitor and record, but also to help and intervene as and when necessary.

I parked in the car park at the front of the centre and we all got out. Adrian and Paula had been before and knew the routine. I never left them in the car, as it was out of sight of most of the rooms, and I never knew how long I would be.

'It's bigger than I thought,' Max said, carrying the fruit and surveying the single-storey building. It sprawled round in an L shape and a large outdoor play area was at one end with a slide, swings, a sandpit and wooden benches. Two children were out there now, riding tricycles as their parents watched. The whole centre was surrounded by a six-foot-high security fence.

Paula held my hand and the boys followed close behind as I led the way up the path to the main entrance. Max was looking slightly apprehensive.

'Don't worry, it will be fine,' I said, throwing him a reassuring smile. I pressed the buzzer and the CCTV camera overhead whirred before the door clicked open. Inside, the receptionist sat behind a low partition, working at a desk. She recognized me from previous visits with other children and said hello and smiled at the children. 'Is Max's mother, Caz, here yet?' I asked.

'Yes, and his sisters. They're in Red Room. Sign in, please, and then you can go straight through.' The six rooms are identified by colours. I signed the visitors' book and then pushed open the swing doors and we went down the corridor.

'My sisters have come too,' Max said, pleased, and glancing up at the brightly coloured artwork on the wall as we went. The whole centre was attractively decorated and child-friendly.

The door to Red Room was open and I stepped in with Max while Adrian and Paula waited by the door. Caz was sitting in the middle of the sofa with her feet up on a child's stool and her crutches balanced against the sofa either side of her. Her daughters were sitting on chairs around her, leaning in and talking in a huddle, pretty much as they had been when I'd first seen them at the hospital. But now there wasn't the same air of collusion or hostility; they seemed to be huddling together for moral support rather than present-ing a united front. They looked relieved and pleased to see me.

'Hello, Cathy,' Caz said, ending their conversation.

Summer immediately stood and came over to Max. 'Hello, little man,' she said, ruffling his hair.

The contact supervisor, seated at a table in one corner, looked up and said hello and then continued writing. Good-ness knows what she was finding to write about, as Max had only just arrived – possibly the way they'd greeted him and were interacting with each other, which was often included in the reports.

'Come and give me a kiss, son,' Caz said. 'I can't get up, my feet are bad.'

He plodded over in his usual style, kissed his mother on her offered cheek and set the box of peaches on her lap. 'Cathy says you have to wash them first,' he said.

'Sorry,' I said. 'I was running short of time so I bought them on the way here.' She knew I usually washed the fruit first so it was ready to eat. I glanced at the contact supervisor. 'Could someone show them where the kitchen is?'

'I've already done that and shown them where the bathroom is,' she said.

'I know where the kitchen is,' Kelly said. 'I can wash them.' Standing, and apparently pleased to have a little job to do, she took the peaches and disappeared out of the room, saying hi to Adrian and Paula as she went by.

'We can have drinks and biscuits later,' Caz enthused to Max.

He nodded but was still looking around, rather bemused and a little overwhelmed, not sure what he should be doing. 'There are games and books over there,' I said, pointing to the cupboards and shelves overflowing with boxed games and books.

'Let's go and find a game, shall we?' Summer said to Max. He crossed the room with Summer while Paris stayed where she was, looking rather pensive.

'Are you OK?' I asked her.

She gave a half-hearted nod.

'There's been a lot going on for you,' I said sympathetically. 'I know.'

I didn't want to pry, and having seen Max in and said hello, it was time for me to leave. Contact is the family's time together and I shouldn't impinge on it. 'Bye then, see you at three-thirty,' I said and left, collecting Adrian and Paula on the way out of the room.

I signed out of the visitors' book and we left the centre. There's a small park not far away that I'd visited before while children had been at the Family Centre and we walked there now. By coincidence another foster carer I knew was there.

She was fostering two children from different families and the little girl was in the centre seeing her parents, so she'd brought the five-year-old boy, David, to the park. We introduced the children to each other and then chatted as they played. 'I spend most of my life here at the moment,' she said. She then explained that David had contact Monday, Wednesday and Friday mornings, and the little girl on Tuesday and Thursday afternoons.

I enjoyed her company and the children played nicely, with Adrian, as the eldest, organizing some games. We had to leave before them, as their contact didn't finish for another half an hour. I said I might see her again on Thursday (Max's next contact), but then the following week we were at the centre Monday, Wednesday and Friday afternoon.

We said goodbye and returned to the centre, where I buzzed us in and signed the visitors' book again. Children's voices playing happily could be heard coming from one room and a baby crying in another. Sometimes on the way in or out of the centre I'd heard a distraught parent crying as they'd had to say goodbye to their child, and it always broke my heart. Sometimes I think I'm too soft for this work, but then again you need a lot of empathy to foster.

The door to Red Room was closed. It was exactly 3.30 p.m. so I knocked and went in. Had we been early I would have waited outside, as every moment is precious when you are only seeing your child for a few hours a week. Max and his mother were sitting together on the sofa with a large colourful book about animals open between them. Summer and Paris were sitting cross-legged on the carpet either side of a low occasional table and playing a board game. Kelly, grown up as she was, had a child's colouring book open on her lap and was concentrating on colouring in a picture with wax crayons, possibly an activity she hadn't done since a child. It was a welcoming and convivial scene – a family relaxed and enjoying each other's company – and it supported the centre's policy of not having televisions in the rooms so that families were encouraged to interact rather than stare at a screen. I had never seen Caz sitting with Max and sharing a book, nor the girls playing a game. So involved were they that they'd barely acknowledged my arrival, and the contact supervisor had to tell them twice it was the end of the session and time to pack away.

Max returned the book to the shelf and then went round the room kissing his mother and then his sisters in turn and saying goodbye. I said goodbye and that we'd phone tomorrow evening at six o'clock and then see them again on Thursday. It's usual for the carer and the child to leave the centre first so that long, drawn-out emotional and potentially upsetting goodbyes don't spill out onto the pavement.

I signed us out and we left. Max was far more relaxed now he was familiar with the centre, and said he'd had a nice time without being asked. In the car he told us that he and his mother had read a book together about unusual animals, and did I know that the spiny echidna, found in Australia, is one of only two egg-laying mammals.

'No, I didn't,' I said. 'I don't expect many people do.'

Nor that the buzz a house fly makes is always in the key of F.

'Why?' Adrian asked.

Max shrugged. 'The book didn't say.'

'Perhaps it's the only tune it knows,' I offered.

It took the children a moment to realize I was joking. 'You are silly, Mum,' Adrian said.

But a really cute fact Max shared with us was that sea otters hold hands when they're asleep to stop them drifting out to sea alone.

From Max's overall enthusiasm I guessed he and his mother didn't often sit down together with a book, if ever, and that the girls rarely played games together. So if there was a positive side to the family having to see each other in the confines of the Family Centre, it was that – to use a cliché – they had spent quality time together and enjoyed it.

The next day was Wednesday and I'd kept it free, as I needed to buy the boys their school uniforms. I'd left it until near the end of the summer holiday, as I'd got caught out before, buying new uniforms and shoes in plenty of time and then finding the child had had a growth spurt and everything was too small and had to be exchanged. I was also hoping that this had allowed Max time to come down a size in clothes from all the exercise and healthy eating during the summer holidays. In the department store I didn't draw attention to the sizes as I selected pairs of trousers and tops for Max to try on. Adrian was easy as he was average for his age and I knew exactly what would fit him.

I was therefore very pleased to find that the clothes that now fitted Max were for age eleven to twelve. His last school uniform had been for twelve to thirteen, so he'd come down a whole size. They would still need turning up, but this was real progress, although I didn't draw Max's attention to it in the store. I would note it in my log later and also tell Jill and Jo (or Lorraine) when I next updated them. Whether I would tell Caz or not I was uncertain. Would she view it in a positive light? I didn't want her taking Max's achievement as a personal slight, the inference being that if he could lose weight then so could she. It was difficult to know what to do for the best.

As it was, Max told his mother when we telephoned her that evening. Although I hadn't mentioned it to him, he was smart and had read the size on the label while in the changing room. I couldn't hear her reply, but it seemed positive so when he'd finished the call I praised him and told him he was doing well with his eating.

Max had contact again on Thursday afternoon, then the following week – the last week of the summer holidays – Lorraine had said it would be Monday, Wednesday and Friday. What the arrangements would be when the new school term started I hadn't been told yet, but I quietly hoped contact would remain at three times a week rather than every night, as it had been when Caz had been in hospital. The new school term is always a time for hard work and it would put both boys under a lot of pressure if homework had to be fitted in around nightly trips to the Family Centre. However, what happened next changed contact arrangements in a way no one could have foreseen, and was truly shocking.

CHAPTER TWENTY-THREE

VERY POORLY

After a pleasant weekend (we went to an adventure park on Saturday and my parents came for lunch on Sunday), Max had a dental appointment on Monday morning and he wasn't looking forward to it. I don't think anyone does, but Max had more to fear than most after his previous experiences when he'd had many fillings and then teeth extracted. I reassured him as best I could, although I, too, was anxious. Adrian and Paula were quietly pleased they didn't have to go to the dentist; they'd had their check-ups during the spring bank holiday so weren't due another one until December.

All three children were the quietest they'd been all summer as we entered the surgery – Max had Adrian's and Paula's sympathy. But the dentist, a young Australian woman, had a lovely child-friendly manner. I explained to her who I was and that Max was staying with me for the time being, then I helped him clamber onto the couch. Adrian and Paula stood to one side, still very subdued, as the dentist began examining Max's teeth. With the stainless-steel probe she gently went round his mouth and called out her findings to the nurse, who wrote them down. They were dental terms, but sadly some of what she said was all too obvious, for example, 'lower right two missing'.

The dentist paused partway through the examination and looked at me. 'I'm guessing you've changed his diet and he's not eating as many sweet foods?'

'That's right,' I said.

'Excellent, and his oral hygiene has improved too.'

'Can you tell that?' I asked.

'Yes, there isn't the same build-up of plaque.'

'Fantastic,' I said, relieved.

I was delighted when she came to the end of the examination and said that there was no new decay in Max's teeth. She said she'd monitor the teeth that were already decayed – and might need to be extracted – but if they didn't deteriorate further or cause him pain then she'd leave them to come out naturally when his second teeth came through. It's a traumatic experience for a child to have teeth extracted under anaesthetic. As I helped Max from the couch she told him he was doing well and emphasized the importance of continuing to clean his teeth thoroughly morning and night and not eat sugary foods. The dental nurse gave Max a well-done sticker and the dentist said I should have one too for the part I'd played, so we both left sporting stickers of big molars with happy, smiling faces.

That afternoon Max had contact and I had no hesitation in telling Caz the good news about his teeth. She knew he had a dental appointment – she'd given me the details and had asked me to take him. She was already in the Family Centre sitting on the couch in Red Room with her feet up, but when I told her the result of the dental check-up she just nodded vaguely and seemed very distant and not herself.

'Are you OK?' I asked her.

'Not really.' She shifted uncomfortably. 'I've had to take strong painkillers for my foot and they make me woozy.'

'Oh dear. I'm sorry to hear that. Have you seen a doctor?' I asked, glancing at the girls.

'No, I must,' she said lethargically.

'The nurse told her to see the doctor the last time she came,' Kelly said.

'It's difficult to fit it all in, having to come here as well,' Caz explained.

'I'm sure contact could be rescheduled so you can see the doctor,' I said.

She nodded and rested her head back. I was concerned. She'd been complaining of her foot hurting for some time – not the one that had been operated on but the other one – and it seemed to be getting worse, not better.

'Perhaps Kelly could make the doctor's appointment and then phone Lorraine?' I suggested, for it seemed that Caz was finding it all too much, and Kelly was the oldest.

'I'll phone when we get home,' Kelly said.

Caz nodded again and closed her eyes. Max, recognizing his mother wanted to rest, went over to find a game to play with the girls.

'See you later then,' I said to them all.

'Yes, bye,' the supervisor called.

Outside, Adrian and Paula, who'd waited by the door and had seen Caz, were worried too. 'What's the matter with Max's mother?' Adrian asked.

'Her foot is hurting so she's going to see a doctor,' I said. 'Don't worry, the doctor will make her better.' How naive those words would seem later.

We went to the park, but the carer I'd bumped into the previous week wasn't there, as Monday contact for her child was in the morning. The weather was still fine in late August and it was lovely to be outside. We'd had an excellent summer, but once we were into September the afternoon air would begin to chill, heralding autumn and then winter. How long Max would be with me I didn't know – it would depend on the social services assessment, which I guessed had been slowed due to Jo being off work sick. Lorraine, as her manager, would cover the essentials, but I doubted she'd have time to complete an assessment. Hopefully Jo would recover and return to work soon or, if not, an agency social worker is sometimes used to cover absence.

We returned to Red Room for 3.30 p.m. and as soon as I stepped in I noticed a pungent smell, despite the windows being open. I assumed it was the result of hot bodies being together in one room with the sun shining in. The room felt hot and Caz looked particularly flushed. She was still on the sofa but was now lying with her feet up. The girls and Max had packed away the games in preparation for the end of contact. The atmosphere had changed and seemed more sombre. As I went further into the room I thought the smell seemed to be coming from Caz's direction, then Kelly said, 'It's Mum's foot that smells. She missed her appointment with the nurse to have the dressing change.'

I glanced at the supervisor, who was also looking concerned. 'We've telephoned Caz's doctor and got her an appointment for this evening,' she said. 'The manager here has told her she shouldn't have missed a medical appointment and contact could have been rearranged.'

I looked at Caz as she began to manoeuvre herself into a sitting position, gingerly lifting one leg and then the other to the floor and then righting herself. She grimaced, clearly in a lot of pain. Sweat glistened on her forehead and her cheeks were crimson.

'Caz, you must look after yourself,' I said. She nodded. 'We'll phone you tomorrow.'

She gave another desultory nod. The girls were looking very serious and worried. There was nothing I could do, so I said I hoped all went well at the doctors and, saying goodbye, we left. What I didn't know at the time was that the girls recognized these warning signs, having seen them before, and were desperately hoping they were wrong.

That night I reassured Max (and Adrian and Paula) that the doctor would make his mother better, and then the following morning Jill arrived at eleven o'clock for one of her statutory visits. We were in the living room and I was updating her in respect of Max. She'd seen and spoken to the children as she was supposed to do at each visit, and they were now playing in the garden. The phone rang and I picked up the handset from the corner table. It was Lorraine, Jo's manager. 'I have some bad news, I'm afraid,' she said, her voice tight. 'Caz was admitted to hospital last night. She has gangrene in two of her toes and is at risk of septicaemia.'

'Oh no!' I said, shocked and aware of the seriousness of this condition. 'How is she?'

'They're giving her antibiotics through a drip and they'll operate as soon as she is stable to remove the infected toes. But she's very poorly.'

'She wasn't well at contact yesterday,' I said.

'So I understand. She should have sought medical help sooner. Could you tell Max his mummy is in hospital, please?'

'Yes, of course.'

'We think it's best if he doesn't see her until she's a bit better. We'll take it a day at a time.'

'What about the girls? How are they managing?'

'They're at home and Caz's friend, Bet, is there. They might go to the hospital this afternoon to see Caz, but they won't stay for long.'

'Perhaps I could phone them later when they've been, to see how she is.'

'Yes. That should be all right.'

'I am sorry,' I said. 'I'll tell Max.'

'Thank you.'

Jill was watching me intently as I said goodbye and replaced the handset. She knew from my expression it wasn't good news.

'Caz is in hospital,' I said. 'She has gangrene in her toes and possible septicaemia. They're going to operate to remove the infected toes as soon as she is stable.' It was then I realized the full significance of the smell at contact. It was the gangrene from her rotting flesh. No wonder she was in pain. I told Jill.

'The poor woman,' she exclaimed, as shocked as I was. 'She hasn't properly got over her last operation and now this.'

'I need to tell Max something. He won't be seeing her for a while.'

'Do you want me to stay while you tell him?' she asked.

Jill had a lot of experience in dealing with traumatic news, so I thought her support would be useful. 'Yes, please.'

I stood and went into the garden. 'Max, can you come inside for a moment, please?' I said.

He seemed to be expecting bad news. 'Is it Mum?' he asked, coming over.

'Yes, love. She's in hospital.'

Once we were indoors and sitting together on the sofa, I explained to him that his mummy was in hospital and was being well looked after by the doctors and nurses. But that she would need another operation soon, similar to the last one.

'Will we visit her in hospital like we did before?' he asked.

'Yes, but not just yet. She's very tired. When she's feeling a little better and has had her operation we'll go.'

'And we'll buy her some sweets and fruit to make her feel better.'

Jill threw me a knowing look. 'We'll certainly take her some fruit,' I said. I balked at the idea of taking her more sweets. The amputation of her toes – first from one foot and then the other – was a result of the complications of type 2 diabetes, from obesity and a high-sugar diet. I wasn't going to be responsible for contributing further to what was already a chronic and life-threatening condition.

'OK then?' Jill asked Max. 'So you understand that Mummy is being looked after in hospital. Do you have any questions?'

He shook his head.

'If you think of any, you can ask Cathy.'

'I will,' he said. 'Can I go in the garden now?'

'Yes, love,' I said.

Outwardly, therefore, Max had taken this news as he did most bad news – in his stride – and Jill hadn't had to say much, although it had been reassuring to have her present. Possibly for Max, having his mother in hospital facing another operation wasn't the shock it might have been to another child, as he'd already had experience of it. Maybe at age six he didn't fully appreciate just how serious her condition was. But I knew Max better than that, so I wasn't surprised when, later that day, after Jill had left, he came to me and asked, 'My mummy won't die, will she?'

The short and brutal answer was yes, if not from this then a related condition if she didn't make radical changes to her diet and lifestyle. But that's not what you tell a young child who needs reassuring. If her condition deteriorated then I'd talk to him further, but for now I said, 'The nurses and doctors are looking after your mummy really well. I'm sure she will be feeling well enough for us to visit before too long.'

Which he accepted, as it was what he wanted to hear.

When Lorraine had telephoned she'd said that Max's sisters were visiting that afternoon, so early evening I telephoned Max's home. Paula was in bed and the boys were playing cards in the living room. I made the call in the hall, out of earshot. Paris answered.

'It's Cathy. I was wondering how your mum was. Lorraine said you were planning on visiting her this afternoon.'

'Yes, we all went. She was asleep most of the time so we didn't stay long. Her temperature has come down, which is good. Bet spoke to the nurse in charge and she said the antibiotics were starting to work and should stop the infection spreading further.'

'That's good news.'

'I guess, although she's still got to have at least two toes off. Is Max there?' I recognized that she didn't want to talk about it any more.

'He is, I'll put him on. So you're all managing?' I said, and called Max. 'You've had some dinner?'

'Yes, Bet cooked it for us.'

'Good. All I've told Max is that his mummy is in hospital. I haven't gone into the details.'

'No, I won't tell him about her toes, although he probably knows. Mum says he's got built-in antenna that picks up everything going on around him.'

I smiled. 'Yes, I know what she means.' Max didn't miss much, because he looked, listened and intuited.

Max came to the phone and spoke to all three of his sisters in turn. When he'd finished he hung up and returned to play cards with Adrian.

The following day and for the rest of the week I kept him busy with a mixture of outings and playing at home. Every evening I telephoned Max's sisters to find out how their mother was and he spoke to them. They and Bet visited Caz briefly each afternoon and her operation took place on Thursday. That evening, when I telephoned, Summer told me that Bet had phoned the hospital to see how Caz was and was told the operation had gone well and she was 'comfortable'. They didn't visit as the nurse had said she was still very sleepy from the anaesthetic. They visited on Friday and when I telephoned in the evening Kelly said their mother was awake and doing OK. The surgeon had told her he was satisfied that by amputating two toes he'd removed all the gangrene and had saved her foot. Apparently, the poor woman had been told before the operation that, depending on what the surgeon found, he might have to amputate her foot to stop the gangrene spreading further. He'd also told her that if she'd left it much longer before seeking medical help, her foot would certainly have had to come off. She asked the girls to find out when I could take Max in to see her. Paula and Adrian were out with their father the following day, Saturday, so I suggested I took him that afternoon.

Saturday morning, all the children were excited to be seeing a parent; Adrian and Paula their father, and Max his mother. I made us a cooked breakfast of scrambled egg, grilled bacon and tomatoes, and saw that Adrian and Paula were ready for when their father collected them at 10.30 a.m. Once I'd seen them off I suggested to Max that we walk to our local shop so he could choose some fruit for his mother. I would have liked to take her flowers as well, but most hospitals don't allow them in the wards for fear they might spread germs and aggravate allergies. Max no longer complained when I said we'd walk rather than use the car. The store was just a twenty-minute walk away and it would be the only exercise he'd have that day, as we'd need to take the car to the hospital – it was too far to comfortably walk.

In the shop Max chose a double punnet containing blue-berries and cherries for his mother, but was interested in the display of pomegranates. He said he'd never had one before so I bought some. They're rather a strange fruit and person-ally I'm not a big fan – they seem hard work for very little reward. The last time Adrian and Paula had tried them they'd had immense fun spitting out the seeds with some force (onto the plates I'd provided). I (unwisely) shared this with Max on the way home and he said he'd save his pome-granate for when Adrian and Paula returned home and they could 'all spit seeds together'.

After lunch we set off for the hospital and as I drove,

I warned Max that his mother would probably look quite poorly. It can be upsetting for a child to see a parent ill in a hospital bed, but of course Max had seen his mother like that before and took it in his stride. She was propped up in bed on a mound of pillows with a blanket support cage over her legs and feet, and a drip in her arm. She looked paler than she usually did and her hair was flattened from lying in bed, but considering what she'd been through she didn't look too bad. She managed a weak smile when she saw us.

'No girls?' I asked as Max presented her with the fruit and kissed her cheek.

'No, they're coming later. Thanks for this,' she said, referring to the fruit.

'You're welcome. I've washed them. How are you feeling?'

'Could be worse,' she said, putting on a brave face. She and Max began eating the fruit.

'I'll leave the two of you then and come back later.'

'Stay unless you've got stuff to do,' she said amicably. 'I wouldn't mind a bit of company.' How different this was from the reception I used to receive when she was in hospital the last time.

'I can stay. I haven't got Adrian and Paula with me,' I said, and sat in the chair. Max stood by the bed, eating the blueberries with his mother.

'Is there anything you need?' I asked her after a few moments. 'There's a small shop downstairs.'

'No, thanks, the girls are bringing in what I need when they come later. Nice of you to ask, though.'

As we talked they quickly finished the blueberries and then Caz passed the box to me. 'Put those on the cabinet, will you? I'll save the cherries for later. I can't be running to the bathroom.'

I did as she asked. 'Have you been out of bed?'

'Oh yes, they make you. It's painful and I can't manage with a walking frame yet so they bring a wheelchair. Hopefully I won't have the complications I had last time.' She then talked to Max about school. 'I expect you're looking forward to going back to school on Monday. Are you all ready?'

'Yes,' Max said. 'I've got new school shoes and a new uniform.'

'I know. You told me on the phone,' she said convivially. 'It's a size smaller, so that's good.'

I was pleased she'd mentioned this, as it allowed me neatly to raise the matter of breakfast club. 'I was thinking of not enrolling Max for breakfast club next term,' I said. 'He has breakfast before we leave. What do you think?'

'Whatever Max wants,' she said easily. Which was awkward, because children of Max's age don't always know what's best for them and have to be directed by a parent.

'I like breakfast club,' Max said.

'I know, but that means you'll be having two breakfasts.' I couldn't really stop the one at home when the rest of us would be eating breakfast.

'But I'm hungry when I get to school,' Max protested.

'I don't want him to be hungry,' Caz said.

'No, of course not.' I let the matter go. He could have a small bowl of cereal with semi-skimmed milk at home and then toast at school as he had been doing the previous term. It shouldn't make much difference to his diet.

'How long will you be in hospital for?' Max asked his mother.

'I don't know yet. Not long, I hope. I want to get home as soon as possible.' Which was very different from the last time she'd been in hospital when she'd been in no hurry to go home. I assumed it was because Dan was no longer there, intimidating and assaulting her. 'I've been thinking,' she then said to me. 'When the new term starts I want my kids to work hard and do well. I'm going to tell the girls not to visit me every night; they'll have homework to do. So will Max. I thought that you could come at the weekend and then you and the girls could take it in turns during the week. I don't know how long I'll be in here, so it seems sensible.'

'Yes, I think that's a great idea,' I said, relieved.

'I'll leave you to sort out with the girls which days you want to visit. Just make sure I'm not left all alone with no visitors at all.'

'You won't be,' I reassured her and we both smiled. How different Caz was now from the person I'd first met. Perhaps the shock of everything that had happened to her had given her a chance to re-evaluate her life and realize what was important. Going home to a house where she wouldn't be shouted at, abused and belittled must have been a great relief. I liked her now. She was someone I could be friends with and, of course, it would help Max enormously to see us chatting and getting along.

CHAPTER TWENTY-FOUR

TELL MAX I LOVE HIM

We stayed at the hospital for over an hour and then left when Caz's daughters arrived so there was room for them around the bed. On Sunday afternoon we visited again, but because I had Adrian and Paula with me I left Max with his mother for about an hour while we went up to the hospital café. I was pleased Caz had suggested visiting on alternate nights during the week; it would help me enormously. On Sunday, when we went to collect Max from the ward, the girls were there and we discussed which evenings would suit us best to visit and decided that I'd bring Max on Tuesday, Thursday and at the weekends, and they'd visit Monday, Wednesday and Friday. Caz agreed this sounded fine, but said again that she mustn't be left without any visitors. She seemed vulnerable and needy, which was hardly surprising as she was in hospital after another operation.

When we arrived home I noted the contact arrangements we'd decided on in my diary and fostering log, and would update Lorraine and Jill when I next spoke to them. I thought the arrangements should work well, but then that evening I'd just got the children into bed at a reasonable time, ready for the start of the new school term the following morning, when the phone rang. I answered it in the kitchen, where I'd started clearing up. It was Kelly and she was in a right pickle.

'I forgot to get Mum the stuff she wanted,' she blurted. 'We're all back at school tomorrow and won't have a chance to go shopping during the day. There won't be enough time after school to get it and our dinner before we have to get the bus to the hospital. I asked Bet, but she's back at work now. I told Mum I'd do it, but Paris and Summer should have reminded me. It's unfair to leave it all to me.'

'All right, calm down. I'm sure I can help.' Which I assumed was the reason she was phoning me. 'Tell me what your mother wants and I'll take it there tomorrow.'

'I've got a list,' she said.

I slid my shopping list and the pen I kept beside it towards me. 'OK, read it out.'

'Tissues. Hand wipes,' Kelly began, leaving time between each item for me to write it down. 'Sanitary towels, maxi. Toothpaste, a cheap one. I took in her toothbrush, but we didn't have a spare toothpaste at home.'

'OK. Don't worry.'

'A face flannel. Her one is worn out.'

'All right. Anything else?'

'She needs a new nightdress. She only has the one she's wearing now and that needs washing. It's got blood on it.'

'OK. I'll get one. What sort of nightdress does she like?'

'She said nothing fancy.'

'Cotton?'

'Dunno. But it's size twenty-six. There won't be much choice. There never is in the big sizes.'

'All right, I'll find something. Anything else?'

'Just some sweets. She asked for sherbet lemons to freshen up her mouth.'

I added sherbet lemons to my list. 'Is that everything?'

'Yes. She'll pay you, she has her purse with her.'

'OK. I'll drop them off as soon as I can tomorrow afternoon.'

'Thanks. I forgot about her stuff. I had to get my books sorted for college.'

'Are you managing all right?'

'Yes. Bet keeps phoning and comes in each day. We've got to try and not be late tomorrow on our first day back at school and college.'

'Have you got an alarm clock?'

'Yeah, we've taken the one from Mum's room.'

'Well, good luck for tomorrow. It's bound to be a wrench the first day after the long summer holidays. It will be for us.'

'Yeah, I know. Thanks for getting Mum's stuff.'

'You're welcome. Just as well I had a free day.'

So Monday wasn't to be the 'free' day I'd originally imagined when, having dropped off the children at school and nursery, I'd planned to return home, have a cup of coffee, tidy up and then do a spot of gardening. As it was, the girls weren't the only ones struggling to get back into the school routine. I had to chivvy along Max, Adrian and Paula so that we left the house on time. I met traffic taking Max to breakfast club and on the way back. I saw Adrian into school and Paula to nursery, where I spent longer than I should have done chatting to other mothers I hadn't seen during the summer holidays. I didn't return home but drove straight into town to the shopping mall. I found all the toiletries Caz wanted under one roof in the large chemist, and also the bag of sherbet lemons. Why a chemist should stock sweets I had no idea, but I added them to my basket. Caz had been through a lot and she'd specifically asked for these sweets, so it would have been cruel to deny her them, even though they were solid sugar. I thought that, given the number of bags of sweets she was used to consuming every night, it was showing some restraint only asking for one.

Choosing a nightdress for Caz proved more difficult. It's quite a personal piece of clothing and although there wasn't a massive selection in her size – as Kelly had warned – I had no idea what her style and colour preferences were. I ummed and ahhed and dithered, and as I held up the various nightdresses, trying to decide what would suit her best, I had an over-whelming sense of sadness for Caz and momentarily choked up. Being alone in her hospital bed, with only one nightdress and a worn-out face flannel, and asking for cheap toothpaste, seemed to demean her, leaving her frail and exposed.

I eventually chose a knee-length cotton nightdress with short sleeves in a pretty, delicate floral print. If Caz didn't like it, I could always exchange it. I headed back to the car, buying a bottle of water on the way, and then went straight to nurs-ery to collect Paula. I anticipated us going home for some lunch and then to the hospital with Caz's shopping, from where we'd probably have to go straight back to school to collect Adrian. However, when Paula came out of nursery she was hand in hand with one of her friends whom she hadn't seen over the summer. Her mother, Kay, whom I'd been chat-ting to, then asked if Paula would like to go home with them for some lunch and I could pick her up on my way to collect Adrian from school.

'I'm sure she'd love to,' I said. We took it in turns to have the girls to lunch, but this offer was perfect. Paula could spend the afternoon playing with her friend rather than coming with me to the hospital.

I kissed Paula goodbye, told her I would see her later and thanked Kay. Then I drove home, had a quick soup and sandwich lunch and went to the hospital with the carrier bag containing Caz's shopping. Visiting hours were from 1.30 p.m., which would allow me an hour if Caz wanted to chat before I had to return to collect Paula and Adrian.

Arriving outside the ward, I gave the sanitizer on the wall a couple of pumps and rubbed the antiseptic gel onto my hands, then went through the double doors and onto the ward, followed by a few other early visitors. Caz was in bed, awake and propped up on her pillows, her gaze trained on the double doors. She was surprised and, dare I say it, pleased to see me and heaved herself into a more upright sitting position.

'What a nice surprise,' she said and, without thinking, offered her cheek for kissing as she did to Max. I kissed it. 'I wasn't expecting to see anyone until this evening.'

'No, well, I had an urgent call from Kelly,' I said as I pulled up a chair.

'About what?' she asked, immediately concerned. 'What's wrong?'

'No, nothing bad,' I quickly reassured her. 'Kelly phoned me yesterday evening, worried because she'd forgotten to get the things you wanted.'

'Again!' she sighed.

'They've all been busy getting ready for school and college today,' I explained.

'Well, that's something, I suppose.'

'Don't worry, I think I've got the things you wanted. I hope they're all right.' I placed the carrier bag on the bed beside her.

'Thank you. That's kind. Did they give you the list then?' she asked, opening the bag.

'Yes, Kelly read it out over the phone.'

'Oh, you are good.' She rummaged in the bag. 'You've got everything. Even the nightdress.' She took it out and held it up.

'I can change it if you don't like it,' I said.

'No, it's beautiful. I do like it. It's really, really pretty and in my size.' But then her face crumpled and her eyes filled with tears.

'Oh, Caz, what's the matter?' I took the box of tissues from the carrier bag and, tearing off the lid, passed it to her.

'Thanks,' she sniffed, wiping her eyes.

'What is it?' I asked gently.

'It's your kindness. You're so thoughtful. I don't deserve it.'

'Of course you do,' I said, touching her arm, and ridiculously I welled up too. 'Stop it or you'll have me in tears.'

She managed a small smile and wiped her eyes again. 'Thank you, the nightdress is lovely. I badly needed a new one. I do like it.'

'Good. You're welcome.'

'My purse is in that drawer,' she said, pointing to her bedside cabinet. 'Can you pass it to me?'

I hesitated. 'Caz, let me treat you to this.'

'No, you can't do that,' she protested.

'I'd like to and the toiletries didn't cost much. It makes up for the fruit I haven't bought you.'

'It cost a lot more than fruit!' she said.

'I'd like to treat you, so let me. It would make me happy. OK?'

She gave a small nod, but her face clouded again and she rested her head back on the pillow with a sigh.

'What's the matter, love? You seem a bit tearful today.' I leaned in closer. There wasn't much privacy on the ward and the next bed was just the other side of the partially drawn curtain. She shrugged. 'You've had to cope with a lot – two big operations.'

'I need to get home,' she said. 'I'm worried it won't be long before the social services kick off over the girls being there by themselves. Kelly's not eighteen yet, not for another two months.'

'They seem to be doing all right,' I said. 'And Bet is there quite a bit.' Although Caz was right. The girls, while teenagers, were still minors, so they wouldn't be allowed to live alone for very long.

'Bet said if the social services said anything she'd move in temporarily.'

'Good. So try not to worry.'

'The trouble is, in here you have too much time to think and worry.'

'I can imagine. What else are you worrying about?' I asked gently.

'Everything,' she sighed. 'The girls, Max and me. I'm not going to make old bones and I worry what will happen to them.'

'Caz, you're doing fine,' I said. 'You've got a bit down, feeling unwell and with the operations. But you're recovering now.'

'I hope so,' she agreed. 'Max is only young. If anything happened to me, would you keep him?'

'Caz, don't say that!' I said, taken aback. 'You're getting stronger each day. You'll be out of here very soon, I'm sure. And what would the girls say if I kept Max?' I added with a smile, trying to lighten her mood. 'They wouldn't be very pleased.'

'No, you're right there,' she said. 'They miss him. They didn't really have much to do with him when he was living at home – he was always in his room. But since he's not been there they've really missed him. They'll appreciate him more when he comes home. We all will.' She paused.

'Yes?' I prompted.

'I need to try to help the girls like you're helping Max,' she said. 'I don't want them ending up like me. I blame my step-father for the way I am – a big fat blob who's eating herself to death. But the only person to blame for how my kids are is me. I don't want them to lead the life I've led. I want them to be happy, do well at school and find partners who treat them nice. Not have to put up with being treated like dog's dirt because they think they don't deserve any better. Paris had the courage to stand up to her father, but I'm not sure Kelly or Summer would have. They're more like me. Paris is feisty, but even so she overeats. What must they think? I've given my kids a death sentence.' Her eyes filled and she reached for another tissue.

'Caz, I'm sure they don't blame you,' I said. 'They love you, very much. I see it when you're all together.'

She shook her head. 'I need to talk to them, try to explain why I'm like this, the person I am. They need to understand that because I can't show them affection it doesn't mean I don't love them. I've never talked to them about what happened to me; I should. I also have to help them lose weight so they don't end up like me. I'm beyond help, but there's time for them to change and make something of themselves.'

It was heartbreaking to hear her talk like this and I felt tears sting my eyes. 'Caz, of course you're not beyond help,' I said. 'That's ridiculous. You will get much better with time.'

'I'm an invalid and will be for the rest of my life, and if I don't lose a lot of weight soon, I'll be dead. The surgeon said as much. You see that woman in the bed over there?' she said, lowering her voice. 'She thought I was the same age as her, sixty-eight. I'm not forty yet, Cathy, but look at the state of me. I don't want the same for my children. I've got to try and help them.'

It was pitiful to hear, although sadly much of what she said was true. Obesity and the ill health resulting from it had aged her, made her an invalid and would kill her if she didn't act fast to help herself. I wanted to reach out and hug her, comfort her as I would a child, but I knew how uncomfortable she was with physical contact – a legacy from all the years of sexual abuse she'd suffered as a child.

'Caz,' I said after a moment. 'Have you thought about going into therapy – as a family? It does help some people.'

She gave a small nod. 'The social worker before Jo mentioned it, but Dan was with us then and put a stop to it. Once I'm home I'll ask Jo or Lorraine. I'll try anything that might help. Thank you for your concern. You're very kind. If I'd had you in my life, how different it might have been.' She let out a heartfelt sigh and her eyes filled.

'You were a victim, Caz. You've suffered a lot, but it's not too late to undo some of the harm that was done to you so you can move on with your life. You sent Dan packing and that took a lot of courage.'

'With Paris's help.' She was silent for a moment, then gazed down at her new nightdress lying across the bed, lightly running her fingers over the material. 'It's a very pretty fabric,' she said presently. 'I wouldn't have had the confidence to choose it. I'd have thought it was too pretty for me. I grew up believing I was unattractive and no one has told me any different.'

A lump rose in my throat. I swallowed hard and struggled to find the words that would make Caz feel better about herself. 'You know beauty comes from within.'

'I know,' she said with a small, ironic smile. 'But it helps if you don't look like a barrel.' She continued to finger the delicate print of the nightdress. 'I'm going to put it on now,' she said, tearing off the store's tag that I'd left on in case it needed to be changed. 'It'll make me feel better. Could you help me? I'm well covered up underneath.'

'Yes, of course.' I stood and drew the curtains further around her bed so she had some privacy. Then, as she raised her arms above her head, I helped her out of the nightdress she was wearing and into the new one. 'It looks good,' I said. 'Really suits you.' She smoothed it down under her. I opened the curtains and sat down again.

'Shall I take this one home for washing?' I asked, picking up the nightdress she'd been wearing.

'You're not doing my washing as well,' she said. 'Leave it in the cabinet and I'll give it to the girls when they come this evening.'

I folded up the nightdress and placed it in the cabinet, and then glanced at the clock on the wall. I'd have to go soon. Caz was still looking at the material of her new nightdress.

'It suits you,' I said again, 'so don't tell me you can't wear attractive clothes.'

She managed a small smile. 'Does it really? I've never worn a delicate floral print before. I've always gone for plain and drab. When I get out of here perhaps I'll treat myself to some new clothes when I have the money. Give me something to look forward to.'

'Yes, do. It's nice to have something to look forward to. And the most important thing is going home to your family.'

She nodded.

'Is there anything else you need before I go? I have to collect my children soon.'

'Just a couple of new feet,' she joked. 'Thanks for coming. I promise I won't eat all the sherbet lemons in one go.' She threw me an old-fashioned look, then suddenly and completely unexpectedly she reached out and took my hand. It was so out of character that I started. It was a very courageous gesture for someone who avoided all physical contact, seeing it as a threat.

'Thank you for everything,' she said, giving my hand a little squeeze. 'Please tell Max I love him lots, and once I'm home I'll make it up to him. Tell him I'm sorry I haven't been a good mummy. I'll try my best to be better in the future. Tell him I'm proud of him and I should have told him sooner.'

'I'll tell him, Caz, although I'm sure he knows how much you love him, as all your family love you.'

'If they do, I don't deserve it. I pray I get the chance to make it up to them.' She wiped away a tear, as did I.

CHAPTER TWENTY-FIVE

BITTERSWEET

I was pretty choked up as I returned to my car and then drove to collect Paula. The image of Caz, childlike in the pleasure she'd gained from the new nightdress but feeling she wasn't pretty enough to wear it, had moved me deeply. All children need to be loved, protected, praised and adored. To go through life as Caz had done, believing she was worthless, was soul-destroying. Partly due to the abuse she'd suffered as a child and then perpetuated by Dan, her self-esteem was non-existent. I hoped that one day, once Caz was settled at home again with her children, if they began therapy then some of the harm done to her could be undone, otherwise she ran the risk of passing her issues on to her children. In respect of comfort eating, she already had.

I was served a timely reminder of how lucky I was when I collected Paula and saw the smile on her face. She'd had the confidence to spend time with her friend and was now over-joyed to see me, as I was her. As soon as I stepped into the hall she flew into my arms and covered my face in kisses, innocent and unreserved. I picked her up, hugged and kissed her, and then, thanking Kay for having her, we made an arrangement for her daughter to come to us for lunch. I then had to leave to collect Adrian and Max.

The first day of the new term and both boys had a lot to tell me. Max knew I was going to the hospital to see his mother and I told him she was fine, sent her love and would see him tomorrow.

I told him again at bedtime that his mother had specifically asked me to tell him she loved him loads, was proud of him and was looking forward to going home so they could be together again as a family.

'So am I,' he said. 'I love my mummy lots.'

'I know, and I think you should tell her that when you see her.'

'Should I?' he asked, slightly surprised. They weren't a family who showed affection either verbally or physically, largely due to the abuse Caz had suffered. Natural affection had become confused and warped by abuse for her.

'I think your mother would like to hear you say you love her.'

'OK, I will. I'll remember,' he said. It wasn't spontaneous as it is in some families.

The following day when we arrived on the ward he walked up to the bed, presented his mother with the fruit, kissed her cheek and said, 'Mummy, I love you.' And added, 'You've got a new nightdress. You look pretty.'

Which, of course, brought Caz close to tears.

'Thank you, love,' she said. 'That is kind.' She managed to give him a small hug.

* * *

Our new routine of hospital visiting continued for the next two and a half weeks. We took it in turns with Max's sisters to go on alternate evenings, and then at the weekend we all went. Bet had moved in, as Lorraine had said the girls weren't old enough to live alone and would have to go into short-term foster care otherwise. I hadn't met Bet. She'd been visiting Caz, but not at the same time we did. She sounded like a really good person, selfless, and a loyal and supportive friend, not only to Caz but the whole family. When Caz was discharged from hospital Bet took the day off work so she could help her settle in and make sure she had everything she needed. Caz left hospital in a wheelchair and was taken home by ambulance, although she used a walking frame inside the house. We kept the same contact going – Tuesday and Thursday evenings and Saturday and Sunday afternoons.

Jo returned to work ten days later and when she telephoned, I said I hoped she was feeling better, although it soon became obvious she was no less stressed than the last time I'd spoken to her. Her voice was tight and she spoke quickly. She told me that Max would live with me while Caz continued her recovery at home and she completed an assessment. The social services had concerns that Dan could return to live at the house, which would make it an unsafe environment for the children, although they were partly reassured that as far as anyone knew Caz hadn't let him back in since he'd left. I said I didn't think she would. They also needed to be satisfied that Caz could provide a reasonable standard of parenting for Max – for example, by making simple meals, establishing a bath and bedtime routine and by meeting his emotional and intellectual needs. I told Jo of the present contact arrangements and she was happy for them to continue, while adding that in future Max would be allowed to stay at home all week-end, which was good news.

Despite all that was going on, or perhaps as a result of it, Kelly and Paris asked their doctor for a referral to the health centre so they could follow a diet and fitness plan similar to the one Max was on. Summer didn't, claiming she had too much homework, and Caz said she'd go once her feet were better and walking wasn't so painful. Max was still following the plan, although it lapsed at weekends when he was at home. He'd tell me on a Sunday evening when I collected him what he'd been doing and what he'd had to eat – the good news first: 'Cathy, Paris and me went for a walk, then I had scrambled eggs on toast with tomatoes for lunch.'

'That sounds good,' I'd say.

'And in the afternoon I had crisps, a chocolate bar, three biscuits and a big bowl of ice cream all to myself.'

'Good heavens!' I'd say lightly, wondering if he was trying to wind me up. 'It's a wonder you didn't burst.'

But despite the lapses at the weekends Max continued to lose a little weight each week – around a pound or two – and was generally much fitter. The rotund portliness that had given him the air of a Charles Dickens character was dimin-ishing, and without rolls of fat getting in the way he could now move more easily and was more agile. He could also skip, work a swing, kick a football with some force and ride a skateboard and scooter, but he hadn't mastered a bike yet. Mrs Marshall, his teacher, made a point of telling me one day that she'd seen a big improvement and that Max was far less self-conscious now in PE, and had recently started joining in and playing with other children in his class at break time, rather than sitting by himself reading. He still loved reading, but joining in was a big step forward; he now had the confidence to play with his peer group. His breathing had improved and he didn't get out of breath so easily when exerting himself. He hadn't used his inhaler at home or school, although he still kept it in his school bag. At night I only heard him snore if he was lying flat on his back and in a very deep sleep. So he was fitter all round, and I hoped the improvements in his health, diet and general wellbeing continued once he was home permanently, but of course that would be his mother's responsibility.

Eventually, in December, the social services were satisfied that Max could return home and the moving date was set for Saturday, 19 December, the day after the schools broke up for Christmas. His leaving was bittersweet. Yes, of course I was pleased he was able to go home, as were Adrian and Paula – it was the best outcome possible – but we'd been imagining Max with us at Christmas, so in that respect we were disappointed. I packed all his belongings, including his Christmas presents, which I asked Kelly to hide until Christmas morning. There were his 'Father Christmas presents' and presents from me, Adrian, Paula and my parents.

The girls had really done a good job of decorating the house for Christmas; they'd put a lot of effort into it. Outside a large illuminated reindeer and sleigh stood by the pathway, and inside festive garlands, balloons, sparkling decorations and 'Happy Christmas' signs adorned the walls and ceilings. The light bulb in the hall had been replaced, and a waist-high illuminated Perspex laughing Santa stood just inside the hall and greeted visitors with a booming 'Ho! Ho! Ho! Merry Christmas!' before bursting into song. Adrian and Paula enjoyed running past and activating it and asked if we could have one. I said we had quite a lot of decorations already. In their living room a tall, glittering artificial Christmas tree stood majestically in the window so it could be seen from outside. Three different sets of coloured lights flashed on and off in various random sequences, multifaceted baubles glinted as they turned, and chocolate novelties and gaily coloured candy bars hung in abundance from the branches of the tree.

It took two trips to move all Max's belongings, although I left him at his house after the first trip and returned with Adrian and Paula for the rest of his things. Then it was time to say goodbye. The three of us stood in their living room surrounded by the trappings of Christmas, and I wished them all a Merry Christmas before saying a personal goodbye to Max, who had gone very quiet.

'So, young man,' I said. 'You have a lovely Christmas. I know you will now you are home. Your mum and I are going to stay in touch, so I'll find out how you're doing, and hope-fully we'll see you before too long. It's been great having you stay with us and you've done really well. So a big hug, please, and then we'll be off.' There was a second's hesitation before he stepped forward to hug me – any spontaneity of affection he'd developed while living with us already waning. But he gave me a hug, and then Adrian and Paula said goodbye to him.

I also said goodbye to his sisters and Caz. It felt odd not hugging or kissing cheeks when saying goodbye, as we did in my family. I'd packed a Christmas present for each of them in the bag containing Max's presents. Caz then told Adrian and Paula to choose a chocolate each from the tree. They all had one too. Using her walking frame, Caz hauled herself to her feet and, leaving the girls in the living room, came with us down the hall to see us out. As we passed the singing Santa he burst into a loud 'Ho! Ho! Ho!' and one of their cats shot by in a frantic panic to hide.

'You have a lovely Christmas with all your family,' Caz said, opening the door. 'And thanks again for everything.'

I smiled. How different this parting was to our first one. 'Take care and we'll speak after Christmas,' I said.

We stepped outside. Caz gave a little wave and then closed her front door. As we went down the path she was returning down her hall and 'Ho! Ho! Ho! Merry Christmas!' burst robustly from within, followed by a verse of 'Jingle Bells'.

Adrian laughed. 'You can even hear it out here!' he said.

'Yes. Ho! Ho! Ho! Merry Christmas!' I returned loudly, and in the same tone as the Santa, much to Adrian and Paula's embarrassment.

'Mum, stop it. I can't take you anywhere,' he admonished with a grin.

CHAPTER TWENTY-SIX

TRAGEDY

When a child leaves a foster carer and returns home it's usually left to the child's parent(s) to keep in touch with the carer. Many do for a short while because they appreciate that the child needs the contact, having established a bond with the carer and their family. Then it often peters out as memories fade, day-to-day living takes over and the family moves on with their lives. Caz had said she wanted to stay in touch with me, not only for Max's sake, but she also felt, as I did, that we'd become (unlikely) friends. We agreed we'd phone each other and get together when we could. In the New Year we got into the habit of taking it in turns to phone every week. Caz was the one who did most of the talking and seemed grateful to have an understanding ear, as she put it.

After Caz and I had spoken and she'd told me all her news, I passed the telephone to Adrian and Paula so they could talk to Max. Sometimes we all said hello to the girls too. The family was being monitored by the social services and Jo's visits would continue for at least a year, longer if there were any concerns.

As time passed our calls grew less frequent – about once a month. During that first year we also visited Max three times while the schools were on holiday – Easter, summer and the following Christmas, when I took them all a little gift and Caz gave us chocolates. Chocolate Santas for Adrian, Paula and the child I was fostering, and a box of chocolates for me. Caz's feet had healed and no further operations were planned, so her mobility was as good as it was going to get. She never went out alone and got around at home using a walking frame. She didn't use crutches, as she said they made her feel unsteady. She still had regular check-ups at the hospital, including attending the diabetic clinic, and ambulance transport was provided.

Caz took a lot of medication, much of which she would have to take for the rest of her life. As well as tablets for type 2 diabetes, she took tablets for reducing her cholesterol, lowering her blood pressure and for water retention, antibiotics if there was any sign of infection, and so on. The list was endless and even she didn't know what some of them were for. Yet when she talked about the tablets and showed me the dosette boxes full of them it was with a certain pride, as if she wore a badge of honour. Yes, it was sad, her world seemed to have closed in and now consisted of hospital appointments and taking medication. She was old before her time.

I didn't ever bring up the subject of food or dieting, but occasionally Caz volunteered that she'd seen the dietician at the hospital who'd given her a diet plan. If she did lose any weight, it couldn't have been much, for it didn't show and certainly her general health didn't improve. Max maintained his weight loss during his first year at home and didn't significantly lose or gain weight. Kelly and Paris began attending the diet and fitness classes at the health centre, and while Paris noticeably slimmed down during the year, Kelly stayed the same, claiming it was her genes. Even Caz gave a snort of laughter and said it was more likely all the chips, cakes, chocolates and ice cream she ate. Certainly, whenever I saw Kelly she was eating. It was such a pity, and I feared she was following in her mother's footsteps. Of all three girls she was the most similar to her mother in appearance and character.

Caz and I continued to keep in touch for the next two years, phoning each other every couple of months, and we still visited her during the school holidays. Kelly left college and got a job locally working for a small printing firm. Paris and Summer continued their education by studying vocational courses at the same college Kelly had been to. Paris maintained her weight loss, but despite her good example Kelly, Summer and Caz remained morbidly obese. During this time Max had continued to grow upwards, which had helped redistribute his weight, so he was now what I would describe as chubby rather than obese. He continued to excel at school and I had little doubt he would do well. When we visited he took Adrian and Paula to his room to play, while I talked to Caz – and the girls if they were at home – in the living room.

On one of our visits we met Bet, who was the lovely person I'd imagined her to be. She was mid to late fifties, so about fifteen years older than Caz, with a very big heart. She lived a few doors away and seemed to act as a motherly figure to Caz and her family, and had taken them all under her wing. I thought she looked familiar when I first saw her but couldn't place her until she said she'd worked at Beeches for twenty years, the large department store in town, and I realized that's where I'd seen her. She said her husband also worked there, in the store's warehouse. We got on very well and the next time she knew we were visiting Caz she made a point of calling in to see us, which was kind. She had five children, who were all adults now and had moved away, apart from one of her daughters who lived at home with her partner and two young children. Bet was of average weight for her height, and I saw her shake her head sadly when Kelly, having made tea, ate most of the cake and biscuits she'd set out on a plate for us all.

'I can only say so much,' Bet confided quietly to me when Caz left the room to use the bathroom. 'Caz needs to be firmer with the girls or they'll all go the same way. I've told her what I think, so there's not much more I can do.' She was obviously worried, not only about Caz's health, but that of her children too.

Bet asked me about fostering, as many people do, and she said it was something she and her husband would consider if ever they had a spare room, but of course at present they had a full house with their daughter and her family living there.

As it turned out Bet got her wish, but sadly not in a way she could have foreseen or wanted.

At the end of January, three years after Max had left us, when Kelly was twenty, Paris eighteen, Summer sixteen and Max just nine, I received a telephone call the like of which I hoped I'd never receive. It was ten o'clock on a Tuesday morning and there was just Toscha and me at home, as the children were at school. It was a cold day – we'd had a frost that morning – and Toscha was curled up in her usual place by the radiator. I was in the living room with a file open on my lap, completing some paperwork for the part-time clerical work I did from home. When the phone rang I was tempted to let it ring, as I really needed to get on with the work while I had some time. I reached out and picked up the handset, ready to dispatch the caller as quickly as possible. 'Hello?'

'Is that Cathy?' The woman's voice sounded familiar, although I didn't know where from.

'Yes, speaking,' I replied.

'It's Bet, Caz's friend.' Her voice broke and immediately I knew something bad had happened. But nothing could have prepared me for how bad it was. I thought that Caz might be in hospital again.

'Cathy,' Bet said after a moment, having collected herself, 'I'm sorry to be the one to have to tell you this, but Caz passed away yesterday.' She stopped as her voice broke again.

'Oh no.' My eyes filled and my throat closed. 'Oh no,' I said again.

Time stood still and I suddenly became acutely aware of everything around me. The discarded toy on the floor waiting to be put away, the small spider's web hanging just outside the patio window, the little twitch of the cat's ear and the framed photographs of the children on the walls that had been there for years, but now seemed suddenly vivid and real.

'Yesterday?' I asked at last.

'Yes.'

Bet sniffed, fighting to regain composure. I swallowed hard and wiped my eyes. Neither of us spoke again for some moments.

'I'm so sorry,' I said. 'So very sorry. It's a dreadful shock. I can't believe it.'

'No, neither can we. The girls are too upset to talk to anyone, so I said I'd phone you.'

'Thank you.' It was impossible to know what to say as, shocked and reeling, I tried to make sense of what had happened. 'I didn't know Caz was ill,' I said, struggling to get the words out.

'She wasn't. It was very sudden. It seems she got up as normal yesterday morning after the kids had gone out, and went into the kitchen to make herself a cup of tea, then collapsed. Kelly found her at lunchtime when she went back to make her some lunch, as she had been doing.'

'Oh, the poor girl.'

'Yes. Her mother was on the floor. Kelly called an ambulance, but there was nothing they could do. She was already dead. It's likely she died from a massive heart attack, but there'll be an inquest.'

I let out a long, heartfelt sigh as her words hung in the air. Then my thoughts went to her children. 'How are Max and the girls coping?'

'They're devastated as you can imagine. They're taking time off. Max is staying with me for now, I've told the social services. I've taken the rest of the week off work, and then we'll see how it goes. They've got no one else to make all the arrangements.'

'Have you told Dan?' I asked.

'Yes. A fat lot of good he was. I didn't expect anything better. He didn't offer to help, so I said I'd let him know when the funeral was.'

'Bet, is there anything I can do to help?'

'Thanks, but not really. My hubby is helping. Sadly, we know what to do – we buried both my parents last year.'

'Oh, I am sorry.' The poor woman had recently lost both her parents and now she'd lost her best friend.

'Will you phone me if there is anything I can do?' I said again. 'Obviously, I would like to come to the funeral.'

'Yes, of course. I'll call you with the details.'

'Thanks, Bet. And please phone if I can help at all.'

'I will.'

You feel so helpless when tragedy strikes and sometimes it can make you feel a little better to help out in the aftermath, but I didn't hear from Bet again until she'd made the funeral arrangements. Needless to say, during that time Caz and her children were never far from my thoughts, and while Caz wasn't an especially old friend, I felt deep compassion for her. I'd seen her at her most vulnerable, been her confidante in past suffering and witnessed her recent struggles first hand. I think what depressed me most was all the heartache and suffering she'd experienced in her short life. If someone old dies you can usually console yourself with the words that they'd had a long, happy and fruitful life or similar, but that couldn't be said of Caz. Don't get me wrong, I'm sure she'd had some happy times, and she obviously loved and got pleasure from her children, but overall her life had been very challenging and sad – abused by her stepfather and then her husband, she'd taken comfort in food, which had ultimately led to her death. It all seemed so futile. I thought she deserved better than that and it plagued me, kept me awake at night and increased my sense of loss and upset.

Caz's funeral took place at our local crematorium and thankfully – a small mercy – it was a sunny day, although cold. Steeling myself, and with a wodge of tissues tucked into my coat pocket, I followed other mourners into the small chapel, where I was handed an order-of-service sheet by an usher. On the front of the booklet was a lovely head-and-shoulders photograph of Caz with her full name, date of birth and death printed beneath. I guessed the photograph had been taken when she'd been in her mid-twenties. Already noticeably chubby, but smiling brightly before ill health had set in. My eyes welled as I sat in a pew on the right of the chapel, third row from the front. It was a truly charming photograph, a brief snatch of happiness and not at all like the person I had known. My bottom lip quivered and I took a deep breath, looked up and tried to concentrate on what was around me as a diversion for my thoughts: the chapel walls, the arrangement of flowers in a vase on a small table at the front, the wooden cross above the simple altar, the modern stained-glass window. Other mourners were slowly filing in and a woman slid into the end of the pew where I was seated. Recorded organ music played softly in the background.

I guessed about thirty of us were gathered to pay our respects when the service started and the minister's voice came from the rear of the chapel and asked us all to stand. The organ music changed and a slow, mournful dirge began. I rose to my feet and braced myself for what I knew would happen now, turning my head slightly towards the centre aisle. Caz's coffin, borne on the shoulders of four pallbearers, began its slow journey towards the front, followed first by Kelly and Paris, both already crying, then Summer holding Max's hand and being so brave, then Bet and her husband. It was piteous and broke my heart, as it did others. I heard sniffing behind me and a man clearing his throat. The woman on my left took a tissue from her handbag and wiped her eyes. The children were too young to be leading a funeral procession, too young to have lost their mother. Everyone looked to the front as the pallbearers carefully lowered the coffin onto the plinth, took a step back, bowed respectfully and then, turning, left the chapel. Caz's children, Bet and her husband took their places in the two rows in front of me.

The minister asked us to be seated and then opened the service by saying we were here to celebrate the life and mourn the passing of Caz. I looked at Max seated between his sisters, concentrating on the minister, listening intently to the words as he spoke of the pain of losing a loved one, the journey we all made from birth to death, and specifically about Caz and her family. He included a couple of little anecdotes about Caz, personal touches that I guessed Bet must have told him, as Caz wasn't a church-goer and as far as I knew didn't know the minister. Paris sobbed as he made reference to the children having lost their mother young and asked for God's blessing and said they were in our thoughts and prayers. Out of the corner of my eye I could see Dan, sitting alone at the end of the pew closest to the door. I wondered what his thoughts were as he listened to the minister's kind words about the wife he'd abused and cheated on. Did he have any regrets or, like many abusers, was he able to justify his behaviour? Whichever, I felt pretty certain he would have little or no involvement in the lives of his children in the future. Bet had said he hadn't been near them since Caz's death, which was probably for the best.

I managed to keep a rein on my emotion and hold it together reasonably well until Bet paid her tribute. Standing, she went up to the rostrum, clearly nervous; her hand shook as she looked at the sheet of paper she held in front of her. I thought she was very brave. Her emotion was palpable as she began by saying that Caz's children had lost their beloved mother and she had lost a dearly beloved friend. She spoke of

Caz's sensitivity, warmth and generosity and how she always had time for a chat over a cup of tea. She said she had many treasured memories of their little chats together that she'd remember always. She said Caz hadn't had the easiest of lives and spoke of her braveness during all the years of ill health that had plagued her for most of her adult life. She said Caz didn't often share her innermost thoughts – she wasn't that type of person. But Bet wondered if she'd had a premonition that she might leave this world soon, for only last month, during one of their chats, Caz had made a point of talking to her about what would happen if she died.

'At the time I told her not to be silly,' Bet said, her eyes glistening with tears. 'But now I'm glad we had that chat, as I was able to reassure her and carry out her last wishes. Caz was worried what would happen to her children and I promised her that my husband and I would make sure they were well looked after. She told me she wanted a simple funeral service at this crematorium and then handed me a poem she wanted read out. This poem,' Bet said, referring to the sheet of paper she held, 'Caz had come across it in a magazine and copied it out. She felt it applied to her, especially the verse that begins, "Those of you who liked me ..."'

She paused and took a breath. 'It's called "One at Rest". For you, my dear friend Caz, rest in peace.

'Think of me as one at rest,
for me you should not weep;
I have no pain, no troubled thoughts,
for I am just asleep.

'The living, thinking me that was,
is now forever still,
and life goes on without me now,
as time forever will.

'If your heart is heavy now
because I've gone away,
dwell not long upon it, friend,
For none of us can stay.

'Those of you who liked me,
I sincerely thank you all,
and those of you who loved me,
I thank you most of all.

'And in my fleeting lifespan,
as time went rushing by,
I found some time to hesitate,
to laugh, to love, to cry.

'Matters it now if time began,
if time will ever cease?
I was here, I used it all,
and now I am at peace.'

Bet stopped. There was silence. You could hear a pin drop. All Caz's children were crying silently, as was Bet's husband. Wiping her eyes, Bet stepped from the rostrum and returned to her seat as I took a tissue from my pocket. Rest in peace, Caz, you deserve it. We all liked and loved you.

CHAPTER TWENTY-SEVEN

CRUEL TO BE KIND

Those of you who liked me,
I sincerely thank you all,
and those of you who loved me,
I thank you most of all.

Caz was grateful if someone liked or loved her because she didn't believe she deserved it, which was heartbreaking. Her words, spoken by Bet through the poem, remained with me years later.

The last time I saw Kerry, Paris, Summer and Max was straight after the funeral service at Bet's house. All the congregation were invited back for light refreshments and about twenty of us went. Bet's daughter, the one who lived with her, had put out sandwiches and other savouries and there was a cup of tea or a beer to drink. The wake, as it's sometimes called, is often looked upon as the start of the healing process, where mourners gather together, share their happy memories of the deceased and start the journey of recovery. But because Caz's children were relatively young, I didn't feel this and I wasn't the only one. The atmosphere of sadness and grieving continued. I said a few words to each of Caz's children, but it was clear they were struggling and didn't want to talk. I talked to Bet, her husband, Harry, and also some members of her family – all lovely, warm-hearted people just as Bet was. Harry told me that he was helping the girls to sort out their finances and making sure the rent and other bills were paid. The girls wanted to stay in the house if possible and he was looking into the welfare benefits that were available. Kelly and Paris were now adults (just) and Summer was nearly seventeen, and they'd all made it clear to social services that if they tried to put Summer into care they'd block it. Max would continue to live with Bet and her husband for the foreseeable future, and the social services were hurrying through a foster carer assessment so they could be passed to foster him. Jo and Lorraine had both left – Jo, after a number of absences due to ill health, and Lorraine to work for another authority – so they were now dealing with someone called Katrina, who Bet said was helpful.

I didn't see or hear from Bet, Max or the girls after that. There was no reason why I should. I'd only met Bet a few times and she led a busy life just as I did, with fostering, bringing up my own children and working part-time from home. Of course, I thought about Max and his sisters often, and wondered how they were all doing, especially Max. Foster carers never forget the children they look after and I secretly hoped that I might bump into one of them in town, as had happened before with children I'd fostered. Or possibly a child I was fostering might go to the same school as Max, so I could find out how he was doing and even see him. But that didn't happen. Occasionally a foster carer finds out by chance how a child is doing through another carer or social worker, but once the child has left, the social services don't usually keep the carer updated. It would be impractical to update all foster carers on all the children they'd fostered; there just aren't the resources available. So the years passed without any news.

Part of me felt that Max would be OK. He was intelligent, motivated to learn, self-reliant (too much so sometimes) and resourceful, and he had Bet and her husband looking after him. How much his early life experience had impacted on him was another matter, though. Those years are so important in shaping a child's future, even into adulthood. Max had coped while at home by shutting himself in his bedroom and burying himself in books and learning, which wasn't really a long-term solution. Or was it?

Ten years after Caz's death, on Monday, 12 December, I was standing in the kitchen opening the mail while waiting for the kettle to boil so I could make a cup of coffee. The mail contained a wonderful selection of festive Christmas cards, beautiful snow scenes with reindeer and robins, Father Christmas carrying sackfuls of presents and nativity scenes. I savoured their bright, glittering images; they brought joy to my heart. I love Christmas with all its trimmings. The next card I opened contained a photograph – not unusual, as some of my friends and relatives who lived a long way away and whom I saw infrequently often included a photograph of their family so we could keep up to date. However, this one was slightly unusual. It wasn't a family group. It was of a young man standing beside a bicycle in front of an historic building that looked familiar. Yet while the building looked familiar, the young man did not. Intrigued, I turned over the photograph and read the handwritten words.

Hi Cathy. Remember me? Just completed my first term at King's College, Cambridge. Had to learn to ride a bike, as everyone here rides bikes!
Max x

Max! Good gracious! Of course I remember you! I quickly flipped back to the photograph and examined the image of the young man. Yes, I could see it was Max now, just. His features showed a passing reference to the young boy I'd fostered all those years ago, but he was so very different. Apart from natural maturity redefining his features, he was no longer chubby – not in the least. He had grown into a fine, tall young man and looked toned and fit. So different from the child I'd last seen that I'm sure I would have walked past him in the street without recognizing him. And he'd secured a place to study at King's College, Cambridge – one of the most prestigious universities in England! Well done, Max. What a fantastic achievement. He'd also finally learnt to ride a bike.

I smiled as my thoughts went back to the six-year-old Max who'd been so overweight he'd struggled to even kick a foot-ball, let alone ride a bike, during that long, hot summer when he'd played in the garden with Adrian and Paula. Yet now he was confidently cycling around Cambridge on his way to and from lectures like hundreds of his fellow students. Cambridge students are renowned for using bicycles to get around, and cars are banned from many areas in the city centre. But had he made friends, I wondered? There would be a good social scene at Cambridge, but was Max part of it? Or after lectures did he return to his lodgings to sit alone and read and study as he had done at home? It was impossible to know from looking at the photograph. He appeared self-assured, but photos are only a snapshot of a person's life, not the whole picture.

Setting the photograph to one side, I now read the words he'd written in the card beneath the printed Christmas message.

Cathy, if you remember me I'd love to visit you during the Christmas holidays.
Best wishes,
Max x

He'd included his mobile phone number. Ignoring the boiling kettle, I picked up my phone from where I'd left it on the work surface and, creating a new contact, entered Max's number. I didn't need to think about what to say in the text. *Hi Max. Thanks for the card. Of course I remember you! Would love to see you. When r u free? Cathy & family x*

I pressed send and began making the coffee, still in a daze of wonder and amazement. Before I'd had a chance to add the milk my phone bleeped with an incoming text message. *Great! Is next Saturday any good? Max x*

I texted back: *Perfect. Around 2 p.m. would suit me x*
See you then. Max x

The following Saturday afternoon saw Adrian, Paula, Lucy (my adopted daughter) and me eagerly awaiting Max's arrival. I'd baked a cake and made some sweet mince pies, which are a traditional Christmas favourite of ours and were warming in the oven. Although Lucy had never met Max, when I'd shown her his photograph and explained who he was she'd become as excited as Adrian and Paula were to meet him. Paula had been so young when Max had lived with us that she only had the haziest recollections of him, but Adrian, that much older, remembered him clearly, as of course I did.

It was Adrian, now aged twenty and home from university for Christmas, who went to answer the front doorbell when it rang at five minutes to two, while Lucy and Paula immediately came out of their bedrooms and down the stairs.

'Adrian, good to see you!' came Max's voice, no longer that of a little boy but a man.

'Max! Good to see you too, come in.' As I entered the hall the boys were warmly shaking hands.

'Max! Look at you!' I said, going up to him.

'Hi, Cathy,' he said. 'Great to see you again.' Smiling broadly, he kissed my cheek and then presented me with a beautiful bouquet of flowers.

'Thank you, they're lovely. But you shouldn't have done that. How kind.'

'A rather late thank you present for looking after me,' Max said. Physically he was so different, but he was still the kind-hearted and good-natured lad I'd known all those years ago.

'They're lovely. You remember Paula?' I said as she arrived at the foot of the stairs.

'Yes, of course. But not like this,' he said with a laugh.

She smiled, a little embarrassed, and they kissed cheeks.

'And I have another daughter now. Meet Lucy.'

Max looked slightly puzzled, but I let Lucy tell him, as I thought she would. 'Adopted,' she said as they kissed cheeks too.

'Oh wow,' Max said. 'So am I.'

It was Adrian's, Paula's and my turn to look confused.

'Didn't you know Bet and Harry adopted me?' Max said.

'No, I didn't. But that's fantastic.'

'Yes, about two years after Mum passed. They thought it would give me greater security.'

'It does,' Lucy readily agreed.

'Let's go through to the living room,' I said, for we were still in the hall. I turned and led the way.

'I remember this so clearly,' Max said, glancing around as we went. 'And you guys.'

'I remember you being here clearly,' Adrian said. 'Although you looked a bit different back then.'

'I did,' Max laughed. 'Very different.'

We went into the living room where Paula and Lucy settled on the sofa and the boys sat in the easy chairs. I said I'd make us a drink and asked them what they'd like. They all wanted tea. I left them chatting and took the flowers into the kitchen, placed them in a vase of water and then filled the kettle. As I made the tea and arranged the sponge cake and mince pies on plates, I could hear them talking about university life. Adrian asked him why he'd chosen Cambridge and Max replied that he'd wanted to study philosophy and they offered a really good course, and that many famous philosophers had studied there. Max's manner wasn't at all boastful, which it could have been considering the intellectual nature of the subject he'd chosen to study and that he'd been accepted by a top university. He sounded as down-to-earth and stoical as I remembered him being as a child, just wiser, and more mature and confident. Paula asked him what he would do with his degree, which had rather crossed my mind, as there was no career in philosophy as far as I knew. Max replied that he hadn't decided on a career yet but enjoyed the subject and a philosophy degree was a good basis to go on to train for a career in law, teaching, media or business.

I carried the tray containing the tea and side plates in first and set it on the coffee table, then returned for the plates of cake and mince pies. I handed each of them a cup of tea and a side plate and then offered round the cake and mince pies, to Max first as he was the guest.

'What can I tempt you with?' I asked him, proffering the plates enticingly. Then I had the uncomfortable feeling that I shouldn't be encouraging him to eat these foods when he'd clearly done well to shift all the weight and keep it off.

Perhaps he saw my dilemma, for he said, 'They look lovely, Cathy. I'll just have one mince pie. Thank you.'

I then offered the plates around before taking my tea and slice of cake to an easy chair. The young people were now talking about Christmas and Max was admiring our tree.

'What are you doing for Christmas?' I asked him.

'I'll be at home with my parents for Christmas Day. Then I'll try to see as many of my family as I can before I have to return to uni. But there are a lot of us now. My sisters all have families and then there are Bet and Harry's children and grandchildren. Last count, I had fifteen nieces and nephews – it may be more now!'

We laughed. Adrian helped himself to another mince pie and offered the plate to Max, but he refused.

'So your sisters are all doing well?' I asked. 'They must be in their late twenties now.'

'Yes, Summer and Paris are late twenties, Kelly is thirty-one. I've got some photos on my phone if you'd like to see them.'

'Yes, please,' I said.

Setting his cup and saucer on the coffee table, Max took his phone from his shirt pocket and I went over to where he was sitting so I could see.

'Can we look too?' Lucy asked.

'Yes, of course,' Max said.

Lucy, Paula and I grouped around Max and Adrian leant over from his chair so he, too, could see. 'This is a recent family photo,' Max said, bringing the first photo onto the screen. 'It was taken this summer before I went to uni. There's Kelly and her three children,' he said, pointing. 'That's her husband. There's Paris, her husband and their two children. That's Summer and her two boys. Her husband isn't there, as he had to work. The others are some of Bet and Harry's children and grandchildren.'

'What a lovely family gathering,' I said. Although there were so many squeezed into the photo and it had been taken from a distance, so it was difficult to make out individual features.

'Here's a better one of Kelly and her children,' Max said, pulling up the next photo. 'Bet says Kelly is the spitting image of Mum.'

'Yes, she is,' I agreed, looking at the photo of Kelly.

'She's got Mum's weight problems too,' Max added reflectively. 'I worry about her most of all. She's always at the doctors and already has to take tablets for high blood pressure and cholesterol.'

I nodded solemnly. It was sad. Kelly would know only too well the risks she was running if she didn't lose weight from the tragic example of her mother.

'This is Paris,' Max said, moving to the next photo.

'She looks very well,' I said. This photo was of just her, dressed up, hair styled and I guessed ready to go on a special night out.

'She had one of those gastric bands fitted and it helped her lose weight,' Max said. 'The doctor told her that they didn't normally do them in people as young as her, but given what happened to Mum and that Paris had tried dieting but was already showing signs of type 2 diabetes, he put her on the waiting list. She had the operation eighteen months ago and has lost over six stone. There's still a lot of willpower involved if you want to lose weight, even when you have a gastric band. She's done well.'

'Yes, she has,' I agreed. 'Very well.'

'And this is Summer, her husband and their children,' Max said, bringing up the next photograph. 'I see her the most. Although she's still struggling with her weight, she's determined her children won't go the same way and watches carefully what they eat. She's strict with them, as Bet was with me.'

'They look good,' I said. Two very healthy-looking boys with cheeky grins stood either side of their parents, although Summer was clearly still badly overweight.

'The rest are group photos and some of uni,' he said, flipping through them. He came to the end and closed his phone.

'Thank you. It's lovely to see you are all doing well,' I said. The girls and I returned to our seats.

'I have Bet and Harry to thank,' Max said. 'They encouraged me in my studies and also kept me on a diet until I was old enough to do it myself. Bet used to say it was tough love and sometimes you had to be cruel to be kind, as kids don't always know what's best for them.'

'Very true,' I said with a smile. 'Bet is a lady after my own heart. Do you ever see your father?'

'Only in the street. He says hello sometimes, but that's it.' Max shrugged. 'As they say, you can't choose your family.'

'I did,' Lucy put in, meaning she chose us by asking me to adopt her. I threw her a smile. (I tell Lucy's story in my book *Will You Love Me?*)

Max stayed for over two hours, talking generally and keeping us amused with tales of university life, including his first attempts at learning to ride a bike. I was pleased to hear he had made friends and socialized with them when he wasn't studying. Eventually he said he needed to go but promised to keep in touch. I offered to give him a lift home, but he said he'd prefer to walk to the bus stop as it was good exercise. We all saw him to the door, where I gave him an envelope containing a book voucher. 'A little something to go under your Christmas tree,' I said. 'It's not very imaginative, but it should come in useful.'

'Thank you, that is kind. I'm sorry I didn't bring you guys anything.'

'Seeing you again is a gift in itself,' I said, and he kissed my cheek.

He then said a warm goodbye to Adrian, Lucy and Paula and I opened the front door. The temperature had dropped as the sun had set and the air was very still. Max glanced up at the sky. 'I wouldn't be surprised if it snowed,' he said. 'The conditions are perfect.'

'A white Christmas!' Paula exclaimed excitedly.

'Snowball fight!' Lucy added.

Max smiled. 'Have a good Christmas.' Then he paused on the doorstep. 'Do you remember it was Christmas when I left you to return home?'

'Yes, I do,' I said.

He looked thoughtful. 'Strange life, isn't it? Well, thanks again for everything.' He turned and with a small wave began down the path.

We watched him go. No longer the self-conscious, chunky, uncoordinated boy we'd said goodbye to all those Christmases ago, but a healthy, personable and confident young man who'd overcome a difficult start in life to do well – thanks to Bet, Harry and Max's own determination and willpower. Fantastic. Well done, Max.

For the latest on Max and the other children in my books, please visit www.cathyglass.co.uk.

SUGGESTED TOPICS FOR
READING-GROUP DISCUSSION

Why do you think the child's contact must always take priority over a foster carer's family arrangements? Is that fair?

What challenges does Cathy face when she tries to change Max's diet to a healthier one?

Obesity is indirectly the second-biggest killer in Europe and America after smoking. Are governments doing enough to help families like Max's? If not, what more could be done?

The paediatrician believes that allowing a child to become morbidly obese is a form of child abuse. Is she right? Do you blame Max's parents? Is Caz any less culpable because of her past?

How does obesity affect Max physically, emotionally and socially?

Max's teacher, Mrs Marshall, likens Max to the Roald Dahl character Matilda. What do you think she means by this?

Caz only finds the courage to separate from her husband when she is faced with losing all her children into care. Discuss the reasons that might have kept her in an abusive relationship for so long.

Jo, Max's social worker, confides that she is thinking of resigning from her post and becoming a foster carer. What are the similarities and differences between the two roles?

Cathy refers to forming an 'unlikely' friendship with Caz. What do you think she means by this?

The ending of the book is both sad and uplifting. Discuss in respect of Max and other members of his family.

Cathy Glass

One remarkable woman, more
than **150** foster children cared for.

Cathy Glass has been a foster carer for
twenty-five years, during which time she has
looked after more than 150 children, as well
as raising three children of her own. She was
awarded a degree in education and psychology
as a mature student, and writes under a
pseudonym. To find out more about Cathy
and her story visit www.cathyglass.co.uk.

Happy Mealtimes for Kids

A guide to healthy eating with simple recipes that children love.

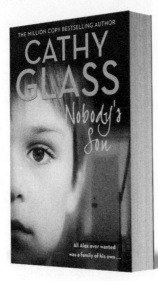

Nobody's Son

Born in prison to a drug-dependent mother and brought up in care, seven-year-old Alex has only ever known rejection

He is longing for a family of his own, but again the system fails him.

Can I Let You Go?

Faye is 24 and pregnant, and has learning difficulties as a result of her mother's alcoholism

Can Cathy help Faye learn enough to parent her child?

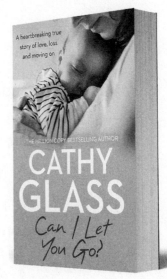

The Silent Cry

A mother battling depression. A family in denial

Cathy is desperate to help before something terrible happens.

Girl Alone

An angry, traumatized young girl on a path to self-destruction

Can Cathy discover the truth behind Joss's dangerous behaviour before it's too late?

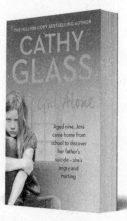

Saving Danny

Danny's parents can no longer cope with his challenging behaviour

Calling on all her expertise, Cathy discovers a frightened little boy who just wants to be loved.

The Child Bride

A girl blamed and
abused for dishonouring
her community

Cathy discovers the
devastating truth.

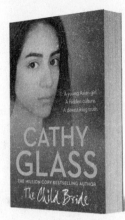

Daddy's
Little Princess

A sweet-natured girl with
a complicated past

Cathy picks up the
pieces after events take
a dramatic turn.

Will You Love Me?

A broken child desperate
for a loving home

The true story of Cathy's
adopted daughter Lucy.

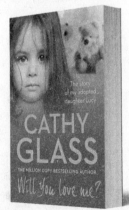

Please Don't Take My Baby

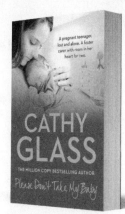

Seventeen-year-old Jade is pregnant, homeless and alone

Cathy has room in her heart for two.

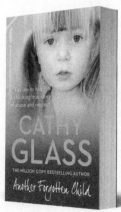

Another Forgotten Child

Eight-year-old Aimee was on the child-protection register at birth

Cathy is determined to give her the happy home she deserves.

A Baby's Cry

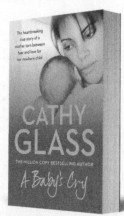

A newborn, only hours old, taken into care

Cathy protects tiny Harrison from the potentially fatal secrets that surround his existence.

The Night the Angels Came

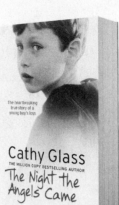

A little boy on the brink of bereavement

Cathy and her family make sure Michael is never alone.

Mummy Told Me Not to Tell

A troubled boy sworn to secrecy

After his dark past has been revealed, Cathy helps Reece to rebuild his life.

I Miss Mummy

Four-year-old Alice doesn't understand why she's in care

Cathy fights for her to have the happy home she deserves.

The Saddest Girl in the World

A haunted child who refuses to speak

Do Donna's scars run too deep for Cathy to help?

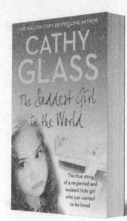

Cut

Dawn is desperate to be loved

Abused and abandoned, this vulnerable child pushes Cathy and her family to their limits.

Hidden

The boy with no past

Can Cathy help Tayo to feel like he belongs again?

Damaged

A forgotten child

Cathy is Jodie's last hope. For the first time, this abused young girl has found someone she can trust.

Inspired by Cathy's own experiences...

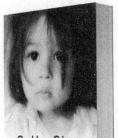

Run, Mummy, Run

The gripping story of a woman caught in a horrific cycle of abuse, and the desperate measures she must take to escape.

My Dad's a Policeman

The dramatic short story about a young boy's desperate bid to keep his family together.

The Girl in the Mirror

Trying to piece together
her past, Mandy uncovers a
dreadful family secret that
has been blanked from her
memory for years.

Sharing her expertise...

About Writing
and How to Publish

A clear and concise, practical
guide on writing and the best
ways to get published.

Happy Adults

A practical guide to
achieving lasting happiness,
contentment and success.
The essential manual for
getting the best out of life.

Happy Kids

A clear and concise
guide to raising
confident, well-behaved
and happy children.

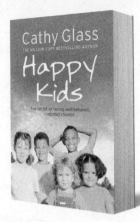

CATHY GLASS
IS BACK IN A BRAND NEW CRIME VOICE WRITING AS
LISA STONE

You know your son better than anyone.
Don't you?

Be amazed
Be moved
Be inspired